White Niggers of America

White Niggers of America

by Pierre Vallières

Translated by Joan Pinkham

McClelland and Stewart Limited
Toronto / Montreal

The Canadian Publishers
McClelland and Stewart Limited
25 Hollinger Road, Toronto 374

Printed in Canada

To the memory of my father

Contents

Foreword

In reading this book it is important to remember the following facts.

1. The book was written in prison, immediately after a twenty-nine-day hunger strike, under particularly difficult conditions. It was written in the midst of the constant noise of cells being opened and closed by an iron hand and of guards and prisoners shouting back and forth, and within the framework of an absurd discipline (called prison rules), invented and applied for the purpose of brutalizing the inmates as much as possible.

The section in which Charles Gagnon and I are still held as these lines are written is reserved chiefly for the mentally ill, drug addicts, men accused of homocide and facing possible life imprisonment, prisoners in depressive states and, lastly, "political" madmen, like Charles and me, whom the officers regard more or less as "deranged."

Very often one or another of our jail mates slits his veins out of despair, or simply to attract attention. For one of the chief characteristics of prison life is the boundless solitude each of us feels, especially during those hours of depression when it becomes impossible to communicate with others.

In addition to this profound and unnamable suffering that constitutes our daily human environment, I must particularly mention the howling stupidity of the radio and television during "lock-out" and "rest period," the fact that we are forbidden to go outdoors to get a breath of fresh air and an occasional look at the sun, and the thousand petty annoyances that are deliberately imposed on our most elementary activities: eating, pissing, sleeping (in the cells in our section

9

the lights are *never* turned out), receiving mail, doing laundry, shaving, etc.

In short, this book was written in a universe of cunningly organized dehumanization . . . which drives more than one prisoner to suicide—or murder, if he is set free again.

2. This book is first of all a *political act*. It is necessarily biased. It contains not so much answers as questions, and facts, that I want to set before men—in particular the men of Quebec—who are capable of consciousness, social responsibility, and revolutionary action.

It is the political act of one member of the Front de libération du Québec (FLQ), of a militant who is still young, who has not had a long experience of revolutionary struggle, and who has no monopoly on truth.

This book, moreover, was not written with the intent of "shaking revolutionary thought and action to their foundations," but of performing an act whose meaning is given by the book itself, which comes from my guts as much as from my head.

3. In this essay, which is no doubt badly put together, and which I shall probably not have the leisure to revise before it is sent to the printer (unless my extradition to Canada or deportation to another country is postponed to the spring or summer of 1967), the reader will find many faults, repetitions, and awkward constructions, side by side with limpid passages where the words "flow." For driven by the constant threat of deportation or extradition that has hung over Charles Gagnon and me ever since we were arrested in New York on September 28, 1966, I have had to scribble down in haste my memories, impressions, ideas, my short but brutal experience of life and my boundless conviction that it is possible to build a better world *now*, if we all agree to roll up our sleeves and set to work. The world is waiting to be transformed.

All this necessarily makes for a book that is unfinished, imperfect, and full of words which, in this age of "relativity," may have different meanings for the author and the reader according to the camera that each focuses on them (his vision of the world). I have tried to write simply, with everyday words, but I have not always been successful; and in certain parts (Chapter 6 in particular) you may find "indigestible" passages. Furthermore, certain categories, such as the words "objective" and "subjective," may now be out of date. I have sometimes used them as convenient tools for making what I have to say more understandable to men who are not primarily concerned with language.

It is also possible that I have given certain words a meaning that is rather personal or a content that is difficult to grasp for anyone ignorant of certain historical facts or systems of thought, thus contradicting my first intent, which was to write a book that would be easy to "digest." (But sometimes the precise expression of what one means, thinks, or wants to make understood does not lend itself to simplification . . . although—another contradiction!—in places I have doubtless succumbed to the temptation to simplify.)

For that matter, you will surely find more than one contradiction in this book. At least, that is my impression. The "literary" and autobiographical pages will probably seem clearer to you—perhaps because of the acid in them—than the pages devoted to a partial definition of "our ideal" of an egalitarian social structure. Certain of my analyses may be disconcerting to some readers, just as certain positions that I take will no doubt be shocking to more than one discriminating mind.

But I think that the unity of the book and its "meaning" (in the phenomenological sense of the word, in the sense of "truth" or relative "essence"—relative both to the experiences, feelings, and ideas of the author and to those of the reader) lie precisely in this complexity of the writing, which is only a very awkward expression of the complexity of human behavior, individual and social, personal and collective. An expression, furthermore, peculiar to one man, restricted to a given number of experiences and acts, formulated by a mind which is, when all is said and done, limited, and conditioned by a milieu—Quebec—which has just leaped from the Middle Ages into the twentieth century.

I believe that the unity and meaning of any activity lie in its complexity and that they cannot exist, develop, and become complete outside the contradictions inherent in reality as we perceive it, reality as we live it, reality as we transform it according to the present, changing state of our knowledge and means of action, reality as to a great extent we also undergo it, under the influence of the forces of nature whose "secrets" we do not yet possess and which we are not yet able to control for purposes really our own.

Contemporary scientists are convinced that the physical and human universe (can one really separate *physical* from *human*?) of which we are a part and which, in each generation, is at a given but not fixed state of development, of evolution, is "essentially infinite." I do not know what meaning they give to the word "essentially." But in any event, if they are right, as I believe, in affirming that the universe is at once infinite and relative—which is fundamentally the same thing—and if, as they likewise affirm, our knowledge of reality can only be partial and must constantly be re-examined; if, finally, our action can only be *biased*, that means that our activities— whether in the domain of thought, of scientific research, or of political engagement—will always contain contradictions.

In other words, every new affirmation calls forth a new set of questions. Every scientific discovery gives rise to hypotheses that were hitherto unknown. Every political action calls forth a reaction ("reaction" being understood here as an effort to prevent man from becoming so identified with his creation or his revolution that he remains *fixed* at that point and becomes fossilized).

But none of this, as I say somewhere in this "rough draft," prevents men—us—from using practical, constantly modified affirmations and negations of the contradictions around us to *make* history, to evolve, ever more conscious and free, by means of "revolutions."

4. This book contains a considerable number of footnotes, some of which are of respectable length. These footnotes should be read *in their place*, that is, at the end of the sentence, expression, or paragraph where they are indicated by the usual numbers.

With a few changes, some of these footnotes could have been integrated into the text, if I had had the time and means to do three or four drafts. But under present conditions I am obliged to turn over to the reader a rough draft expanded here and there by explanatory notes.

5. I am neither a scholar nor an accredited philosopher. I am only a proletarian who has had the good fortune to read a great deal (but without method, since there was no money to buy method at a university) and who has also had the opportunity to act, who is acting and wants to go on acting. For whom it is enough to be honest with himself and to try, as best he can, to put his convictions into practice.

6. This autobiographical essay is a conscious witness and a con-

scious appeal that I have made freely and for the same reason that I have made my political choice, my choice of the revolution: the conviction that the relations between men must be radically transformed and that imperialism must be definitively overthrown if—in this age when biologists, biochemists, physicists, astronomers, and so on are on the verge of discovering the "mysteries" of matter both living and inert, conscious and unconscious, and therefore the "secrets" of life and death—if, I say, we do not want humanity, on the threshold of tremendous progress, to become, in spite of itself, the victim of a universal nuclear catastrophe which would turn it back to the stone age.

We must wrest the vast resources and gigantic possibilities of this century (which are due in large part to contemporary technological discoveries) from the grasp of the businessmen—the businessmen of state capitalism as well as the businessmen of private-corporation capitalism—by practical, revolutionary, and collective action.

Today, as in the time of Lenin, this action, which began as far back as the eighteenth century with the first rebellions of the English workers and the organization of the Chartist movement, must advance to new stages. It must do so not only in Quebec but in the entire world. For it must be recognized that with the present expansion of communications and of population movements, etc., which is based on the international organization of the market, of competition and class struggle, our true country is increasingly becoming the world. This, far from destroying nationalities and the individual, actually provides an opportunity, if we succeed in overcoming certain individual and collective fixations on outmoded "categories," of coming into our own, perhaps for the first time in history.

7. The author of this book is a Québécois, a French Canadian, a proletarian, a colonized man and a baptized son of the Church. Hence, an extremely frustrated individual for whom "freedom" is not a metaphysical question but a very concrete problem.

My consciousness and activity (what I sometimes call my responsibility) are bound up with my frustrations and my need to free myself from them completely, once and for all.

I believe that my experience of life has much in common with that of many individuals, both in Quebec and in other countries, in my own class and even in the upper classes, which are better off, richer economically and intellectually.

That is why I spontaneously chose to write an essay that would be at one and the same time an autobiography and an attempt to reflect upon and sum up acts which have already been performed and others yet to be performed, acts which concern you just as much as me.

8. I have no diplomas or medals. The one thing I take pride in is something I owe to the American police, who arrested me at the request of the Canadian police. By so doing, they in a way forced me—and my friend and comrade Charles Gagnon—to bear witness publicly to the determination, not only of a little nucleus of individuals but of the immense class of the oppressed (peasants, workers, students, young people, intellectuals, white-collar workers, and even scientists and researchers harnessed to the interests of big capital), to free their human activities definitively from the dictatorship of the "sharks of high finance."

The increasing number of letters that Charles and I receive offer us daily proof that we will not have borne witness in vain.

9. I take advantage of this foreword to give infinite thanks to all those (students, workers, journalists, militants in unions and popular movements, housewives, friends known and unknown) without whom this work would have rotted in the many garbage cans of the Manhattan House of Detention for Men into which, often enough, we throw the whole plate of dogfood they serve us at mealtime.

To me, as to Charles Gagnon, the disinterested devotion and uncalculating support of all these friends is material proof of the existence of human *solidarity*. Solidarity which will be the cement of the new classless society, as money is the cement of the present society based on the exploitation of man by man.

There is already a growing number of people for whom solidarity has replaced money as the "reason for living," as the principal "value" in life.

That is why I have chosen—that is why *we* have chosen—to work for the revolution.

As in the physical universe, so perhaps in the revolution there are neither straight lines nor curves. One can act in many ways, just as there are many ways of seeking and discovering the "secrets" of the universe. But there are constant *relations* among these many different ways of acting on the world and on society. And I have an increasingly clear impression that through these relations, which at first glance are difficult to grasp and comprehend because they are complex and integrated with a universe that is perpetually changing, we are approaching a unity unprecedented in known human history, a unity which will not be monolithic or subject to the hegemony of any one group. A unity which we will make concrete only through a long revolutionary struggle, collective and multinational, conducted by the majority of the men who people this planet: the peasants, workers, white-collar workers, students, young people, progressive intellectuals, and researchers.

It is this unity of *conscious, responsible* men, bound together in solidarity, that will create the new society humanity needs in order to progress. Yes, to progress, for this unity is not an end but a beginning, the first act of a new world, of a human history that will at last be determined by the majority of men.

10. Finally, this book, as is clearly indicated in the introduction which follows this long foreword (!), was conceived first of all in terms of the practical tasks which today confront the workers, students, and young revolutionaries of Quebec.

Nevertheless, perhaps it may also have something to say to the men and revolutionaries of other countries, colonized or even imperialist.

—*Pierre Vallières*

Manhattan House of Detention for Men
New York, fall-winter 1966–1967

By Way of Introduction

In writing this book I claim to do no more than bear witness to the determination of the workers of Quebec to put an end to three centuries of exploitation, of injustices borne in silence, of sacrifices accepted in vain, of insecurity endured with resignation; to bear witness to their new and increasingly energetic determination to take control of their economic, political, and social affairs and to transform into a more just and fraternal society this country, Quebec, which is theirs, this country where they have always been the overwhelming majority of citizens and producers of the "national" wealth, yet where they have never enjoyed the economic power and the political and social freedom to which their numbers and labor entitle them.

This book is the product both of day-to-day experiences in a given social milieu at a given time, and of a conscious political commitment which today seems to me irrevocable. My life experience has always been an integral part of a collective experience. Necessarily. And my political commitment also is an integral part of the awakening of the Québécois collectivity, more particularly of the working class. That is why this autobiographical account is also an account of the evolution of a whole social milieu. And that is why the ideas developed in this book reflect the evolution of the ideas of many men and many groups, an evolution that has in turn been brought about by the social transformations that have taken place in Quebec during these last years and which have been summed up in the expression "the quiet revolution."

This book is therefore not, strictly speaking, the product of an individual but of a milieu. The milieu is contemporary Quebec, but more especially Montreal and the metropolitan area. A man from the Gaspé would probably have written a quite different book.

This book is not perfect and does not pretend to be. Its observations are necessarily limited and incomplete. The ideas expressed lay no claim to the objectivity of a neutral person: they are biased and political. (It is often forgotten that in certain areas such as politics, "objectivity" too is an ideology—the ideology of the status quo.)

I mention men by name and I take sides concerning them. I denounce certain institutions highly respected in Quebec, and I have no pity or "understanding" for the Church and the ruling classes. But I do not seek controversy and I have not the slightest inclination to play the game of "impertinences," as the functionary Desbiens once did.° I describe the things I see, I note facts and draw simple conclusions from them, conclusions that are, so to speak, natural and that any unprejudiced man who is not compromised in the present system of exploitation can easily understand and remember if he observes the world around him, the world in which he moves and in which sooner or later he must determine his true place, take sides, and assume his responsibility.

Social responsibility is a virtue not often practiced in Quebec, even today. One does not hear much about it in sermons, lectures, and editorials. One hears only about order, social peace, and respect for laws. The social responsibility of the class presently in power is so missing from its order, its peace, and its laws that workers who demand the most elementary justice are forced to resort to physical violence to make themselves heard, merely *heard* (because of the noise they make) and not respected.

The ruling class has social responsibility only for its own interests. It doesn't give a damn about the 90 percent of the population who have nothing to say and no decisions to make in "their" democracy.

° This is an allusion to the great bestseller of the "quiet revolution," *Les Insolences du frère Untel* (*The Impertinences of Brother Anonymous*), by a teaching brother from north of Quebec. The author, who was later identified as Jean-Paul Desbiens, became an educational reformer in the civil service under the Liberal premier Jean Lesage. (Trans.)

The workers have already wasted too much time waiting for the "conversion" of those who have always robbed them and scoffed at them. The workers have already been deceived too many times by all the "pure" men of traditional politics, all the redeemers from the old parties, the René Lévesques, the Marcel Masses, and their kind.° The workers and all the clear-thinking people of Quebec must take *their* responsibilities in hand and stop relying on the Messiahs who are periodically thrown up by the system to fool the "ignorant." † Of course it isn't easy. There is a long and arduous road to travel. This book bears witness precisely to the efforts, the trials and errors we must be willing to go through in order to free ourselves from all the balls and chains that capitalist society attached to our feet as soon as we were born, chains which are sometimes so deeply embedded in our flesh that it is impossible to shake them off completely.

But determination can overcome anything at last, even the dictatorship of capitalism over the bodies and minds of the majority of Québécois. It is the responsibility of the workers of Quebec to learn to stand erect and to demand, to *take* what rightfully belongs to them. For it is abnormal, unjust, and inhuman that the economic and political power which governs the entire life of the workers should belong not to the workers themselves but to others, to parasites whose sole function, sole ambition, and sole interest is to accumulate unlimited profits out of the labor, the energy, the sweat, the life of the majority of citizens.

The true reason for the insecurity of the workers is not that their wages are inadequate, that jobs are scarce, or that they are ignorant; it is essentially that they have no control over economic and social policy. That is what the workers of Quebec have to get through their heads, as the saying goes. Because otherwise they will continue to remain for generations the "white niggers of America," the cheap labor that the predators of industry, commerce, and high finance are so fond of, the way wolves are fond of sheep.

° René Lévesque is the leader of the centrist, pro-independence Parti québécois and a former minister in the Liberal Party government. Marcel Masse was Minister of Inter-Governmental Affairs in the National Union government. (Trans.)

† This is an allusion to a remark by Jean Lesage, Quebec premier, who made the mistake of replying to a reporter who asked if he intended to hold a plebiscite on the Constitution: "How are you going to explain that to the ignorant?" (Trans.)

Let us kill Saint John the Baptist! ° Let us burn the papier-mâché traditions with which they have tried to build a myth around our slavery. Let us learn the pride of being men. Let us vigorously declare our independence. And with our hardy freedom, let us crush the sympathetic or contemptuous paternalism of the politicians, the daddy-bosses and the preachers of defeat and submission. It is no longer time for sterile recriminations but for action. There will be no miracles, but there will be war.

° John the Baptist is the patron saint of French Canada, and in the folklore Jean-Baptiste is the old, traditional first name for a French Canadian. In many cities and villages there is a parade every year on his feast day, June 24. In the 1969 parade in Montreal, demonstrators tore the papier-mâché figure of St. John from its pedestal and hacked it up. (Trans.)

1
The White Niggers of America

To be a "nigger" in America is to be not a man but someone's slave. For the rich white man of Yankee America, the nigger is a sub-man. Even the poor whites consider the nigger their inferior. They say: "to work as hard as a nigger," "to smell like a nigger," "as dangerous as a nigger," "as ignorant as a nigger." Very often they do not even suspect that they too are niggers, slaves, "white niggers." White racism hides the reality from them by giving them the opportunity to despise an inferior, to crush him mentally or to pity him. But the poor whites who despise the black man are doubly niggers, for they are victims of one more form of alienation—racism—which far from liberating them, imprisons them in a net of hate or paralyzes them in fear of one day having to confront the black man in a civil war.

In Quebec the French Canadians are not subject to this irrational racism that has done so much wrong to the workers, white and black, of the United States. They can take no credit for that, since in Quebec there is no "black problem." The liberation struggle launched by the American blacks nevertheless arouses growing interest among the French-Canadian population, for the workers of Quebec are aware of their condition as niggers, exploited men, second-class citizens. Have they not been, ever since the establishment of New France in the seventeenth century, the servants of the imperialists, the white niggers of America? Were they not *imported*, like the American blacks, to serve as cheap labor in the New World? The only difference between them is the color of their skin and the continent they came from. After three centuries their condition remains the same. They still constitute a reservoir of cheap labor whom the capitalists are completely free to put to work or reduce to unemployment, as it suits their financial interests, whom they are completely free to underpay, mistreat and trample underfoot, whom they are completely free, according to law, to have clubbed down by the police and locked up by the judges "in the public interest," when their profits seem to be in danger.

1

Our ancestors came here with the hope of beginning a new life. They were for the most part soldiers or day laborers. The soldiers came, a long time after Champlain, to fight the English, and they remained in New France because they did not have the money to return to the metropolitan country. They became traders, artisans, or *coureurs de bois* in order to subsist. The others came as "volunteers," especially under the Talon administration, about a century before the English conquest. They were unskilled laborers who could find no work in Colbert's France and no reason for living. They belonged to the growing number of idle men and vagabonds who filled the towns of mercantile France. In Talon's mind, these "volunteers" were to be added to the unemployed to serve as a permanent local source of labor. Married by force, as soon as they arrived in New France, to orphan girls imported from Paris, the "volunteers" were given the task of laying the foundations of an independent society. They were to work at building an indigenous industry and developing agriculture, and they were to have as many children as possible in order to rapidly expand the labor force and the market. Those who refused to obey the directives of the intendant were put in prison or sent back to France. Many colonists preferred to become *coureurs de bois* rather than be forced to marry a woman whom they did not know and often did not want because she was ill-tempered, homely, or stupid.

The colonists, or Habitants as they later came to be called, were thus placed at the service of the ambitious projects of Colbert's protégé. But these men, who were sent from France by the hundreds, had learned no trade in the metropolitan country. They possessed no technical knowledge and had nothing to offer Talon but their muscle, good will, and taste for adventure. In the mother country they belonged to that mass of unemployed workers whom the development of manufacturing, the concentration of capital in the towns, and overpopulation had driven out of the rural areas and reduced to idleness and vagrancy. In the towns of France they constituted that increasingly large and threatening class of pariahs who could find no other way to survive than to turn to highway robbery. The king had outlawed brigands and vagabonds, but the only result of the law was to send a considerable number of innocent men to prison or to death, because the state, whose revenues were devoted to financing incessant wars and the splendor of the court, was unable to provide work for the growing number of the starving. The ruling classes had three ways of getting rid of this cumbersome burden: the army, prison, or the colonies. Tens of thousands of these "paupers"—as the aristocrats called them—were therefore sent to the battlefields of Europe, America, Asia, and the Middle East. Tens of thousands more died in prison, had their throats cut, were hanged or decapitated. The rest were abandoned to their fate or exported like cattle to the colonies, where they were to serve as labor or cannon fodder. When the prisons of the metropolitan country were filled to overflowing and the people were growing a little too restless, the "hotheads" were often exiled to the colonies instead of being hanged: it was more humane. Periodically the strongest prisoners were "freed" to be turned into mercenaries or "colonists." The same policy was applied by the English ruling classes, especially with regard to the Irish and Scotch *bastards* (English *dixit*). Furthermore, France and England were then engaged in an unrestricted and lucrative trade in black slaves. The pirates (the gangsters of those days) made fortunes by assisting the ruling classes of Europe in their work of "civilizing" and "evangelizing"!

Talon had little success in endowing the colony with an independent economy. He lacked not only qualified labor but capital. The French merchants were not in the least interested in sacrificing their monopoly in order to develop an independent economy which would sooner or later be prejudicial to the interests of the metropolitan country—that is, which would increasingly restrict their freedom of trade and their profits. For these merchants, colonization in the sense in which Talon understood it did not deserve to be encouraged. New France was to remain a trading post, a source of raw materials and profits for France. The theocracy Bishop Laval was trying to estab-

lish, Talon's industries, and the rapid increase in the number of immigrants irritated them. The money "swallowed up" in colonization
and evangelization brought no returns to France. And all the "volunteers" who were taking root in New France appeared to them as so
many potential rivals and enemies. Decidedly, this Talon had become their chief enemy. They demanded that the king recall him to
France. Which was done in 1672.

No intendant dared pursue Talon's work. The "volunteers," desti-
tute, disappointed, prisoners of their poverty, resigned themselves to
clearing an ungrateful soil on the seigneuries granted by the king of
France; they had to become hunters, fishermen, and woodsmen in
order to feed their numerous children. In 1689 there were 10,000
French Canadians in New France.[1]

The fur trade was monopolized by a few French merchants—"the
French of France," as they were already beginning to be called by
the Habitants, who hated them. All the profits went back to the metropolitan country. The little money (many times devalued) that remained in the colony was concentrated in the hands of a minority of
speculators. The people lived in the most extreme poverty, under the
amused eyes of the François Bigots of the administration. Sometimes
the Habitants were called to the colors to defend the American pos-
sessions of the king of France, while their women cleared the land
and tended to the sowing and harvesting, raising their broods at the
same time. At times, alone or in groups, these women even had to
arm themselves with rifles to confront the Iroquois guerrillas, while
far away their husbands were fighting the English in the name of the
king.

With each war reinforcements arrived from France. And after
each treaty, the penniless demobilized soldiers stayed to swell the
ranks of the Habitants, marrying their daughters and perpetuating
their rough existence. Only a few officers had the signal honor of
being admitted to the society of the nobles.

Soon the seigneuries were overpopulated. Abandoned by the seigneurs, who were more interested in speculation and trade than in agriculture, the land deteriorated and the misery of the Habitants became unendurable. A great many of them abandoned their fields,
cursing God for having led them to this country of forests, rocks, and

water where man wore himself out in vain trying to build a life consistent with his dreams of freedom, happiness, and peace.[2]

The towns of the colony, like those of the metropolitan country,
overflowed with idle, hungry men. A few years before the English
conquest, the "hunger riots" broke out nearly everywhere; Bigot replied with an edict ordering all the unemployed to return to their
land. "Take your hunger off our hands," Bigot said to them. "We
don't know what to do with it. Instead of idling away your time in
the towns and stinking up the place with your poverty, go cultivate
the land, work harder. There is no work for you here. But all the land
belongs to you. Go where you please!" But the Habitants could not
work miracles and change rocks into arable land. Besides, all the land
did not belong to them, as Bigot claimed. The best land had long
been reserved for the handful of merchants and nobles who had obtained control of the wheat trade.[3] The riots broke out again worse
than ever, and even under the intendancy of the saintly Hocquart,
the Habitants became more and more of a threat.

The last war between England and France, which was to give
New France to the English, made it possible for the ruling class to
enroll the rioters in the French king's army. Many Habitants died in
combat, and once the war was over, the people, exhausted, again
withdrew to the seigneuries.

The English merchants took over from the French merchants who,
before surrendering the colony to the English, had had time to effect
some profitable sales of arms. The conquerors had no difficulty in
gaining the collaboration of the clergy and those impoverished seigneurs who had remained in the colony despite the defeat. Together
they divided up the power: the English monopolized economic
affairs and the executive power, the clergy continued to control education and collect the tithe, the seigneurs retained ownership of their
land and obtained the right to hold certain administrative posts.
Nothing changed in the frugal and monotonous life of the Habitants.
They were still beasts of burden, despised in a hostile country. But,
God be praised, the clergy received the order from Heaven to make
this resigned and silent collectivity into a nation dedicated to the
Church. At last the life of slavery would take on meaning by becoming redemption. This people, planted in America by an accident of

history, suddenly found itself invested with a supernatural vocation. Its task, in the pagan world of the savages and the English, would be to save souls by patiently bearing poverty, hard labor, and isolation. The clergy organized the embryonic nation into parishes, created elementary schools and *collèges*, arrogated to itself the right to regulate the lives of individuals and groups, and defined the ideology which was to fashion a vision of the world consistent with the interests of the Church. The higher clergy became the true ruling class, while every day the self-complacent nobility sank a little further into decay.

The population continued to increase at a very rapid rate. The land, which was already inadequate and impoverished, became less productive and more overpopulated. The young people left the countryside to try their luck in town, where the number of unemployed was constantly growing. In the meantime, in its classical *collèges* the clergy was educating an indigenous petty bourgeoisie, composed mainly of lawyers, notaries, doctors, and journalists. Toward the end of the eighteenth century, this petty bourgeoisie began to develop its own class consciousness and, in the name of the nation, set itself up in opposition to the clergy, the decadent aristocracy, and the English. By establishing a Legislative Assembly for Lower Canada (Quebec), England gave the petty bourgeoisie a forum which it used to the fullest to identify its class interests with those of "the people" as a whole. After a few years of apprenticeship, the French-Canadian politicians entered into open rebellion against the masters of the economy, the English, and their allies, the higher clergy and the seigneurs. The Habitants, who had been completely dispossessed, were hypnotized by the fiery Patriots and, despite the opposition of the higher clergy, demonstrated with increasing violence their will to overthrow the ruling classes. Papineau, more than any other man, inflamed the imagination of the Habitants and became almost a god to them. Nevertheless, some of the Habitants who were skeptical or discouraged were already beginning to set out for exile, seeking a more hospitable land. In 1820 there began an exodus of French-Canadian families to the United States. This exodus was to last a century.

French-Canadian Christendom was suddenly transformed into a vast insurrection, which was just as frightening to the Church as to the conquerors of 1760. The French-Canadian population of Lower

Canada had reached 500,000 and was growing rapidly. For many months unrest had been spreading across the country.[4] In 1837 and 1838 the people rose up without asking permission from their Leader. The Leader, Papineau, fled with his chief associates to the United States. The Habitants had to confront the English soldiers alone and practically unarmed. After having met the savage counteroffensive of the English with heroic and desperate resistance, they were crushed and massacred.

The Patriots, the petty bourgeois led by Papineau, had not wanted a popular revolution. In mobilizing the people they had only sought to bring pressure on the English in order to obtain for themselves, for their class—and not for the Habitants—a new division of power which would bring them certain additional revenues and a greater share in the economic advantages of the system. Thus, they demanded control of the trade in wheat and domestic consumer goods in Lower Canada. They wanted to participate in the financial activities which had up to that time been reserved for the English and to take back from them the rights which they declared had long been their due. But they did not want to overturn the system or to drive the English out. They demanded nothing more than a redistribution of privileges between themselves and the English. They wanted the victors of 1760 to recognize them as the ruling class and to admit them as equal partners within the same political institutions, the same economic system, and the same social organization. The discontent of the Habitants had only been exploited as a means of applying pressure. The people, taken in by Papineau's eloquence and driven to desperation by their economic difficulties, had let themselves be "had."

The popular revolution took the Patriots by surprise. It upset their plans. For now the English were justified, from a capitalist point of view, in granting no concessions to the French Canadians. Worse yet, the English still had the support of the clergy, who everywhere began to preach obedience to the established authority and submission to the "just punishment" which had been brought upon the people by the Patriots' rationalism, atheism, and spirit of revolt!

The defeats of 1837–1838, the defection of Papineau, and the many sentences of excommunication handed down by the upper clergy struck a hard blow to the hopes of the Habitants, who, like their ancestors, took refuge in bitterness and resignation to "God's will." The exodus of French Canadians to the United States increased.

For the petty bourgeoisie, once the English hysteria in response to the rebellion had passed, the defeat was quickly turned into a new compromise. The popular rising had alarmed those of the English who understood what was happening. They decided the time had come to integrate the petty bourgeoisie into their system of class collaboration and to meet some of the Patriots' demands. Lafontaine and Baldwin were the instruments of this compromise. The French-Canadian petty bourgeoisie renounced Voltaire the way Christians renounce Satan "and all his works and pomps," and became reconciled with the higher clergy. Even Papineau made honorable amends before being officially rehabilitated and becoming the seigneur of Montebello (a fine career as a revolutionary!). England granted Quebec and Ontario "responsible government," and a few years after the rebellion the French-Canadian petty bourgeois, with few exceptions, were only too happy to be paternally invited by London to play at being statesmen and to become "English." But affairs remained under the exclusive control of the British.

Since 1760 the British and their English-Canadian agents had monopolized the trade in furs and wheat and had been the sole beneficiaries of the sale of English products on the Canadian market (Ontario and Quebec), as well as of the export of Canadian raw materials (furs, lumber, wheat) to England, via the ports of Quebec. These capitalists, anxious to preserve the social peace that had been regained, began to buy the services of a few Québécois lawyers and by giving them prestigious posts, to co-opt them into their companies and into the political parties whose "machines" they had controlled from the beginning. So it was that after the departure of Lafontaine, Georges-Etienne Cartier became a dominant figure, both as solicitor for the Grand Trunk Railway, the most powerful financial institution in the country (controlled by British interests), and as "national" leader of the Tory party. The Grand Trunk used him as chief propagandist for the projected confederation, which was to be approved by London in 1867.[5]

The petty bourgeois had managed to come out all right, but the working class of Quebec was none the better for that. The clergy began to worry about the exodus of French Canadians to the United States. The petty bourgeoisie, which often controlled trade in the countryside, was also growing nervous. If the rural areas continued to be depopulated, to be drained of their youngest and most dynamic elements, would not the clergy and the petty bourgeoisie lose the base of their power and profits? Montreal was then a city more English than French, and in the eyes of the French-Canadian élite, the rural milieu represented the *true* nation, the *true* people. But if the people refused to live in this rural milieu, would not "the nation" (that is, the petty bourgeoisie and the clergy) sooner or later disappear? What would become of the Church and small, family industry?

It was then that the instinct of self-preservation inspired the clergy and the petty bourgeoisie with the ideology of a "return to the land" and the "colonization" of the vast undeveloped regions of Quebec. This unexpected find was welcomed by the English Canadians and by the French-Canadian bourgeoisie of the towns, who saw it as the most practical and economical means of solving the problem of urban unemployment created by the rural exodus. Business circles and the government hastened to finance the colonization projects, and a whole literature began to circulate inviting the French Canadians to remember their "glorious" past, deliberately falsifying history so as to idealize the life of the Habitants under the French regime, making the words "rural," "Catholic," and "French" synonymous and preaching the crusade of a "return to the land" as the sole solution to the grave social problems of the French-Canadian nation.

Thousands of unemployed were despatched with their families to Saguenay–Lake St. John, to the Laurentians, to Upper St. Maurice Valley, to certain remote corners of the Eastern Townships, to the Portneuf region, and to the interior of the Gaspé peninsula. Later, colonization was to extend to Abitibi and northern Ontario. The colonists were given plots of land to clear without anyone's bothering to find out if the land could really be cultivated. Some colonists were lucky enough to be granted land of excellent quality. But the majority of these "pioneers" were innocent victims of the stupidest, most antisocial, most inhuman enterprise conceivable. Only a clergy and a petty bourgeoisie as backward as ours could have dreamed up and carried out such a "reform." For decade after decade, hundreds of thousands of Québécois, left to themselves, were to wear themselves out like convicts trying to convert acres of rocks into productive, profitable farms. The miracle never took place. And the result of colonization was even greater misery than any the French-Canadian workers had known until then. But listening to the curés' preaching, we could console ourselves with the divine thought that so much suffering could not fail to win us entrance into Heaven. Were we not on earth to expiate our sins and to "earn" a place in paradise? This absurd philosophy was again presented to the people as the essence of the most perfect happiness. Does the history of mankind offer other examples of collective masochism as tenacious as the Catholic religion of Quebec?

While the French Canadians toiled in pain and anxiety and expiated sins whose exact nature they did not know, the businessmen of Montreal and Toronto, with the advice and support of the businessmen of London, were organizing the infrastructure that would enable them to grow rich. The compromises which Lafontaine and Cartier had reached with the English millionaires had left the Habitants totally indifferent. Since the insurrections of 1837–1838, they had only contempt for professional politicians. The politicians did not dare to stir up the indifference of the masses by submitting the plan for confederation to the popular verdict. The Confederation was established the way a law is passed in the House, in complete disregard of public opinion.

The Confederation of 1867 institutionalized the domination of business over Canadian economic, political, and social life as a whole, "coast to coast." Today we know the real motives that guided the Fathers of the Confederation and the economic considerations hidden behind the sentimental speeches about the unity of the two "founding races" of Canada. The Canadian Confederation was nothing more than a vast financial transaction carried out by the bourgeoisie at the expense of the workers of the country, and more especially the workers of Quebec. At the time the Confederation was established, the railroad companies, which had invested large amounts of capital and were finding it very difficult to meet the competition of the American lines, were on the brink of bankruptcy. The Montreal businessmen were afraid of losing their monopoly on the trade between England and Canada, a large part of which was beginning to pass by way of New York rather than Montreal. Since railroads were considered at the time as the principal economic agents of progress, the Montreal businessmen concluded that as much capital as possible must be invested in the construction of a railroad which would link the Atlantic to the Pacific, Toronto to New York and Quebec via Montreal, and the west to the commercial capital of Canada—Montreal. In order to reduce the risks of private enterprise, they decided that this money should be taken from the state coffers; that is, from the pockets of the taxpayers, from the greatest possible number of citizens. As the heads of the Canadian government, Cartier and Galt in particular, were also administrators of the Grand Trunk, the most important of the railroad companies, the operation was relatively easy to carry out on the legal level. The Maritime Provinces (with the exception of Newfoundland), Quebec, and Ontario were inundated with romantic speeches about "Canadian" unity and the prosperity that this unity could not fail to bring to the "privileged" inhabitants of the vast country.

Once Confederation had been voted by the House and approved by London, in complete disregard of popular opinion, Quebec, which thirty years earlier under the influence of the Patriots had dreamed of becoming a republic, was *de facto* turned—by the disciples of those same Patriots—into a minority within the fictitious bicultural and bilingual "Canadian nation." Quebec patched together a government from the few jurisdictions left to the provinces, in the fields of education, social security, and natural resources (hardly developed at the time). The federal government retained control of currency, banking, commerce, customs, immigration, foreign policy, etc., and applied from the beginning a policy of centralization that worked to the advantage of the financial circles concentrated in Montreal and Toronto. The capital that was gathered together by uniting the provinces was invested in the private railroad companies, which thereupon experienced unprecedented expansion. The Confederation was no sooner born than it set off down the road toward its first bankruptcy, its first economic crisis, for which the workers would, as always, pay the bill.

Already in 1840, the Anglo-Saxons, who possess a keen sense of their own interests, had taken advantage of the climate of hysteria generated by the French-Canadian rebellion to proclaim a provisional union of the two Canadas (Ontario and Quebec) and to merge

.the debts of the two provinces. Quebec (which had a larger population and no debts, since the ruling classes had invested nothing in the development of an infrastructure) was thus made to pay for the considerable deficit created by the construction of many costly canals in the Ontario of the Loyalists.[6] In 1867 the Confederation effected a similar merger, in more attractive guise. Quebec and the Maritime Provinces were made to serve the economic interests of the Anglo-Saxon bourgeoisie of Montreal and especially of Ontario. Once this conquest was complete, the Fathers of the Confederation undertook to annex the west. The railroad, accompanied by the army, conquered each of the western provinces and bloodily crushed the least signs of resistance on the part of the local populations, in particular the Metis (a people formed by the intermarriage of Indians and French Canadians from Quebec). The result of crushing the Metis was to unify all classes in Quebec against the Confederation, the central power, and English Canada only a few years after the provinces had been united. The Québécois turned to their own state, the State of Quebec, and tried to make the best of their forced annexation to the rest of Canada. The federal government, for its part, granted them subsidies in order to avoid a resurgence of nationalism. The premiers of Quebec, in particular Honoré Mercier, cultivated this nationalism and turned it into an instrument of blackmail, to the profound irritation of the federal government. Daniel Johnson, like Lesage and Duplessis, is only doing what Mercier did.

But French-Canadian nationalism did not necessarily provide a living. The petty bourgeoisie, of course, turned it to good account (while at the same time making deals with the English Canadians and the Americans behind the people's back). But the condition of the workers hardly improved, even if Honoré Mercier did his best to make them believe in the greatness of their "mission" as Frenchmen and Catholics in North America. An estimated 700,000 French-Canadian workers were forced into exile between 1820 and the end of the First World War. For the people do not readily resign themselves to dying of hunger . . . even out of patriotism! Today the descendants of these Habitants are to be found in Louisiana, New England, New Brunswick, Ontario, Manitoba, and even British Columbia. (Even now, in the period of the "quiet revolution" and Expo 67,

Québécois workers are abandoning their homeland to go chop pines in British Columbia or bury themselves alive in the mines of northern Ontario and Manitoba: a sure sign that, since the time of Honoré Mercier, the petty-bourgeois nationalists of the State of Quebec have still not found solutions to the agonizing problems of the French-Canadian working class. The workers of Quebec are fed up with speeches, flags, hymns, and parades. They want to have their own industries, control over the sale and consumption of their products, political power and economic security, the privilege of studying and sharing in the discoveries of science, etc. They no longer want to sit like beggars on either side of Sherbrooke Street every June 24 to behold, with joy befitting the occasion, the allegorical floats of an artificial "national pride" bought on credit at Household or Niagara Finance. The people are going to rise to their feet, parade in the streets themselves, and make of this country something other than a medieval masquerade organized by grocers who can scarcely see beyond the borders of their own parish.)

If Confederation made no immediate change in the traditional life of the people of Quebec, "rural, Catholic, and French," it did create the economic and political conditions for the invasion of Quebec and the rest of Canada by the American entrepreneurs and financiers. Preparations for the "real" conquest were being made in the polished offices of the executive boards in New York, which were in continual contact with London and in whose service a whole army of lackeys, in Toronto, Montreal, Quebec City, and Halifax, were working feverishly and spending millions to buy local politicians and businessmen and, with the complicity of the bishops and journalists, to lull the masses to sleep. Already the British imperialists controlled a large sector of the Canadian economy. But every year the United States was taking a bigger slice of their powers and privileges. The progressive transfer of financial, industrial, commercial, and political hegemony to the Americans could not be effected without provoking crises and liberating (for the time being at least) new, independent energies which were under the illusion that they could compete with imperialism. That is why, in order to avoid clashes that would be pointless (between capitalists) and politically dangerous (they might set the stage for popular revolts) the English and American businessmen engaged in a gigantic underground bargaining operation of which the people, and sometimes even the majority of politicians, unaware of the economic reality, were totally ignorant.

Leaving the imperialists to silently invade the country, Honoré Mercier, for example, converted "colonization" into a policy of national salvation and, with the help of the clergy, made the "return to the land" into a veritable mystical epic. This absurd nationalism was dubbed a "Christian miracle," and the misery of the people was sprinkled with holy water. Shanties were decorated with dried palm leaves, effeminate Sacred Hearts, and bloodless Virgins. "Blessed are the poor, for theirs is the kingdom of Heaven." The religion of degradation, of the vicious circle, of unremitting sacrifice and resignation to misfortune became "The Imitation of Jesus Christ." But the forces of life were not to be so easily gainsaid by the requirements of atoning for sin and saving souls from Purgatory.

Even in this society dedicated, in spite of itself, to the interests of the Holy Church of God and of His poor servants—cardinals, bishops, and canons—men were still men, basic needs were still basic needs, and money was still a vital necessity. For the bakeries, hardware stores, groceries, and clothing stores, the doctors, lawyers, notaries, and merchants of grain, hens, and livestock did not fatten their bank accounts on indulgences. Even the curés liked to collect the tithe—in hard cash! Because it took a lot of money to build cathedrals and presbyteries—those lowly houses of God—out of Italian marble! So you always had to get more money, by working if possible. Or by stealing from others. Or finally, in desperation, by giving yourself up to the money-lenders of every village and county, who asked nothing better than to "get you out of the hole," the better to take the shirt off your back.

Thus, while God looked on amused, a new social category became more important every day: the money-lenders. These "realistic" Christians (who would have made excellent Calvinists) placed in circulation the money that was to enable the petty bourgeoisie (professionals, tradesmen, and clergymen) to prosper during the end of the nineteenth century, which marked the high point of our collective misery, our virtues (the virtues of baptized slaves), and our impotence, sublimated by Catholicism. The French-Canadian petty bourgeoisie (doubtless less Christian than we, the blessed poor) took full

advantage of our docility, first by developing trade in everyday consumer goods, especially in the countryside, and later by creating
those thousands of small, family manufacturing enterprises which are
so justly celebrated for the low wages they have always paid and still
pay—in the name of patriotism.

Toward the end of the nineteenth century, the English, American,
and Canadian capitalists became aware of all the advantages and
profits to be drawn from Christian Quebec.

Already, in order to build their railroads, they had begun buying
up a number of seigneuries and driving the farmers out. Shortly
thereafter they demanded the abolition of the seigneurial regime,
which restricted their freedom to build roads, speculate in real es-
tate, and exploit the rich forests of Quebec for export. It will be remembered that at that time the English forests had been devastated
and the British demand for lumber was constantly growing. They immediately obtained satisfaction, despite the opposition of certain
French-Canadian seigneurs, including the "revolutionary" Louis-
Joseph Papineau, then seigneur of Montebello!

Seeing the abundance of cheap labor standing idle in the towns,
suburbs, and even remotest "colonies," businessmen said to themselves that they must take advantage of all these hands begging for
work and use them to exploit cheaply Quebec's vast resources in tim-
ber, minerals, and hydraulic power; and at the same time to develop
in Quebec certain industries based on the exploitation of cheap
labor, such as the textile industry, which was flourishing at the time.
In this way they could create and develop, with a minimum of expense and a maximum of profitability, a "Québécois" economy that
would complement the dominant economies of the end of the nineteenth century, those of Great Britain and the United States.

After buying up the best land, these capitalists obtained broad
lumbering and mining concessions from the provincial government.
And almost for nothing. The sawmills multiplied. The forests were
devastated in record time. Thousands of "colonists" became lumber-
jacks. Little by little the lumber industry reached out to every region
of Quebec, and the great majority of farmers began to sell their labor
to the lumber companies, at least for several months of the year. The
French Canadians, peasants in spite of themselves, became "a people
of hewers of wood and drawers of water." The textile industry began

to develop in turn, particularly in the Montreal region and in the Eastern Townships. A whole army of workers—men, women, young people—were turned into slaves of the spinning jennies and looms in factories where there was neither light nor air nor safety. Wages were low, accidents frequent, diseases numerous and sometimes fatal. (These conditions have not changed.) Finally, at the beginning of the twentieth century, asbestos began to be mined in the Eastern Townships, and gold, copper, and zinc in Abitibi; hydraulic resources were exploited for the manufacture of newsprint on the St. Maurice and of aluminum ingots in Saguenay–Lake St. John.

The proletarianization of the "rural, Catholic, and French" French Canadians and the urbanization of medieval Quebec became irreversible. The "return to the city" needed no propagandists; it happened of its own accord, like any natural phenomenon.

While continuing to preach "return to the land," "buy at home," and the "call of the race," the clergy and the petty bourgeoisie were taking advantage of the industrialization of Quebec, particularly in the region around Montreal where a considerable number of industries were being installed, close to the financial and commercial institutions, communications, and the headquarters of the masters of the economy (most of them foreigners). The petty bourgeois paid court to the Anglo-Saxon businessmen and, on the periphery of the fiefs reserved for the bigshots of imperialism, began to establish hundreds of small, family industries for the manufacture of products for domestic consumption: furniture, clothing, shoes, candles, food and drink. (Later, around 1920, they would secure additional revenue by taking control of the food, dairy, and loan cooperatives, and especially of the cooperative credit unions.) Around the turn of the century a few French Canadians launched out into big industry: railroads (Sénécal), lumber (Dubuc), textiles (Hudon), wholesale trade (Paquet). But their rise was as short-lived as it was rapid. They were unable to resist the formidable American financial offensive launched at the beginning of the twentieth century and not yet ended.

In fact, a number of Americans had already undertaken the economic conquest of Quebec in the middle of the nineteenth century, without being too sure whether they should rely on British imperialism, which was still very powerful, or on the new American imperialism, which was much more dynamic. These "knights of industry," these adventurers of the dollar, had neither patriotism nor "national interests." They had only class interests and all they cared about was their own fortunes. Capital was at one and the same time their religion, their politics, and their reason for living. Their language was the language of business. Their empire was the world market of capital and goods produced by an anonymous mass of cheap labor for which they had only contempt. They manufactured Law, Justice, Democracy, and the Rights of Man from day to day, as these served the unlimited growth of their investments and profits. Their great ambition was to take possession of the world in the name of the Dollar, which God gave to businessmen so that (along with the Pope and the Archbishop of Canterbury) they might worship Him, love Him, and serve Him in the gilded basilicas, abbeys, and cathedrals of the Church of poor little Jesus.

These American Christians, who constantly invoked the name of God in their apologias of capitalism, made friends with the higher clergy of Quebec and the heads of the Quebec government just as quickly as with the financial circles of Montreal. Religious communities were invited to join them and invest in banks, commerce, and industry. (It was at this time that the Montreal clergy began to demand that Rome give them a cardinal, who, with the prestige and financial powers attached to his rank, would be in a position to promote the interests of the Church by negotiating the most advantageous transactions possible. All that, of course, for the propagation of the Faith: in China, the Congo, and Peru. Still, it cannot be said that the Vatican bureaucracy hastened to give satisfaction to the tonsured bourgeois of the Canadian See!)

From the time they arrived in Canada, the Americans, who came from New York, Pennsylvania, or the New England states, practiced a "double allegiance" to English capitalism and American capitalism, waiting to see which country would in the end eliminate the other in the frantic competition they were carrying on as they multiplied agreements, understandings, and treaties on matters of "common interest." These great entrepreneurs—who were often men of genius in their specialty—gave a vigorous stimulus to the exploitation of Quebec's natural resources, took control of the most profitable sectors of the infant French-Canadian industry, and soon bought the allegiance of almost all the premiers of Quebec who came after the nationalist Honoré Mercier and of most of the prime ministers of Canada, starting with the French-Canadian "Sir" Wilfred Laurier. At the end of the nineteenth century, they were convinced that England would continue to lose ground and that in a few years the United States would be master of the world—which the evolution of imperialism in the twentieth century was to confirm.

The Americans encountered no opposition within the Quebec government, no matter which party was in power. Nearly all the successive premiers of Quebec were invited to sit on the executive boards of one or another of their enterprises. The electoral machines of the two traditional parties were also well provided for, and the business circles got on as well with the "reds" as with the "blues."

At the federal level, the Americans rapidly took control of the Liberal Party, while *"les British,"* who had a sentimental attachment to the English Crown and managed British interests in Canada, had the Conservative Party well in hand. The struggles between the two parties only reflected the extension to Canada of the competition between English and American imperialism for control of the world market. But while Great Britain increasingly alienated public opinion by its openly imperialist and racist policy, its colonial wars (such as the Boer War), its ridiculous attachment to the gilded remains of a sanctimonious and conservative monarchy, its contempt for the French Canadians and for "colored" peoples, its hypocritical and inflexible legalism and so on, the United States, equally racist, imperialistic, and hypocritical—but more intelligent and wily—quietly effected the economic and, I might say, the "spiritual" conquest of Canada, especially Quebec and Ontario.

The French-Canadian petty bourgeoisie, in particular the "thinking" élite, ignorant of economic and social reality, of its origin, its historical development, and the direction of its evolution, and perceiving the world through the *idées fixes* of an immutable system, as in the Middle Ages, spoke to the people in a language that did not correspond in the least with the reality of the daily life of the worker. Henri Bourassa and his disciples were still talking about "return to the land" and "Canadian independence" vis-à-vis Great Britain at a time when the urbanization of Quebec was an irreversible phenomenon and the Americans were taking control of the economic activity and even the politics of Quebec. The tutelage legally exercised over

Canada by London was now only symbolic. The Dominion of Canada, already shaky, was changing into an economic colony of Yankee America. And within this vast colony, Quebec was no longer anything but the poor appendage of a foreign economy.

Bourassa's speeches were of no use to anyone except the small-minded petty bourgeois for whom attachment to the values of the past meant the subjugation of the people to their own narrow economic interests.

It is thanks to this parochial mentality that the French-Canadian petty bourgeoisie was not completely swept away by the economic offensive of the Americans in the twentieth century. Supported by one of the most powerful clergies in the world, this class of professionals, small industrialists, small tradesmen, and small financiers has succeeded in preserving and even strengthening its role as an intermediary between the people, on the one hand, and, on the other, the foreigners who hold the economic power and the English-Canadian bourgeois who control federal politics. The provincial state was (and still is) its licensed instrument of domination and betrayal, a means of perpetually bargaining over the collective wealth and auctioning it off, an enterprise for hoodwinking the masses and debasing the whole political life of Quebec. For the last hundred years the State of Quebec has been nothing more than the legal form of the dictatorship of the most reactionary strata of the French-Canadian petty bourgeoisie—and their silent partners of the Rue Saint-Jacques—over the vast majority of the population of Quebec, for whom the sole political activity permitted by the system is the famous "right to vote," the absurd freedom to choose which of two, three, five, or eight thieves will be granted the privilege of exploiting the masses!

The industrial revolution of the beginning of the century radically changed the way of life of the Québécois, or rather it urbanized and modernized their three-centuries-old slavery. The population became concentrated in the cities which, with the exception of Montreal, were—and still are—only huge underindustrialized villages, poor and without a future. Montreal rapidly became the center of attraction for the "hewers of wood and drawers of water." Many found work there and a little security, but Montreal alone could not absorb all the unemployed and poor of Quebec. Already in 1920 the proportion of unemployed in Montreal was steadily rising. And when the crisis of 1929 broke, the unemployed and the poor of the big city experienced a misery even more terrible than that of the countryside. Social agitation expanded with the depression of the thirties. The union movement made enormous progress, and socialism began to recruit sympathizers and propagandists in Montreal. Strikes and demonstrations of discontent multiplied. In 1937 riots broke out in Sorel, leaving dead and wounded. The port of Montreal was more than once transformed into a battlefield, and the textile workers rose up against their exploiters. Finally, when the second "conscription crisis" broke out during the war, insurrections occurred all over, and Quebec experienced the beginning of a popular revolution.[7] Already, during the First World War, the draft had provoked violent outbreaks, and every night for three months the streets of Montreal had been invaded by thousands of angry workers demanding the overthrow of the system and trying to procure arms.[8] But these spontaneous uprisings had not given birth to any popular, political, revolutionary organization. On the one hand, the workers' leaders were for the most part dominated, if not terrorized, by the clergy, who systematically blocked every attempt at revolutionary organization of the working class. On the other hand, the "anti-draft" leaders of the forties were petty bourgeois who had no real influence over the workers. They were disciples of Bourassa and Canon Groulx, intellectuals who were often sympathetic to Mussolini and Hitler, anti-Semitic and racist. They were incapable of mobilizing popular discontent around a concrete program of social reforms, and all they did, in sum, was to prepare the ground for Duplessis by their exacerbated nationalism.[9]

After the war, apathy, withdrawal, and indifference followed once more upon the disappointed hopes that had been raised by the unionists, the Communists, and the anti-draft groups. Duplessis entered upon his reign without opposition. He took advantage of the fact to cede the rich iron deposits of northern Quebec to the Americans and, with their financial assistance, to endow his party with the most formidable political machine Quebec and Canada had ever known.

The cooperative movement and the union movement, both of which (with few exceptions) were controlled by the Church and the traditional petty bourgeoisie, were put into the service of the slogans "buy at home," "French-Canadian thrift" (monopolized by the

Desjardins Credit Unions), and the "preservation of faith, language, and religion." Certain union leaders even preached "return to the land" and the abolition of any policy favoring immigration, because in their eyes the immigrants were only "stealing jobs and land." The chaplains exercised a despotic reign over the unions and cooperatives, as did the curés over the parishes and the bishops over the dioceses. For the Church, while it had been struggling against the rural exodus ever since the beginning of the century, had had the wisdom to provide priests for the thousands of workers in the cities who were "exposed to vice, pernicious ideas, and Communism." The laymen who dared tell the priests to concern themselves more with God and a little less with politics and union affairs were automatically called "rebels" and "Communists," calumnied and persecuted. The Middle Ages would not be the Middle Ages without a well-organized Inquisition.[10] And despite the efforts of the American capitalists, God did not want Quebec to lose its medieval character. It's a wonder the Holy Virgin did not appear to some child, the way she did in Portugal, to entreat us to obey those who were carrying on the work of the schizophrenic Bishop Laval who, in the seventeenth century, had laid the foundations of the madhouse we were living in.

The American unions with branches in Quebec were less dominated by the obscurantism of the chaplains but they were more subservient to the economic interests of the United States, which in the end was just as bad for the workers of Quebec.

In 1949 striking asbestos miners took control of the city of Asbestos for a few days and refused to obey their leaders, including Jean Marchand, and even their curé. Duplessis' police crushed their revolt, and this action aroused the people against the monarch of "the great darkness." [11] The Asbestos strikers received sympathy, support, and material aid from all sides. A few years later, in 1957, the miners of Murdochville, on the Gaspé peninsula, rose up in turn, and the opposition to Duplessis grew deeper and more widespread. Spontaneous strikes broke out in various corners of Quebec, and Duplessis' political police became increasingly hard on the workers. The union movement got rid of the chaplains and the advocates of blind obedience to the Very Catholic Leader—who went to Mass and took communion every morning. Some of the Quebec intellectuals began to concern themselves with "social sciences" and founded "left" reviews. Weeklies like Jacques Hébert's newspaper *Vrai* revealed the true face of Duplessism to the people. The "Coffin affair," ° among others, forced tens of thousands of Québécois, accustomed to the cunning demagogy of Duplessis, to open their eyes and reawaken to their responsibilities. It was no longer possible for anyone to accept injustice without protest.

Quebec awoke only very slowly from its long winter. In 1960, after years of obscure and difficult struggles, of lost strikes, rigged trials, legal assassinations, censorship and inquisition, eleven years after Asbestos, the unexpected victory of the Liberals and the coming to power of the "socialist" René Lévesque marked the end of "the great darkness" and the beginning of "the quiet revolution." All the institutions of Quebec were publicly called into question. Secularism, separatism, and Marxism shattered the apparent unanimity. The traditional monolithic ideology was broken. Pressure groups, patriotic organizations, and political parties separated into opposing factions. New groups and parties were founded. Political reviews and newspapers multiplied. Young people were seized with a desire to read and to know, and the book trade enjoyed an unprecedented expansion. A hearty appetite for truth and a fierce need for freedom took hold of the nation. God made a terrible grimace and the bishops called an urgent meeting to invoke the Holy Ghost.

The gospel of resignation and the apologia of slavery were ripped up with an enthusiasm mixed with an obscure instinct for vengeance. And more than one man who had helped to manufacture the traditional ideology and had profited from it began to suffer from insomnia and break into sweat dreaming of civil war. "Like in Spain . . . Is it possible? . . . Rich men and priests executed . . . Factories in the hands of workers . . . Churches burned to the ground . . . The socialists in power . . ." The simple announcement by the Liberals that they intended to modernize—that is, "bring up to date"—the teaching dispensed to the youth of Quebec sowed panic among most of the venerable and undisputed "bosses" of traditional education; especially among the bishops, who finally succeeded in quietly sabo-

---

° Wilbert Coffin, a prospector from the Gaspé, was accused of the murder of three American hunters from Pennsylvania. Coffin, whom many believed to be innocent, was convicted on circumstantial evidence and hanged on February 10, 1956. (Trans.)

taging educational reform, with the complicity of Ti-Jean-la-Taxe-Lesage,° who had only defended reform (which his Minister of Education wanted very much) in order to win re-election in 1962. But the bishops' sabotage was a partial defeat for the Church, which has never been so discredited in the eyes of the people as it is today. To be sure, the churches are still filled with the faithful on Sundays, and most people believe in God. But the Québécois are disgusted with the comfortable priests who lead the lives of millionaires in their richly furnished presbyteries and drink Scotch on the money of the poor. As for the young people, not only are they anti-clerical, but the majority of them refuse to go to church on Sunday to watch the empty and incomprehensible rituals of another age and to pay for the show besides, if only so much as 25 cents. Do they believe in God, in Jesus Christ, in Mohammed or Buddha? I don't know. But I have the impression that they believe first of all in themselves and in humanity, and that, unlike their parents, they are not prepared to sacrifice their earthly life for a hypothetical celestial happiness.

Notwithstanding the opposition of those who had formerly profited from obscurantism, the "quiet revolution" completely upset the habits of thought of the Québécois, who for the first time in their history—thanks partly to the prodigious development of television, radio, and the press—witnessed a "national" debate that enabled them all to ask questions, discuss their problems openly, and take sides. The "quiet revolution" liberated hitherto unsuspected energies, and the reformist Liberals were the unconscious instruments of unprecedented social ferment. Every level of society, every class, took a position in accordance with its present condition and its fundamental interests. The petty bourgeoisie expressed its traditional nationalism with new vigor. However, a broad faction of the petty bourgeoisie secularized this nationalism and transformed it into a resolutely separatist and lay movement. For the first time since 1837, the petty bourgeoisie set itself political, economic, and social objectives that were precise enough to constitute a complete political program (a program for the petty-bourgeois class and not the working class). Today there remains no doubt that the entire petty bourgeoi-

---

° Jean Lesage earned his nickname by imposing heavy taxes to finance his reforms, notably new schools. This policy helped defeat him. (Trans.)

sie, from the traditional nationalists to the separatists, are demanding a new division of power. The Canadian Confederation is at the point of death at the very moment when it is beginning to celebrate its centennial in an effort to believe it will survive, like a half-unconscious victim of cancer who refuses to make his will and persists in denying the death that is devouring him.

In Ottawa, only a small minority of Québécois who are either behind the times, blind, or ambitious for their own careers (I'm not sure which) still believe that Lafontaine, Cartier, and Laurier were not traitors and are desperately calling for a constitutional miracle that will save the Confederation. How, without denying history, can these intelligent men believe and declare that it is in the interests of French Canadians to perpetuate a "pact" which in reality they never concluded and which was imposed on them in the same way as the recent Canadian-American treaty on free trade in automobile parts? Can Messrs. Marchand, Favreau, Sauvé, Pelletier, and Trudeau tell us *when* the French-Canadian people were democratically consulted on this famous "pact of confederation," for love of which these gentlemen were willing to compromise themselves with the stinking, scandal-ridden Liberal stable? And with the Liberals' impotent leader, that darling of President Lyndon B. Johnson, that insipid prime minister for whom it would be worth instituting a Nobel Prize for Incompetence? Decidedly, the great men who lived through (*sic*) Asbestos must have gone through some pretty traumatic experiences under the reign of Duplessis. They are still haunted by "the great darkness." And their *"politique fonctionnelle"* is thrashing around like a man who is suffocating from having swallowed too much smoke.°

° The phrase *"politique fonctionnelle"* refers to an article entitled "Pour une politique fonctionnelle: un manifeste" ("A Manifesto for Realism in Politics"), by Pierre Elliott Trudeau, Marc Lalonde (now one of Trudeau's chief advisers), and others. This article appeared in 1964, at a time when Trudeau, together with Gérard Pelletier and Jean Marchand (both now ministers in the federal government), was preparing to go into Liberal politics. The manifesto expounded the authors' views on "functional politics" (or "pragmatism in politics," as the phrase is sometimes translated), that is, the necessity of dealing with practical social problems rather than with grand schemes and ideologies (i.e., separatism and Marxism). The Trudeau government still considers itself to be carrying out this manifesto. (Trans.)

While the founders of the *"cité libre,"* ° imprisoned in the Parliament in Ottawa as members or ministers, pace back and forth in their offices like madmen unaware of their madness, ceaselessly turning over in their tired brains ideas that men of healthy minds do not even want to discuss, the French-Canadian workers fix their eyes on Quebec. All the promises of reforms and "revolutions" that the petty bourgeoisie in power (the Liberal Party) waved in front of the people (educational revolution, social revolution, revolution here, revolution there) have aroused new needs and deeply stirred old hopes that have given birth to a feeling of urgency among the most disadvantaged layers of the population. The "ignorant," whom Lesage despises, want their share of the feast, their *ample* share. Do they not constitute 90 percent of this nation that has just been promised a new life free from fear, ignorance, and servitude?

The promises of 1960 are still the promises of 1966 except, in part, in the field of education. Promises are even postponed indefinitely. And with Danny Boy in power, some people are wondering if the promises that are kept by the "new regime" will not be consigned to oblivion tomorrow. Since his surprising election, Mr. Daniel Johnson has been talking a lot about independence, but he also talks about breaking strikes, cutting social expenditures, and granting new privileges to foreign investors. How can Mr. Johnson reconcile his policy of independence with his unequivocal invitation to American investors, whose economic activity, in the words of the economist André Gunder Frank, can only "develop underdevelopment" and impoverish us collectively and individually until Quebec is nothing but a country in ruins? Naturally, Mr. Johnson will not answer you, because it is not in his party's interest to do so. But as my father used to say, "we're not crazy."

In recent years, taxes have been steadily going up in order to finance these so-called reforms which the people have not yet been allowed to see, as though they were state secrets. Where has all this

° The phrase "the founders of the *'cité libre'* " is an ironic allusion to Trudeau, Pelletier, and others. In 1950, these men founded the magazine *Cité libre* (in which the manifesto on *politique fonctionnelle* was to appear fourteen years later). The magazine's point of view was Catholic, secularist, nuclear pacifist, anti-Duplessist, social democratic, and, later, anti-separatist. Since *la cité* is sometimes used in French in the broad, political sense of "the marketplace" or "public life," Vallières is making a play on words to mock the pretensions of "the founders of the 'Free Society.' " (Trans.)

money gone? Into the pockets of the ministers, the party hacks, the Filions?° Swallowed up in Sidbec, the stillborn steel works? Wasted on pieces of road or on gifts to certain school board members? Transferred to friendly capitalists in the form of "industrial loans"? Given to the Americans in payment of interest on the ever increasing "national debt"? Invested in projects for the centennial of the Confederation and the Expo of the capitalists?

In 1962 Social Credit gave the first concrete formulation to popular discontent, and Caouette's party, finding support in the old resentment of the French-Canadian farmers and workers against the capitalists, swept Quebec in the federal elections.† The *créditistes* disappointed the workers by their internal quarrels and incongruous statements, but popular discontent continued to grow. Two years later strikes broke out pretty much all over. Lesage wanted to muzzle the press, and conflicts multipled in journalistic circles. *La Presse, Le Soleil, L'Action, La Tribune* went through difficult times. The very long strike of the employees of *La Presse*, a strike that had a strong political coloration, made the population aware of the problem of freedom of opinion and the right to information. The people understood that in trying to censor newspapers, the Liberals were trying to hide the truth from them, and that this was being done at the instigation of the very men who had launched the reform movement.

Strikes increased in number and intensity. The Liberals became professional strike-breakers and club-swingers. Their speeches boiled down to irresponsible denunciations that were pointless and sometimes even hysterical. The people saw them as their worst enemies. In the elections of June 1966, Lesage's crowd received a vote of no-confidence. The National Union Party was carried back to power in spite of itself—and in spite of the workers, who could not choose their methods. But never fear. The workers of Quebec may have voted against Lesage so as not to go through another period of "great

---

° Gérard Filion, long a Catholic Farmers' Union official and suburban mayor, later director of *Le Devoir*, is now president of Marine Industries, a mixed state-private corporation. He is an anti-nationalist and an advocate of the view that his fellow French Canadians should forget about separatism and acquire the business sense of the English in order to get ahead. (Trans.)

† Social Credit is a right-wing, religious fundamentalist, anti-separatist party with a working-class orientation. It rose from obscurity in the elections mentioned. (Trans.)

darkness," but do you think they are going to let themselves be burdened for long with Daniel Johnson and his clique of upstarts who are in the pay of the Americans and the most reactionary elements of the nationalistic petty bourgeoisie? And do you really think the workers of Quebec are going to go on playing at elections indefinitely, for the fun of it, every four years, just because the system asks them to? Hunting rifles can sometimes be used for other things besides shooting deer.

At the time these lines are written, there is nothing to indicate that there will be a slowdown in popular demands: violence is breaking out everywhere. Farmers, workers, and students make no secret of their profound dissatisfaction and constantly manifest it in one form or another. The government of Quebec is finding it harder and harder to master the situation. Especially since the state coffers are empty and it is impossible for the party in power, whichever it may be, to think up lasting remedies to quiet the muttering storm.

While the working and agricultural class (farmers, however, represent only 6 percent of the total labor force) is slowly and painfully developing class consciousness—without which no revolution is possible—the Americans are seizing more and more of our national patrimony. It is estimated that today they control, directly or indirectly, 80 percent of the economy of Quebec. By means of an increasing number of long-term loans, they capture an ever growing share of the revenues of the State of Quebec in the form of interest and thus hold back any possibility of autonomous development. Even if Quebec gets all the taxes back from Ottawa, this additional revenue will soon pass into the hands of the Americans, who constitute the main obstacle to the economic independence of Quebec. As for paper independence, Washington couldn't care less. What difference does that fiction make so long as American interests are safeguarded? Imperialism is not interested in flags: one flag more or less in no way disturbs its universal system of exploitation of natural resources and cheap labor. An obedient "nationalist" government is the surest ally for Washington, as Latin America shows by many an example. What the Americans fear is socialism, popular revolution. With Daniel Johnson, as with Jean Lesage, they can rest easy.

Seventy thousand in 1760, the French Canadians of Quebec today number more than five million, out of a total population of about six

million. Ninety percent of them belong to the working class, and to
that figure should be added the majority of non-British immigrants:
Italians, Greeks, Spaniards, Poles, *et al.*, who represent an important
percentage of the proletariat of Montreal. Forty percent of the population of Montreal, according to a study made in 1965 by the Montreal Labor Council, is considered "economically weak," and in the
countryside—where two-thirds of the French-Canadian population
lives—the proportion of poor people, unemployed, seasonal workers,
and welfare recipients is considerably higher. With the exception of
the area around Montreal, where all the wealth of Quebec is concentrated and where the headquarters of both indigenous and foreign
exploiters are located, most regions of Quebec are economically
chained to a single type of local production controlled from abroad:
aluminum in Saguenay–Lake St. John, pulp and paper in the St.
Maurice Valley, copper in Abitibi, iron on the St. Lawrence North
Shore, etc. A drop in the world (or American) demand for one or another of these products suffices to bring the whole region concerned
face to face with famine. Moreover, only a minority of workers can
find jobs in these industries, which are sometimes highly automated;
and the great majority of the population "vegetate," as the saying
goes, and spend their time *surviving*.

The Quebec market is flooded with foreign products, and local
production of consumer goods, even food, is reduced every month by
the overwhelming competition of products imported from the United
States, Japan, and elsewhere, a competition that is completely unrestricted. Prices rise steadily and so does the indebtedness of the
workers. "Credit" poisons the life of individuals and insecurity is the
general condition.

Notwithstanding the unprecedented number and long duration of
their struggles, the workers of Quebec have not yet succeeded in
creating an independent political organization with a view to taking
power and radically transforming the society into one of justice,
equality, and fraternity. But the idea of such a revolutionary, popular
organization and the need for it are becoming increasingly clear to
the workers, farmers, and youth of Quebec. The violent demonstrations of May 24 and July 1, 1965, the recent conflicts of workers in
the textile industry, in the ports of Montreal, Trois-Rivières, and
Quebec, in the La Grenade Shoe Company, in the construction
trades, hospitals, railroads, and the post office, and the struggles of

the trade-school students, the teachers, and lastly the employees of Ayers at Lachute°—to cite only a few—show beyond all doubt that the "white niggers of America" are determined to break the yoke of slavery once and for all and to take the control of their destiny into their own hands.[12]

After three centuries of an entire people's mute and useless submission to the interests of you exploiters, the truth is at last throwing a glaring light on everything, and you must not expect the popular revolt that is brewing to concern itself, Messrs. bourgeois and bishops, with what is going to happen to your privileges and your respectable persons when it breaks out—pitiless and inevitable outcome of the system of exploitation and enslavement which you *yourselves* established and developed.

2

While it is no exaggeration to call the people of Quebec white niggers, they are not the only whites in America who "deserve" this degrading title. The industrial revolution of the eighteenth and nineteenth centuries drove from Europe millions of peasants and workers who came to America in search of freedom as well as work and bread. Only a small number of them succeeded in growing rich and enjoying the freedom of enterprise which, on this continent, is bought at great price. The majority of immigrants have remained the hired servants of the "first white men," the entrepreneurs of the superior English race, who ever since the time of the Washingtons, Jeffersons, and Franklins have considered themselves the sole proprietors of North America. These immigrants, despised by the European capitalists, were welcomed with open arms by the founders of American democracy, who badly needed cheap labor in order to make maximum profits out of the labor and capital they had invested in the American colonies since the seventeenth century. The "first white men" became accumulators of profits, speculators and businessmen, while the newcomers were invited to cooperate, by selling their labor by the hour, in the rapid development of this gigantic country which was supposed to belong to them.

The famous "melting pot" was—and still is—a snare and a delusion. There was a "melting pot" at the level of the wage earners, the

---

° "Ayers" refers to three companies: Dominion Ayers Wood, Ayers Blankets, and Beautyrest Mattresses, all owned by Gilbert Ayers. (Trans.)

unemployed, the poor, those who struggled to survive. But there was never a "melting pot" at the level of the American aristocracy, the class of the big bourgeoisie, the financiers and professional imperialists.

Furthermore, American democracy developed a spirit of division in the working class that has enabled the bourgeoisie to dominate the enormous and extremely mobile mass of cheap labor without much difficulty. First, American democracy kept immigrants from the Christian countries of Europe as far as possible from the blacks. It organized black slavery in the South, white slavery in the North. Later, it conquered the West, and the new rich of Texas and California organized Mexican and Indian slavery. In the North, the Yankee élite divided the white slaves into "colonies": Italian, Irish, Polish, German, Puerto Rican, etc. The second industrial revolution, stimulated by the war of 1939, gave rise to an exodus of southern blacks to the big industrial cities of the North. The white slaves, already grappling with unemployment, greeted their black brothers, who were even poorer than they, like enemies. The unions, which were organizations of the white slaves of big industry, were closed to the newcomers. Racism, which had already turned the South into a veritable hell, poisoned working-class life in most of the cities of the North. The blacks were penned up in ghettos where the misery exceeded anything that the various "colonies" of white slaves had known. The workers' struggle against capitalist exploitation was compromised by fierce hatred of the blacks, engendered by the racist ideology. Financed by the exploiters of white and black workers alike, racism enabled capitalism to delay popular revolution in the United States for many decades. By keeping the workers at each others' throats for irrational reasons, racism made it easier for the big bourgeoisie to sabotage the American union movement and protected the millionaires from the disagreeable experience of having to curtail their profits a little in order to finance social reforms. The union movement, controlled by speculators who were tied to the financial and political interests of the "Warfare State," supported the official policy of Washington and became the surest ally of the big corporations. Disgusted and in revolt, thousands of white slaves, who had been ardent union members before the war, set off hundreds of wildcat strikes in protest against the joint dictatorship of the unions and the companies. As for

the blacks shut up in their ghettos, they rose up *en masse* and set fire
to their miserable poverty. Automation brought with it a considerable increase in the number of persons unemployed or on welfare, and
a few years ago the State Department had to admit publicly that
there were fifty million poor in the United States, or nearly a third of
the total population. Today the unemployed number three million,
while the young people, particularly those who belong to the working class, have no idea what the future may hold for them. The
blacks, the Puerto Ricans, and the Mexican-Americans engage in
more and more demonstrations and riots. Thousands of them fill the
prisons, North and South. Black Power is organizing, inspiring the
most conscious elements of the working class with the idea and
the necessity of "Workers' Power." The war in Vietnam has aroused
the youth against the state. Groups opposing the war, fascism, and
capitalism are multiplying across the country. Class consciousness is
developing despite the long history of senseless hatreds that has so
weakened the movement for workers' demands in America in the last
thirty years. It is a slow process, but little by little racism is giving
way to solidarity. The big-business nature of the unions, although discredited, still remains a major obstacle to the emancipation of the
workers, but the workers are beginning to find more direct and violent ways of asserting their rights than collective bargaining and legal
strikes. The blacks are at the head of the movement, followed by the
Puerto Ricans of New York and the agricultural workers of California
and Texas. These slaves learned long ago to mix their blood with
their anger. The white slaves, who are just beginning to awake from
the long nightmare of racism, will not take long to discover that it is
in their interest to follow the "colored" workers who long ago set out
ahead of them on the road to liberation.[13] It is the same in Canada,
where the workers of Ontario and British Columbia and the
"Frenchies" of northern Ontario and New Brunswick are beginning
to turn to violence.

The development of class consciousness among all levels of workers in America is still not clearly discernible because it has not yet
reached the stage of independent, revolutionary political organization, and because there are many unhealed wounds left by long years
of racism. So far as black nationalism is concerned, far from seeing it
as an obstacle to the class struggle, as do certain so-called orthodox

Marxists (who are more obsessed with scholastic orthodoxy than with the urgent necessity of working *practically*, under *given* conditions, for the liberation of the working class), I see it as one of the most positive and progressive manifestations of the development of the American revolution. For that revolution will have to take into account not only the "proletarian" aspect of the worker, but also his culture, his ethnic origin, his traditions and customs, his particular needs and tastes; otherwise it will not be a human revolution, total and liberating.

Black nationalism—like French-Canadian separatism—is of inestimable service to revolutionaries in that it forces them to envisage the liberation of the whole man and enables them to avoid the trap of half-revolutions which, as soon as they are victorious, change into the oppression of racial, linguistic, religious, or other minorities. Black nationalism and Quebec separatism are again teaching people how much is demanded by a true respect for men in the equality of *natural* and *historical* differences (and not of differences in power and privilege created by the unequal division of wealth, by private ownership of the means of production, by free competition, the concentration of capital in the hands of the fiercest exploiters and the division of society into antagonistic classes). This respect of man for man presupposes the abolition of social classes, of capitalism, of the exploitation of man by man. And the nationalism of the poor, the exploited—in contrast to the nationalism of the steel and oil kings, the proprietors of nuclear energy and atomic bombs, the warmongers and the manufacturers of Agena rockets—aims to crush no one. Since they are already the ones who are most oppressed, the poor can only dominate themselves, that is to say, become their own masters. Their enemies cannot be the "dirty niggers," because *they are* those dirty niggers; they cannot be the "French Pea Soups," because *they are* those French Pea Soups; they cannot be the "damned ignorant factory hands," because *they are* those ignorant factory hands. These niggers—who do not all have the same color skin, who do not all speak the same language, who believe in different prophets, live in ghettos that are foreign to each other and experience in different ways the dictatorship of the same economic, political, and social system—all these niggers whom the partisans of slavery, the businessmen, and the politicians have for centuries contrived to set against each other (the better to exploit them and keep them powerless), know today that in this world of money, violence, and oppression, freedom and peace can be won only by the strength of numbers and of arms. They already have the numbers. The arms will come in due time . . . on the day when they are sufficiently united to constitute the invincible army of their own liberation and the liberation of the millions of men on the five continents who are now enslaved to the interests of the "free world." For the niggers of America are one with the niggers of the entire world. One with them in servitude. One with them in the struggle for liberation. One with them, when the time comes, in the final assault on imperialism and in the definitive victory of the human over the inhuman. One with them in the revolution of man and by man, in the grand event that will sweep away all the decay of the old system and prepare all humanity, that is, all men, to begin a new history, without masters or slaves, without war or racism, without banks or thieves.

3

"But how can we, the niggers, who are the ones most deprived (materially, intellectually, technically) of the means of conquering power and keeping it, how can we hope to overcome the greatest economic, political, and military power in the world, overthrow imperialism, and found a new society on a completely different basis from that of the present society, we who possess nothing and who find it hard to understand the workings of the oppression that makes us slaves?"

Every nigger, every worker who becomes aware of the intolerable injustice of the present system, every slave, in short, who educates himself and opens his eyes to the truth—which it is the function of propaganda, religion, and education to hide from him as much as possible—asks himself with anguish and skepticism the famous question: HOW?

A man accustomed to humiliation and forced labor (labor in order to subsist) becomes fatalistic, passive, skeptical. He is tempted to say to himself: "All those dreams only make us even more unhappy and don't change anything. And then, isn't it in the 'order' of things that there should be some people more intelligent than others, more hard working, more thrifty, less given to drink, less lazy, who succeed more easily because they are more 'capable,' soberer, better educated . . . richer too, you have to admit?

"But doesn't someone become 'capable' because he is educated? And that education that he got at the university, didn't he pay a lot for it? Where did he get the money? Where did his father get the money? How does it happen that his father has a higher income than the average person? How did he get to be a doctor or an industrialist? Where did his father's father get the money to have his son educated? And where did his father's father's father . . .

"And then, why couldn't *my* father have *me* educated, send *me* to the university? Why have *my* father and my father's father always been so hard up? And why are the schools in the working-class quarters dirty, ill equipped, damp, as if they had been built on purpose to make you hate studying? (You do better taking lessons from the gangsters, you know. And it pays off fast, too! But I'd be afraid of that . . .) And why are workers' wages so low, and the cost of living so high, that at fourteen or sixteen you have to look for work like your father, sell your labor by the hour or the week and accept the hardest job like a gift from Heaven because it brings in a few bucks —which you will immediately spend at the clothing store, the corner grocery, the movies, the doctor's . . . and at the tavern when, at the end of six months of this dog's life, you go there to drown the dreams of your youth in beer and noise? Can you explain to me, dear doctor, how it is that there are so many taverns in Montreal and so many drunkards inside? Can you explain to me why you meet mostly workers there, "ignorant" men and the unemployed? And why there are more of these taverns in the French East than in the English West?

"There must be an explanation for all that," Joe says to himself over and over. "It's not possible that all of us from the East End of the city, and from Saint-Henri and the Pointe Saint-Charles, are mentally retarded. And that all of those damn rich men from Westmount, Outremont, and Mount Royal are more intelligent than the rest of us. Here, take my boss for example: he doesn't even know that Cartier made political deals for the railroad companies. He doesn't know the first thing about the history of his country, and he believes in fairy tales. The other day he said to me in all seriousness that his father knew Ringuet well, 'the author of *Maria Chapdelaine*,' says he! ° How can those damn fools get rich so fast while I, who am still taking courses at night and am interested in everything that's going on and everything that's being written, I'm still paying back my debts? In the middle of the twentieth century, my wife has to go to work as a cleaning woman to pay for the schooling of my oldest, who's at the *collège*, and I'm not even sure I can send him back next year. And while the rest of us are busting our guts, those bastards tell us to get an education! (Of course there's Arthur, my brother-in-law, who's a contractor—he has money and no education. But he makes it off patronage, damn him, he steals from his own people.) I'm sick of hearing them preach to us. If this goes on, I'm going to send one of those bourgeois to the next world. If I haven't done it already, you see, it's because I'm not sure it would help much. A lot of us would have to get together and settle their account once for all, all that gang of damn heartless exploiters, of . . . There's enough dynamite in Quebec to blow them all up at the same time. But the men are afraid. When I get worked up at a union meeting, the president cuts me short, because he doesn't want the men to do something foolish, he says. And the men fall for it, because *monsieur le président* is a great friend of the business agent! The business agent, he's a lawyer. He knows a lot about the law, but he doesn't know much about life. He's not one of us. He doesn't understand what you say to him. And then he complicates everything with his Labor Code that you can't understand a word of . . . But things are going to change, I'm telling you. Take a worker's word for it! At the next elections we're going to kick all the old ladies off our Executive. We're going to take our affairs in hand. And then to hell with the regulations on this and the regulations on that. The sparks are going to fly! We're fed up with having the bosses and the union treat us like children. From now on either they listen to us or we smash their faces for them. I hope the men will stick together. It's damn well time we took our responsibilities and stopped making our revolutions in taverns and started making them in *our* factories. I can't wait for the day when one of our

° *Maria Chapdelaine* is a well-known novel written in 1913 by Louis Hémon. It deals with the life of the Habitants around the turn of the century. Ringuet is the pen name of Philippe Panneton, the author of another novel on the same theme but set during the Depression. (Trans.)

boys, a longshoreman, say . . . or a lumberjack, yes, a lumberjack, a big strapping fellow, stands up in front of us, thousands of workers assembled in Lafontaine Park, and strikes up the *Marseillaise* or the *Chant des partisans*—because we don't have any songs like that yet in these parts—and then this lumberjack shouts to us: *'Aux armes, Québécois!'* And all together, like one man, we repeat: *'Aux armes, Québécois!'* And then we get out our rifles and grenades and decide to make an end of . . . But that great day, it won't be tomorrow. We'll have to rouse the men. If we can get rid of the moss-backs and the ass-lickers, that will help. Those idiots are worse than the bosses. By the way, you know the little newspaper *La Cognée*? I don't know who writes it, but they're right on target! Read it. If *I* could write, that's the way I'd do it. They're just right when they say the bigshots in the union are rotten. But we're going to change that, and no later than this year, whether *they* like it or not. We're sick of being spat on. I for one, anyway, I've made up my mind. Nothing is going to stop me. If the men can act like men . . ."

It is through such reflections, based on a daily experience of exploitation, that every conscious worker reaches the conclusion that the heart of the problem is not the alleged "capacity" of some (the few) and the incapacity of others; that it is not a question of "competence," much less intelligence, but basically a question of privileges unequally divided, of powers unjustly acquired through centuries of violence during which the weaker have always been pitilessly crushed by the stronger (stronger because richer).

4

The heart of the problem is neither metaphysical nor moral. It is material; it is at the same time economic, historical, and military. Consequently its solution must be of the same nature. Since the evolution of humanity is not a philosophical system, there is no theoretical solution to the problems that it raises. There are only practical solutions.

Theory is an instrument of research whose usefulness is measured by the practical actions it enables us to perform. A theory is progressive and revolutionary insofar as it enables men to perform acts which *transform* their world by *radically changing their social relationships.*

That is why every worker who comes to realize the injustice of his condition, the condition of his fellows, and consequently of the vast majority of men, is immediately confronted with the most gigantic practical problem that has ever presented itself, first to men, then to collectivities: *How* to transform thousands of years of exploitation of man by man and of incessant murderous wars, how to transform centuries of accumulation of capital and concentration of wealth at the expense of men's progress and freedom, how to transform this long history of massacre, pillage, and slavery into a new history of peace, justice, and freedom? *How* to transform a world dominated and perverted by money, hatred, and violence into a world without money, hatred, or violence? *How* to make a world without niggers?

How . . . ? It is not a theoretical problem but a practical one, because it is solely a problem of the relationship of forces. It is a question of overturning the present relationship of forces; of seeing to it that the weak—the vast majority of the two billion inhabitants of the planet, whose numbers give them a natural, inalienable right to control their own affairs—become the stronger, the sole masters of their fate, the sole artisans of their social universe; of seeing to it that the powerful—the small minority who make up the international business bourgeoisie and who monopolize economic, political, and social affairs, the means of communication, the engines of war and the reigning ideologies—are reduced to impotence, held in check, prevented forever from exploiting human labor for their profit.

It is a question of making men equal, not only in law but in fact.

It is necessary to create the material conditions for this equality, that is, to abolish everything that makes the present social relations the relations between masters and slaves, sellers and buyers, rich and poor, exploiters and exploited. It is necessary to replace all that with new social relations which are no longer based on force, money, and systematic injustice, but on all men's right to equality, on justice, fraternity, and the collective enjoyment of the wealth, both material and cultural, that belongs to every man from birth.

Humanity, like everything that is natural, can find within itself the "self-regulators" necessary to its survival and progress, without needing a class of businessmen to act as policemen. Perhaps, up until now, humanity needed to be run by a minority class of "entrepreneurs" (in the broad sense). But today every man is in a position to become his own entrepreneur, because science and technology have already reached a sufficient level of development to enable all the collectivities on earth—and through them, all men—to acquire the material and intellectual means of achieving freedom, social equality, and the happiness of working through personal and collective creation for the progress of humanity.

Only the usurpation by the international business bourgeoisie (businessmen, manufacturers of automobiles and rockets, warmongers) of the instruments of research, the industries, the discoveries, the universities, the means of disseminating knowledge, etc.—only this usurpation by a handful of financiers and their army of technicians, scientists, and intellectuals prevents humanity today from taking the most gigantic step in all its history, from making the most profound and human revolution the earth has ever known. Only this class of businessmen, to whom must be added the bureaucrats of Soviet and East European state capitalism, prevents humanity from coming out of its long prehistory.

The point of departure of all revolutions has been that a broad faction of a given population has recognized the conservative and parasitic nature of the dominant class, which enjoys everything without doing anything, without producing, while the majority is reduced to servile obedience to the dictates of the guardians of Order. The great revolution for which humanity is ripe will really get under way on the day when the workers, scientists, technicians, and intellectuals meet in joint opposition to the gold-plated obscurantism of the bankers and monarchs of the universe. In this century more than one revolution, civil war, insurrection, riot, general strike, and war of national liberation has demonstrated the will of the peasants, workers, and youth of the entire world to transform this world, pillaged by the international race for profits, into a world of peace, social justice, and fraternity. But too few scientists, technicians, and intellectuals have as yet come to understand that their discoveries and labor will always be subjugated to the class interests of the great financiers (to their wars, to their exploitation of the labor of hundreds of millions of men, and to the systematic development of underdevelopment in the majority of the countries of the "third world") until the day when, instead of assisting the capitalists in their enterprise of dehumanization "made in U.S.A.," they turn toward those whose toil, over the centuries, is precisely what has enabled them to make discoveries that are the pride of the twentieth century, and who, for their part, are ready to join together to build a world commensurate with the imagination of the scientists.

Unless they renounce all dignity, unless they cynically flee from their tremendous social responsibility, the scientists, technicians, and intellectuals of the twentieth century must consent to become politicized, to get their hands dirty along with the millions of "ignorant" men, the starving, the illiterate, the beggars, the peasants, the unemployed, the little office clerks, the sales clerks, and the wage-earners, to whom science has so far brought only new and more refined forms of oppression and alienation.

The same remark holds true for that faction of the petty bourgeoisie, of the middle class, which does not aspire to live in the orbit, or on the periphery, of the great multinational corporations, but which wishes to give its existence a meaning more worthy of man. This progressive part of the petty bourgeoisie must lose its illusions about the alleged ability of the system to put an end to injustice without itself disappearing. You cannot abolish slavery without abolishing the power of the master and the relation of master to slave.

For the progressive petty bourgeois, as for those scientists, intellectuals, and "technocrats" who have not sold out to the present holders of economic and political power in the world, the *only choice* that makes sense objectively is *to ally themselves with the workers, farmers, students, and all young people*—with the great majority of mankind.

By allying themselves, I mean that they must take over the profound aspirations, the demands, and the economic, political, and social objectives of the mass of men, not as "enlightened" and paternalistic guides of the "ignorant" but as responsible and conscious auxiliaries of men and women equal by rights, to whom history at last offers the opportunity and the means to organize, in every country, for their definitive liberation from oppression, from their thousand-year-old status as niggers, as cheap labor, as exploited and humiliated beings.

5

At first glance, the problems raised by the evolution of humanity at each historical stage always appear insurmountable. The picture one paints for himself, and describes to others, of this society without exploitation, for the achievement of which one is ready to take up arms, is like something out of science fiction.

And in the beginning, your utopia makes some people pity you, others ridicule you, and the majority look upon you as a kind of mystic without God! It is not long before you have acquired a reputation for being a dreamer—a fellow who is "sincere" but "idealistic." If, on top of that, you intend to go on to action, then you become *ipso facto* a "communist," an "anarchist," an irresponsible and dangerous man who, in the interest of society, should be locked up as soon as possible in a prison or insane asylum. As long as you only preach your utopia, the established order is content to take note of your "dissent" with contempt or indifference. But as soon as you begin to act, the old system hastens to turn you into a public menace and a criminal, so as to be able to bury you alive before your "idealism" puts Molotov cocktails, dynamite, and rifles into the hands of the workers and the young people, who are very receptive to the idea of Utopia, which is all they are waiting for to rise up *en masse* against those who organize, profit from, and defend oppression. For no matter what the ideologists of capitalism, neocapitalism, and imperialism may say about Utopia, it is not a philosopher's utopia: it sums up aspirations which cry out not only to be perceived and understood, but above all to be *realized*. Nor is Utopia the final point, the terminus of human evolution. On the contrary. It is only the point of departure, the beginning, the first stage of the new history which men will embark upon together once they are liberated from their present condition as niggers, as sub-men.

The worker or petty bourgeois who has one day confronted himself and become personally implicated in the unprecedented challenge which the liberation of hundreds of millions of men on the five continents represents, cannot help feeling that he is a visionary and a madman. And this is so even after the Russian, Chinese, Vietnamese, and Cuban revolutions, for we all know that these revolutions are still only first, stumbling steps. Much greater changes will have to occur if human freedom is to become not just an essence of the philosophers but an act, if it is to pass from being an ideal of the moralists to concrete existence, from desire to practice, if it is to become the individual and collective reality of life.

6

The author of this book is an idealist who, from childhood on, learned from his father to long for a better world in which the men who work anonymously from day to day—the farmers, workers, day laborers like my father—could enjoy life after having toiled so hard to subsist, to endure . . . and to perpetuate the species. Enjoy life not by getting drunk on the weekend, by "drinking up their pay," beating their wives and children and destroying themselves in useless fits of anger, but by possessing the material and intellectual means of creating something in this world, of giving of themselves to others and of exchanging with them something other than curses, sarcasms, and humiliations.

"I wonder when we'll be able to take it easy for a bit and enjoy life without worrying about tomorrow," my father often said. And with a bitterness mingled with resignation, my mother would answer: "When you're born for half a loaf, you can't expect . . ." My mother was learning to forget all the dreams of happiness that, like all women, she had had in her youth. And she did not want to discuss fantasies with my father. What was the use? You hurt yourself by hoping. You increase your disappointments and life becomes unbearable. Better to expect nothing and take what comes, as it comes.

My father would say nothing, suppressing his hopes the way one holds back sobs. I would look into his deep, gentle eyes and read a mixture of immense kindness, silent suffering, and perhaps also grief. Sometimes he would smile, just long enough to tell me, without opening his lips, that his dreams could be realized, that one had to believe that.

My mother would complain about her headaches, the dullness of the radio broadcasts, the slovenliness of such and such a neighbor . . . while I, trying not to hear anything that was going on around me, would listen to the revolt that mounted inside me and heated my blood.

They say that silent suffering is the most terrible. (I read that in a prose poem of Baudelaire's, I think.) I learned very early to question fate in silence. Especially on those long rainy days when it seemed to me that the whole universe had withdrawn into the depths of a swamp of misery. There, men seemed to have given up, abdicated, as if it was their destiny to go around in circles in the slimy mud of their impotence. Rainy days soon became unbearable for me. With eyes darkened by loneliness and hunger, I would appeal to the sun. For the sun gave me back playmates and made me forget my hunger. Life very early posed for me the questions that are hard for men to answer. It took me many years to begin to find the elements of an answer, and even more time to discover what had to be done to provide a concrete solution, a real solution, to servitude, passivity, alienation, and poverty.

My itinerary from working-class slums to the FLQ was long and tortuous. For a workingman's son, nothing in life is laid out in advance. He has to forge ahead, to fight against others and against himself, against his own ignorance and all the frustrations accumulated from father to son, he has to surmount both the oppression laid upon his class by others and his own congenital pessimism, to give his spontaneous revolt a consciousness, a reason and precise objectives.

Otherwise, he remains a nigger, he turns into a delinquent or a criminal, he consents to becoming at the age of thirty the ruin of a man . . . a bitter and disenchanted slave.

The entire experience of workers shows them that the explanation for their poverty and impotence lies in the brutal fact that there are, on the one hand, those who possess everything and, on the other, those who possess nothing. That is something they all know, they live it every day. But, they say to themselves, what can you do when you are one of those who possess nothing?

If revolt is natural to workers, hope is not. Except in times of crisis and revolution, when workers can take advantage of the weakness of the system to deal it a mortal blow, their long-enforced degradation often engenders fatalism, resignation, and even indifference to everything, including themselves.

When a "great darkness," such as characterized the Duplessis regime from 1944 to 1959, extends over a whole people, those who ask themselves questions about man's destiny are sometimes tempted to despair of others and of themselves. The triumphant reign of Stupidity seems to justify the metaphysics of the Absurd, of individual Anarchy and of Nausea. Before going through its "quiet revolution," Quebec went through the dictatorship of Stupidity; and for a long time the Québécois struggled vainly, in anxiety and despair, like penniless prisoners who are totally ignorant of the procedures that cause them to be in prison one day and in court the next, then in prison again, without ever understanding the working of the machine that shifts them back and forth in a universe from which all light, reason, and meaning are shut out, the universe called Justice, Law and Order, the Public Interest.[14]

Under the reign of Duplessism, it was not easy for the Québécois to resist intoxicating themselves by reading the classics of despair. How could one give a meaning to this society of crushed and silent men? Not even the best of the oppressed knew how to turn their oppression into revolt. Everywhere there was unanimous silence, a conspiracy among all men to remain shut up in their ghettos, to die there as soon as possible and no longer have to breathe the atmosphere of submission mixed with selfishness in which practically no one dared accept the responsibility, beyond his own immediate interest, of working for the *downfall* of Stupidity!

It was as if after the years of struggle during the Depression and the war, the Québécois had become indifferent to their fate. They had no resiliency left.

At that time, a man who chose to give his life for an idea would have stirred no emotion among the mass of sluggish men. Winter had frozen the best minds. Nothing was left but day-to-day living, without a future, without passion, without reason. Once in a while— rarely—a revolt, a burst of anger here or there. But no enduring passion, no firm determination, no precise goal. God the Father governed in Quebec, and while the Québécois did not really justify that government, they did not seek to contest it either. They laughed at it; and took advantage of it "under the counter." Political patronage provided social welfare for the disinherited and profits for the new rich who were manufactured by the regime to compete with the liberal bourgeoisie.

It seemed as if, having come through many years of black misery, the Québécois no longer attached any importance to their future, to what they called their fantasies of the old days. The only thing they looked forward to— and they didn't even really believe in that—was the American money that Duplessis dangled glittering in front of the bishops, deputies, and petty bourgeois; and, when there was any left over, in front of the farmers or workers who promised him their votes and complicity in advance.

And yet, a few years before, these same men had often assembled to denounce the dictatorship of capital and to demand the heads of their exploiters. They had invaded the business quarter and done significant damage to the big buildings of the financiers. They had refused to go and fight to defend the interests of Rockefeller. They had hidden in the woods, armed with their rifles. They had even mobilized their wives and children to organize resistance to the military police. They had been men.

And now here they were, applauding the demagogy of Duplessis and the vulgarities of the drunkard Camillien Houde.° The country was becoming a vast circus where if one still wanted to give a meaning to life, one had to have blind faith and commit one's inner self to a solitary hope, hard as the rocks of the Gaspé, black as the mines of Abitibi, dreary as the faces of the workers of Montreal and cold as the winter of Quebec.

Few were those who dared to believe. Nevertheless, during the war men of this country had spoken to other men of this country in a language of combat and fraternity. A language which men like my father kept in their hearts, in the hope that one day combat and fraternity would give them the homeland they did not have. Yet in those days there was war and hunger.

At the very time when war seemed to be telling men that they were wrong to be bent on living, there were workers in Quebec, as in most of the countries of the world, who were longing more than ever for a change of system.

Notes

1. While the Anglo-Americans numbered 200,000. In 1760, at the time of the English conquest, 1,500,000 Anglo-Americans mobilized their forces against 70,000 French Canadians dispersed over a vast territory.

° Camillien Houde was the mayor of Montreal during the 1940's and early 1950's. (Trans.)

2. ". . . New France sought to evolve a sounder economy than it had yet known, with its sole reliance on the fur trade. Agriculture was encouraged . . . but it did not prosper and misery was often widespread. Commerce and industry fared as badly; the fur trade passed through its customary cycles of poverty and plenty; while inflation, shipwreck, and the profiteering of French merchants kept the prices of imports high, far beyond the means of most of the colonists. Local industry was alternately encouraged and then stamped out when it interfered with French manufacturing interests, under the mercantilist policy which prevailed at court; in 1702 it was still the king's view that *'The Colony of Canada is good only inasmuch as it can be useful to the Kingdom.'* Where noncompetitive industries could be established, they were encouraged with too lavish a hand, so that they never became self-sufficient. Corruption, the shortage of manpower and capital, the difficulties of communication and transportation, and absentee direction all combined to prevent New France from developing a strong and well-rounded economy." F. Mason Wade, *The French Canadians 1760–1945* (New York: The Macmillan Co., 1955), p. 31; emphasis added.

See also the excellent study by Jean Hamelin, *Economie et société en Nouvelle-France,* published by the Presses de l'Université Laval.

As can be seen, the idyllic New France of Canon Groulx never existed outside the imagination of the apostles of theocracy and obscurantism. Moreover, it is false to picture our ancestors as Louis Héberts, professional farmers. Agriculture was developed very belatedly in Quebec, especially in the Eastern Townships . . . under the English regime! The French-Canadian seigneurs took no interest in the development of agriculture, unlike the Anglo-American colonists, who quickly grasped the fact that at this time the development of agriculture was the very foundation of the accumulation of capital, and who instituted slavery precisely in order to accelerate and increase this accumulation by the maximum exploitation of human labor. That is why a bourgeoisie rapidly developed in the United States, while in Quebec the ruling class remained poor and powerless. (The rich did not belong to the country and had come only for as long as it would take them to amass money.)

At the time of the conquest of 1760, more than one French-Canadian seigneur viewed the defeat as a kind of deliverance. These do-nothing nobles would no longer have to *answer for* the country; they would no longer have to feel responsible for its development. They could die quietly in idleness, content with the privileges that protected them from work and insecurity.

The dreams of Champlain and Talon were never realized. Under the

French regime, there existed no economic base for autonomous development. Under the English regime, the economic base (agriculture and commerce) was created and placed at the service of the Anglo-Saxon interests. With the development of banks, canals, railroads, and industry, this economic base expanded, but it continued to serve English and American interests. Today, in the era of the great multinational corporations, the economic base of development is controlled and limited by American imperialism, according to the needs of the world market—that is, according to the interests of the powerful American business bourgeoisie. Today imperialism is working hard to underdevelop the development that already exists, in order to prevent the people from building a solid economic base for the independence and social revolution they want.

That is why, in nearly all the countries dominated by imperialism, even the once powerful "national" bourgeoisies, and most of the petty bourgeoisies, are reduced to the role of policemen and lackeys of Yankee interests. And that is why, when the necessary revolutions have taken place in those countries, everything will still have to be built.

(One of my future projects will be to gather the necessary material for an economic history of Quebec.)

3. The nobles belonged for the most part to the group of privileged, idle men who formed the local ruling class (as opposed to the French merchants who were only "passing through" the colony). In reality, this ruling class had only the power to profit from the general corruption, while the people, who were reduced to the most abject poverty, did not participate in the government in any way. The ruling class was poor because misery was too widespread for the accumulation of wealth to be the basis of the social structure of the time. Apart from the merchants, the only nobles who succeeded were the Jesuits, the Sulpicians, and the priests of the Seminary of Quebec, who did not have to finance the numerous wars (against the Iroquois and the English). Besides, ever since 1659 Bishop Laval, who was a Vaticanist and believed in centralization, had been taking advantage of the absence of civil administration in the colony to make the Church the armature of the emerging nation. The missionaries were imported not so much to convert the savages as to conquer the country in the name of the Church. Four years after the arrival of this holy dictator and aristocrat, the town of Quebec alone had 150 ecclesiastics out of a total population of barely 500, or one for every three inhabitants! Even today, after three centuries, the power of the Church is still one of the greatest obstacles to the development of Quebec. This was proved yet again when the bishops undertook to torpedo Bill 60 on educational re-

form. On this subject see, among others, the recent study by Léon Dion on Quebec pressure groups and Bill 60, published in the *Cahiers de l'Institut canadien de l'éducation des adultes*, No. 1, 1966, and titled "Le Bill 60 et le public."

4. This whole period was dominated by a serious commercial and agricultural depression that affected both Europe and the colonial empires. This depression (which reached its depth in the years 1833–1838) sharpened and precipitated class conflicts in most of the countries of Europe and their overseas colonies. The French-Canadian rebellion of 1837–1838 was thus part of an international movement of revolutions which sowed panic among the ruling classes of Europe.

The economic depression of the first half of the nineteenth century had many consequences for the life of Lower and Upper Canada. Perhaps the most important of these was the massive immigration from the Irish countryside, which was being laid waste by the pitiless industrial revolution presided over by the capitalists of His Very British Majesty. It is estimated that between 1838 and 1849 England sent to Canada 428,000 Irish poor who had been dispossessed of their goods and independence. During this period thousands of French Canadians, likewise dispossessed of everything, emigrated to the United States. According to contemporary historians, twenty years after the failure of the rebellion of 1837–1838, 100,000 French Canadians had left their country. And, according to the first census of the Province of United Canada (created from the union of Quebec and Ontario), in 1851 there were 60,000 more English-speaking people in Canada than French Canadians, out of a population of about two million. Shortly after Confederation, the French Canadians would represent 31.07 percent of the Canadian population, and henceforth everything would be done to convince them that they did not form a nation but a "minority," a "cultural enclave," an "ethnic group." Exceeding five million today, they are still considered by the descendants of the conquerors of 1760, and by the Americans and most foreign observers who deign to take an interest in this curious people, as a "remnant" of medieval society, with no power and no future. Fortunately, the Québécois have a quite different view of themselves, and they firmly intend to carry out the revolution that is ripening in the cities and in the countryside, to the great despair of those who profit from the present regime and their most faithful allies, the politicians and the clergy.

5. Cartier was the only French Canadian, but the cleverest politician, in the group of Hincks, Galt, Merrit, Watkin, Keefer, and Andrews, who created the coast-to-coast railroad network for which the British North America Act was drawn up. Already in 1854–1856 and in 1861–1862 he

had protected the interests of the Grand Trunk by a piece of legislation that provided guarantees and substantial loans for the reorganization of the railroads belonging to the most important financial group in the country. That is what the taxes wrung from the workers were used for.

6. "One powerful force [in London] behind the Union Act was that of the banking firm of Baring Brothers, which had underwritten almost all the Upper Canadian securities. . . . One of the principals of this firm, Francis T. Baring, was chancellor of the exchequer in the Melbourne cabinet, and the Baring interests may have had something to do with the determination of the cabinet to shift the burden of Upper Canadian bankruptcy onto the shoulders of the prosperous lower province." F. Mason Wade, *op. cit.*, p. 225.

   It can be assumed that the same phenomenon occurred again in 1867, if one considers that the Grand Trunk and Intercolonial Railway companies were controlled by British interests.

7. During the summer of 1944 a number of street fights took place in Montreal between French Canadians and the military police. The Saint-Jean-Baptiste Society of Montreal, of which Roger Duhamel was president, publicly condemned violence. "Civilized people should have other methods for finding a common ground for their different viewpoints," he wrote in *La Patrie* of June 10, 1944.

   In the fall, acts of violence multiplied all across Quebec, even in Chicoutimi and Rimouski. There was more talk than ever about independence and revolution. The Rue Saint-Jacques and the "clique of colonels" were denounced on every hand.

   On November 29, after a speech by André Laurendeau, several thousand French Canadians paraded through the financial district of Montreal breaking windows at the offices of the National Selective Service, the "sold-out" newspaper *Le Canada*, the Bank of Montreal, the Montreal Trust Company, and other Anglo-American businesses.

   The riots spread and the English-language newspapers demanded that the demonstrations be repressed. *Le Devoir*, as was its habit, "deplored" the incidents in Montreal, Quebec, Chicoutimi, and Rimouski.

   An angry crowd broke windows at the Quebec residence of Louis St. Laurent, then Canadian Minister of Justice. And eminent English Canadians recommended that machine guns be used to force the "French Pea Soups" to defend the interests of the "free world"!

8. The disturbances came to a head on August 29 and 30, 1917. Orators exhorted the crowds to clean their rifles and take up a collection to buy other arms. The police tried to break up the meetings: at least one man was killed. The wealthy home of Hugh Graham (Lord Atholstan), owner

of the *Montreal Star*, was dynamited. One Lalumière and eleven other French-Canadian workingmen were held responsible for this attack and were accused of having plotted to kill Borden, Senator Beaubien, and other public men who supported conscription. The leaders of the rioters, Villeneuve, Lafortune, Côté, and Mongeau, gave their entire support to Lalumière and his companions. They were all arrested on September 12, 1917. Crowds continued to roam the streets shouting "Borden to the gallows!" and "Long live the Revolution!" and shooting their rifles into the air. Some Paris newspapers began to raise the possibility of Quebec's seceding from Canada, while Bourassa preached more sermons on "sterile violence" and sang the praises of electoralism and dialogue (from Bourassa to Pelletier, the tradition is maintained!). Which did not prevent violence from reigning from one end of Quebec to the other, even in Sherbrooke, one of the most conservative cities in the country.

In March 1918 riots broke out in Quebec. Several thousand persons poured through the city and set fire to the federal police station. The crowd went wild and sang the *Marseillaise*. They sacked the offices of the *Chronicle* and *L'Evénement*, then attacked the office of the registrar of the Military Service Act and burnt it to the ground with all its records. On March 30 the army fired on the crowd, and the next day the entire city rose up. It was Easter. On the 1st of April the crowd in its turn fired on the army from rooftops, windows, snowbanks—any place that afforded cover. Five soldiers were wounded and four civilians killed. Hundreds of workers and young people were wounded and some sixty others were thrown in jail. On April 4 the federal government decreed, by ministerial order, that the rioters should be immediately drafted, the effect of which was to heighten the rioting instead of lessening it. The disturbances ended with the close of the war, but the people's bitterness never ended.

9. Trained in the classical *collèges* of the clergy, where education was based exclusively on the study of the "humanities," these petty bourgeois, stimulated by "the Irish troubles," began to promote a quasi-religious separatism without an economic program. Duplessis was able to take advantage of this to reinforce his power immediately after the war, but once firmly established he wasted little time supporting the nationalists, whom at heart he despised. He became God's gift to the Americans. In the same way, Duplessis took advantage of the clergy's admiration for Franco, Hitler, Mussolini, and especially Salazar (who had set up in Portugal the corporate regime recommended by the encyclicals) to place the bishops and curés at his mercy. Having broken the back of the nationalists, the liberals, and the "Communists," Duplessis built his power on an alliance between Religion and Finance, with a "pro-autonomy" flavor—in order

to save face for the Banana Republic that Quebec had become. His greatest delight was to provide the bishops with opportunities to come and eat out of his hand . . . when he had concluded good bargains with his American friends.

10. The Grand Inquisitor of the time, Cardinal Villeneuve, was the chief architect, along with Duplessis, of Quebec anti-Communism, the French-Canadian and Catholic version of Senator McCarthy's witch hunt.

11. On the occasion of this conflict the Archbishop of Montreal, Msgr. Charbonneau, declared: "We want social peace, but we do not want the working class to be crushed. We are more interested in man than in capital." (*Le Devoir*, May 2, 1949.) Alerted by the Rue Saint-Jacques, Duplessis persuaded Pope Pius XII to force the resignation of Msgr. Charbonneau and exile him to British Columbia.

12. When Charles Gagnon and I went on a hunger strike at the United Nations, a group of Christians from the University of Montreal demonstrated their solidarity with us. One can judge from the contents of their "declaration of solidarity" what a long way social consciousness has come in Quebec, for believers as well as nonbelievers. This declaration has been one of the greatest consolations to us during our detention in New York. Here are a few extracts from it:

"We declare our solidarity with the hunger strike undertaken by Pierre Vallières and Charles Gagnon in New York on September 26, 1966. By this we mean that we are fighting for the liberation of the workers of Quebec, and indeed against all forms of exploitation of man by man; and that we are trying to promote a more just and fraternal society through socialism. If Pierre Vallières and Charles Gagnon thought it necessary to use *violence* by organizing the new terrorist network of the FLQ, they did so advisedly. One may dispute the realism and effectiveness of this method of action. One may also approve it. . . . As one may dispute the realism of a world which 'right-thinking' people believe to be peaceful when it is steeped in' the *violence* that is done to the weakest every day . . . !

"We are united in solidarity with those who are fighting against the chief enemy of Man, which at the present time is *neocapitalism* . . . and imperialism. . . .

"We are aware of the fact that our struggle in Quebec is taking place in the framework of another, much vaster struggle, that of all the clear-thinking, responsible, and fraternal men the world over, atheists or not, Christians or not, Marxists or not, who are fighting for the liberation of Man. . . ." *Le Quartier Latin*, October 24, 1966; and *Le Devoir*, October 25, 1966.

This statement was signed by believers and nonbelievers, students, workers, professors, journalists, writers, priests, and so on.

13. A. *The American blacks:* Increasingly conscious, they are becoming increasingly responsible and active. Black Power, however, is not yet a structured and ideologically defined *organization*. It is a sort of Afro-American equivalent of Quebec separatism and contains all the same shades of thinking. On the other hand, its immediate objectives are more clearly defined. They can be summed up as follows:

(1) The first aim of Black Power is to give the black majorities of certain counties, districts, or great urban centers (in 1970, blacks will be in the majority in fifty big American cities) control over economic, political, and social affairs—first of all, the affairs of the blacks themselves—by putting in force the rights which the American Constitution already guarantees to all citizens of the United States, including blacks. In the beginning, therefore, the struggle is legal, but the blacks are determined to have *all* their constitutional rights *fully* respected. And in the North of the United States no less than in the South, that is enough to sow panic among the white ruling classes, particularly among their richest members, who are almost exclusively of British stock. Nazism and all the other forms of fascism (Minutemen, John Birch Society, Ku Klux Klan, etc.) are organizing the counterattack against Black Power.

(2) That is why the second point of the Black Power program is the organization of *armed self-defense* of American black communities and of such governments as they may in time establish over counties, districts, quarters, cities, and perhaps even states. The blacks also want to take control of their schools, hospitals, playgrounds, etc., and to defend this control, weapons in hand. (There is a striking similarity between this objective and that of the Popular Liberation Committees that the FLQ wants to help organize in the cities and countryside of Quebec. See especially "Les Comités populaires de libération" in *L'Avant-Garde,* No. 2, February 1966, and my pamphlet "Qu'est-ce que le FLQ?," 1st ed., June 1966.) Armed self-defense was organized for the first time by the black revolutionary Robert Williams, who has related his experience in the book *Negroes with Guns* (New York: Marzani and Munsell, 1962). Williams' book, together with *The American Revolution* (New York: Monthly Review Press, 1963) by the black worker and unionist James Boggs, has appeared in translation in the collection "Les Cahiers libres" of François Maspero under the title *La Révolution américaine.* A good part of the philosophy of Black Power has been drawn from the famous lectures of Malcolm X (who was assassinated in 1965). The major speeches of Malcolm X have been published by Merit Publishers (New York) under the title *Malcolm X Speaks.*

(3) In addition, Black Power demands that black leaders democratically elected by blacks to defend the interests of blacks be given the right to represent the twenty million Afro-Americans at the international level. That means that if the whites refuse to apply the majority rule, which they themselves invented, the blacks will simply get along without them. And that is the profound meaning of what is called "black nationalism." The blacks are increasingly refusing integration, because *integration means the subjugation* of the black majorities of many counties, districts, and cities in the United States to rich, white minorities. (Thus, in Lowndes County, Alabama, the blacks constitute nearly 85 percent of the population, and yet in the elections of November 8, 1966, there were in that county as many whites as blacks who had the right to vote! That's integration.) Constitutionally the blacks have the same rights as the whites, but in concrete reality they do *not* have the same freedoms. And when the rich whites cannot crush the blacks with laws, they assassinate them. Personally, I believe that in no civilized country does one find so much violence and hate as in the United States. And this hate-filled violence comes exclusively from the powerful American capitalists.

Since the violent death of Malcolm X in 1965, the most influential and popular leader of the Black Power movement has been the president of SNCC (Student Non-Violent Coordinating Committee), Stokely Carmichael, who is only twenty-five years old. He has already been in prison several times, but he has not yet been assassinated! Working with poor blacks of the rural South, Harlem, Atlanta, or Los Angeles, Carmichael has just launched a campaign against the drafting of blacks, whom the Pentagon sends to Vietnam by the thousands to murder innocent people and be murdered in turn in the diabolical war engendered by imperialism. A great number of American officials are now demanding Carmichael's head.

Black Power is being organized in a climate of riots, bombings, and assassinations and is a strong expression of the class struggle that is developing in Uncle Sam's country and threatening its system. But while Black Power and the Black Panthers—the political party to which it has given birth in the South—are organizing the blacks against the white capitalists, their "nationalism" has a strong socialist coloration and is in increasingly radical opposition to the black bourgeoisie which, moreover, has just publicly condemned Black Power. Of course, there are conflicts of interest within the Black Power movement, but dominated and led as it is by the most progressive (and youngest) elements of the black "nation," "class," or "community," it has every chance of creating, in the near future, the conditions for a revolution of unprecedented scope in the United States. For Black Power, which is a very popular mass movement, one which mobilizes the majority of the most exploited citizens of North America, is developing a strategy which cannot fail to radicalize class struggle in the United States and lead the millions of poor people in this, the richest country in the universe, to rise in revolt. That is why it is in the interest of all the other niggers, all the other exploited people, including the Québécois, to unite with the American blacks in their struggle for liberation.

More than one petty bourgeois in the black organizations dreads the approaching upheaval, but feeling it to be inevitable, is forced either to follow the movement or to ally himself with all the Martin Luther Kings of the black bourgeoisie and of Lyndon B. Johnson's Democratic Party; in short to prostitute himself to the organizers and defenders of colonization at home and colonization of the third world, in the name of "nonviolence"! Today it is no longer Birmingham—that is, the integration of buses, snack bars, and bowling alleys (what a revolution!!)—that symbolizes the fundamental aspirations of the twenty million black workers and young people, but Watts—that is, armed violence, the disappearance of the slums and ghettos, the occupation of factories by the workers, and so forth.

The black organizations that feel most responsible for their class are CORE (Congress of Racial Equality) and SNCC. These organizations, which were originally "nonviolent," are becoming increasingly conscious of what is required to liberate the blacks and are learning in daily struggle *with* the workers that it will be necessary to employ energetic and, consequently, illegal means to transform not only the unbearable condition of the blacks but the whole of American society, which is completely perverted by capitalism and its terrible social consequences: racism, poverty, unemployment, crime, delinquency, etc. With fire and sword, the blacks are regenerating North America and giving back to man what belongs to man by wrenching it from the grasp of the businessmen, the Johnsons, the McNamaras, and the Kennedys (Bobby, Ted, John F., and Co.).

As for the "white" organizations, those that are most aware and most concretely *committed* understood from the beginning that Black Power and "black nationalism," being fundamentally and spontaneously anticapitalist, were therefore not "racist." They saw at once that the blacks were not hostile to cooperation on a basis of *absolute equality* but to the white paternalism that constantly humiliated them—the paternalism of the Marxists as well as the liberals. The blacks loathe that sort of paternalism, and rightly so, but they willingly agree to cooperate with the revolutionary whites, in particular Youth Against War and Fascism, the DuBois

Clubs (a mixed organization that includes both whites and blacks but is predominantly white), Students for a Democratic Society, the Progressive Labor Party, and the Young Socialist Alliance. All of these organizations are young, dynamic, open, and in ideological agreement with Marxism. They differ among themselves only as to means of action. Apart from Youth Against War and Fascism and Students for a Democratic Society, their members still take refuge too often in the clear conscience that comes from giving the blacks "moral" support. But they are all in the process of becoming radicalized and their agitation, like their propaganda, has increasing influence in the cities of the North and the poor rural areas of the South.

The "white" publications which support and even contribute to the development of Black Power are as follows:

(a) *Monthly Review* (of international reputation) which, together with the French review *Partisans* (François Maspero), contributes the most to the renewal of revolutionary thought and to the historical, dialectical analysis of the development of the class struggle throughout the world. By their profound economic analyses, Baran, Sweezy, Huberman, Gunder Frank, and the others are successfully carrying on the work undertaken more than a century ago by Marx and Engels. Together with the *Partisans* group, they are certainly the intellectuals of the capitalist world who are closest to the revolutionaries of the entire world, the most useful to them on the level of revolutionary ideology and strategy and the most listened to and respected by the movements struggling against oppression. (b) *The Partisan*, published by Youth Against War and Fascism, a review more accessible to the masses and, like *Monthly Review*, open to the problems of revolutionary movements the world over. (c) *The Young Socialist*, published monthly by the group of the same name. (d) *Challenge*, the newspaper of the Progressive Labor Party, published in English and Spanish (for the Puerto Ricans and Dominicans "in exile" in New York).

B. *The Puerto Ricans and the Mexicans:* The Puerto Ricans of New York, of whom there are at least a million and whose numbers are growing very rapidly, constitute an increasingly dangerous mass for the capital of "free enterprise" where everything is the "greatest in the world." Unemployment, slums, disease, and ignorance bring them together with the blacks in the same struggle for liberation. Besides, the majority of them live near Harlem, and as nearly all the Puerto Ricans are brown or black, they are coming more and more to form a single community with the Afro-Americans—especially since they share the same living conditions as their Harlem brothers. (A fact to be underlined: in the Manhattan House of Detention, one of the biggest prisons in the state of New York, where Charles

Gagnon and I have been held since September 28, a minimum of 80 percent of the prisoners are black or Puerto Rican. The remaining 20 percent are chiefly Greeks, Italians, Jews, Poles, *et al.*, in short "white niggers." The subordinate prison personnel are in great majority black, while the superior officers—captains and so on—are almost exclusively white. Personally, since I have been here I have seen only one black captain . . . and God knows we see enough captains! They are the only "visitors" we have inside the cell blocks.)

The Puerto Ricans, to whom should be added a few thousand Dominicans, Haitians, Japanese, *et al.*, who live in the same district, have a few newspapers and magazines of their own. But unfortunately, these newspapers and magazines are quite conservative, although not so much so as the Yankee publications. There are a few small groups of revolutionaries (made up chiefly of refugees from Santo Domingo), but as yet nothing comparable to the black organizations. At first glance, it seems that the Puerto Ricans lack the "rediscovered pride" and determination which animate the struggle of the blacks. They seem more completely crushed, more disoriented. Many thousands of them do not speak a word of English, unlike the blacks, who all speak English. Consequently, they are more withdrawn into themselves and more vulnerable to the despotic nature of the system. The prisons of New York are filled with *innocent* Puerto Ricans who have no means of defense. The blacks, in general, do better; not because they are more intelligent, but because despite the centuries of slavery their community is better equipped, because they are more numerous, and because they have rediscovered their collective pride. They have a class consciousness which the Puerto Ricans have not yet sufficiently developed. But the struggle for independence and revolution going on in Puerto Rico makes them more aware every day, and their anti-imperialism is becoming more violent. A number of black and white organizations are presently contributing to the awakening of a Puerto Rican class consciousness that later will spontaneously integrate itself with a broader class consciousness, a class consciousness that is international and multiracial.

As for the Mexican-Americans of Texas and California, they are organized in agricultural workers' unions. In 1966 their demands took on unprecedented scope. Forming a population of a few million disinherited workers, stripped of everything, underpaid and enslaved to seasonal labor, they have begun to invade the luxurious cities of the "new rich" by the thousands. A number of strikes and demonstrations, directed jointly by union leaders and priests, have been repressed by the "Western-style" reigning Order, which did not hesitate to have Kennedy assassinated and which is the brains and heart of the white, millionaire, extreme Right. The "Kennedy" men, who are not very firmly established in this region, are trying to take advantage of the discontent of the Mexican-American "poor" who are beginning to imitate the black "poor." It is possible that the Mexican-Americans will continue to be deceived by the Democratic Party, because their struggle is only beginning and an ideology corresponding to their true interests does not seem to have been formulated yet. It is possible that they will be fooled by a Martin Luther King or a Bobby Kennedy (who is only a fascist disguised as a liberal and who is taking advantage of his brother's "canonization" by capitalist opinion to attempt to succeed him). But the recent and current history of the "decolonization of the American black" (that is the title of a book by Daniel Guérin, published by Editions de Minuit, Paris), demonstrates that all the Martin Luther Kings that capitalism can manufacture, now and in the future, are—like the system itself—not strong enough to resist the will of the majority of men, to resist their vital need for concrete freedom. The Mexicans of Texas and California will also finally come to understand that this freedom is not to be found by marking an X on a ballot.

C. *The "white niggers":* Although their unions are rotten to the core, although most of their parties—including the Communist Party—are conservative and accept the rules of the democratic (i.e., legal) game, the workers, students, intellectuals, and youth of the United States are beginning to recognize the true nature of the system, its *arbitrary* character, which is called freedom of the individual. (Which individuals? The rich, of course, those who can "buy" anything they want, even the right to kill the weak, to jail them, exploit them, etc.; those who regularly spend millions to get themselves elected so as to be able to "democratically" impose on the people laws which will enable them to make even more millions, and to manufacture wars—in Vietnam, the Congo, Santo Domingo etc.—in order to make billions out of the oppression they give themselves the right to exercise over three-quarters of humanity . . . in the name of the Rights of Man, the United Nations, world peace, the great Kennedy, Saint Paul VI, God the Father, and General Motors!) The war in Vietnam, the bloody repression of the Dominican revolution, the intervention of the CIA in Indonesia, in Algeria, and in Brazil in 1965, the struggle of the blacks, the growing number of spontaneous strikes, the widespread and growing unemployment, poverty, delinquency, etc., the increasingly frequent intervention of the State Department in the private lives of members of the opposition, the rising cost of living, etc., are turning the white "American Way of Life" into a veritable hell. Revolt is rumbling among the whites. Housewives boycott the supermarkets; union members go out on wildcat strikes; young people ally themselves with the blacks against the Southern and Northern racists, publicly tear up their draft cards and other symbols of American imperialism, burn Johnson in effigy and choose to go to jail rather than murder innocent Vietnamese. The unemployed and the poor whites, say thirty million Americans, are still unorganized. But out of the present social agitation there should arise a revolutionary organization capable of reaching this mass which now has no voice or power but which, if it rose up united with the blacks, Puerto Ricans, and Mexican-Americans, would soon rid humanity of its worst enemies. Let us hope that the "New Left" in America will soon recognize the urgency of building a revolutionary organization and will devote less energy to publishing seventy-five newspapers that have undeniable value . . . but not the value of a people in arms. (It is interesting to note that most of the leaders of the progressive "white" movements are of non-British origin; they are the descendants of the generations of immigrants from whom the big bourgeoisie, which is of British stock, has drawn its wealth by exploiting their labor to the maximum and by rigorously applying the social philosophy of Adam Smith: give the worker a subsistence, that is, just enough to enable him to go on producing surplus value as long as possible for the profit of the Wall Street birds of prey.)

To that Left which is accustomed to orderly offices and "anti-revisionist" conventions, the day when the whites will take up arms, join with blacks and other minorities, and march on Washington seems far off. But personally, I believe that the American working class is ripe for revolution. Although, like every working class in the world, it is poor in resources and weak in hope, it lacks neither courage nor ingenuity. But since the Left neglects its responsibilities and is still content to wait, it may be up to the black revolutionaries to give the "white niggers" the opportunity and the means of making the revolution, notwithstanding all the difficulties presented by such an undertaking in a society contaminated by racism. But the economic interests of the workers, whatever the color of their skin, always win out in the end, overcoming both racism and religious prejudice. The poor economic health of the American people in this last third of the twentieth century leads me to believe that the American revolution is already on the march.

14. To be convinced of this, one need only read or reread the Québécois literature of the 1950's.

2
The Realm of Childhood

When I was born, a year and a half before the Second World War, there was growing unrest among the working class of Quebec. The year before there had been bloody riots in Sorel, and a number of strikes were turning to violence in Montreal and the other cities of Quebec. After the years of "social peace" which had followed the great conscription crisis of 1917, a degree of hope was appearing for the first time.

A small group of idealists, of "Communists," were trying as best they could to exorcise the people's obscurantism and fear of living, to change their traditional frustration and despair into passion and class struggle. It was not easy. But there was a steadily growing number of people who, like my father, believed that these men, denounced by the financiers and the politicians in power, were right. Yes, it was necessary to change *everything*, tear everything down and start afresh, get rid of the exploiters.

The English and American financiers, the French-Canadian petty bourgeoisie and the clergy—united by common interests despite their continual wrangling—were asking: "What is happening to our people who have always been so peaceful, so industrious, so profoundly religious [read: resigned], so submissive?" The Catholic Middle Ages and capitalist oppression did not want to die.

There was more and more talk of the approaching war. For some, it was an opportunity for awakening and revolt. For others, the material justification of despair. Most people were disoriented, torn by contradictory feelings and unable to take a position.

It is hard for a people to learn to shake off a long period of disenchantment.[1]

"It's all very well to revolt, but what good does it do?"

The Husband, coming home from the factory where the whole day had been filled with the workers' anger against the system, would try to convince his wife. But she, who had spent the whole day alone contemplating the grayness that covered the city—and her life—could not believe in miracles.

"Look," the Québécois Wife would say, "look how wretched we are. Our servitude has become so complicated. . . . There's no cure for it. War is coming. It's going to open up old wounds that are not yet healed and make new ones . . . even worse ones. Because these days they are much better equipped to spread death and suffering.

"Your friends talk about a new society because they want to take advantage of us. . . .

"No, you're right, I shouldn't have said that.

"But why do they insist on reawakening a hope that will soon be dead and will have done no good? Can your friends prevent the war, depression, misery?

"Once again the flesh of millions of men is going to rot in the mud of battlefields, just as yours goes on turning black in the sweaty soot of the Angus Shops of the CPR! °

"Our flesh, which has never known the tenderness or the warmth of . . . what I dare not name, is only good these days for sowing the land with blood spilled for nothing. And you think that out of this universal atrocity there can one day come fraternity? You're dreaming, my friend, or else you like to forget reality. . . ."

The Wife felt like crying aloud the anguish she felt as a solitary slave, a disillusioned and exhausted mother hen.

The Husband, his face hard, his eyes wet, his heart full of kindness and anger, would place his worn hands on the Wife's shoulders.

"That's why I want to fight. You are right to complain. But you are wrong to be resigned."

"I know it won't do any good," she would reply.

"*I* know it *will* do some good . . . to somebody . . . to our children, maybe."

° Montreal is the eastern terminal point of the Canadian Pacific Railway, and Angus Shops are its center for locomotive repair. (Trans.)

He would drop the discussion and say no more. Impatient as a child getting ready for a party, he would wash his face, his neck, arms, hands, consulting the newspaper the while to check the time and place of the meeting. . . .

1

It was a strange marriage, the one between my mother's disenchantment and my father's timid but tenacious hope. I do not know if it was a happy one. But I do not remember having observed in my parents the *joie de vivre* that one sees in people who are secure and self-confident and have no trouble believing in life.

I always saw my parents worried, doubtful, anxious . . . even when they happened to laugh. Men who are condemned to death are sometimes overcome with fits of laughter too. That does not mean anything. And above all, that does not *change* anything.

What their daily problems were I know, for I lived through all their anxieties. But what was their love life like? That is something I can only surmise, only deduce from what I came to know after many years of painful conflict.

The first years of their marriage were doubtless different from those which followed, those which I knew, when with "three boys on their hands" my parents lived in continual fear of *tomorrow*—that is, of possible unemployment, possible illness, possible hunger and want. They could never escape from that fear by allowing themselves to forget their cares once in a while, to let go a little, to have a bit of diversion. No. They had to *economize*. Economize on everything, even affection. They had to make ends meet before they could think about living.

My mother in particular lived in a constant state of insecurity. And her anxiety shut her off from the outside world. My father could free himself at the factory, with his comrades on the job. My brothers and I could free ourselves by playing with our friends or going to school. Then we escaped from the family hell. But my mother never went out. She could have made real friends among her neighbors but refused to do so. It was as if the only thing she lived for was to calculate income and expenditures, wax the floors, wash the windows, cook and do laundry—as if she were forbidden to leave the house.

Nothing roused her interest. Nothing appealed to her . . . except her Sacred Duty, which, in her mind, was the obligation to be continually on guard against any "accident." That was why she did not want my father to get involved in politics, why my brothers and I were not allowed beyond the immediate vicinity of the house, etc.

Anything that disturbed her habits was a terrible anxiety to her. She never ran a risk or took a chance. She was as much afraid of what might help her as of what might harm her, of what might help us as of what might harm us. She wanted to be sure of everything, to have many guarantees, to hold on to what she had. Any prospect of change would keep her awake at night. She always feared the *worst*. "What if there were a change for the *worse*?" That was one of her favorite questions. She clung to the little we possessed and refused to loosen her grip, to relax the tight vigilance that was stretched to the breaking point.

Within a few years she changed into the "boss" of the little family of which she was the principal servant. She became a slave to fear and tried to subjugate my father, my brothers, and me to her need for security.

Security took precedence over freedom, economy over love, resignation over hope.

"Donalda" had made her Sacred Duty into a tyranny from which, insofar as possible, "sentiment" was to be progressively eliminated.° My mother was unconscious of all this, but it was very hard for the rest of us to bear. We suffocated.

That is why I have the impression that my parents never knew love but only pretended to love each other, as thousands of Québécois have done and still do.

There is no doubt that my mother suffered a great deal. She was disappointed in her condition, her poverty, and perhaps also in her marriage, her husband, and her children. In any case, she loved no

---

° Donalda is the heroine of a novel by Claude-Henri Grignon, *Un Homme et son péché* (A Man and His Sin) (1933). The novel was a bestseller and was later made into a movie and into highly successful radio and television serials. According to the story, Séraphin, an aging miser, has made a bargain with Donalda's father (a peasant who is in debt to him) for the hand of his daughter. Donalda is secretly in love with young Alexis, but being a good French-Canadian Catholic, represses her love and remains faithful to her tyrannical husband. (Trans.)

one except her husband and children. But I am not sure she loved us as we would have wished to be loved. I can even say that, outwardly, her love seemed to be only a sacred duty, and that it had none of that quality which sometimes makes human love more precious than life itself.

My mother suffered from her insecurity and did not want a still greater insecurity to come and add to her suffering. My father (who likewise suffered constantly from insecurity) would have preferred to join in a struggle against it instead of submitting to it. He knew that it was a social and collective problem that demanded social and political engagement. But my mother saw it only as an individual or, at most, a family problem. For her, other people did not exist. She did not know them and did not want to know them. For my father, on the contrary, other people did exist: they were his comrades at the shop, the neighbors with whom he had long conversations (although he was a very silent man at home), his brothers and sisters for whose sake he had left school at the age of fourteen and gone to work, taking the place of his paralyzed father. My father read the newspapers and was interested in everything they said. But never would my mother have "allowed" him to become involved in politics or social questions.

In *Man's Fate*, Malraux has Kyo say that to recognize another person's freedom is to acknowledge his right to it, even at the cost of one's own suffering. My father acknowledged my mother's right to freedom despite his own need to combat oppression. But what good did that do him? Over the years, his life, which was increasingly identified with his work—the work of an underpaid slave—became a routine made up of silently endured humiliations and useless submission to the arbitrary will of an anxious wife. Can it be said that in this way, through "love" for my mother, he recognized her freedom by acknowledging her right to it even at the cost of his own suffering? Can one recognize another person's freedom to annihilate you, to imprison you in a fear that is irrational and, to put it bluntly, selfish?

In my opinion, there is no love where there is abdication. And my father abdicated. It is true that since the age of fourteen he had been wearing himself out working and that his health was not very good. On weekends I would often urge him to follow his dreams and make haste to do something. But I soon noticed that by the next day he had given up the idea. Between us two, there was always my mother's "No."

How I wish my mother had been a woman with some courage and at least as much hope as my father. I am certain that then my father would have lived better and given a meaning to his life, because he would have fought against oppression instead of submitting to it without a word.

I do not know what my father was like at the factory. From the conversations I had with him I gathered that he and his comrades often discussed their common problems and that they had not forgotten the teaching of the Communists. Since the end of the war, nothing more had been heard of them, but their ideas remained in the air. Everyone at the factory agreed with those ideas and was desperately seeking a party to put them into practice immediately. There was talk of the reforms that had been brought about by the CCF in Saskatchewan,° but the CCF did not know that there were thousands of Québécois workers who would have liked to hear its leaders tell them in French that their party was ready to give them a hand too. The men were alone. They voted for Duplessis because they had to, out of habit, the way they went to Mass on Sunday . . . and waited to be offered a real choice. There was no alternative.

My father was probably impassioned at the shop. At any event, his comrades loved him. But at home he was a defeated man.

He was not the only one in that situation. Many of his friends had been defeated by their wives. But unlike my father, they reacted violently on pay day, getting drunk, beating their wives and driving the whole family out of the house. The next day, however, they would go to confession and become gentle, silent husbands again. Silent at home, but in a constant state of rage at the shop, where they were always denouncing their situation and cursing it.

Why, then, had my parents married, if it was not in order to escape together from their condition? They had married at a time when it was almost impossible for working-class families to provide for their basic needs. Hunger left no time for love and pleasure.

° The CCF (Cooperative Commonwealth Federation), a social democratic party, was the forerunner of the present New Democratic Party. (Trans.)

Earning money, as much money as possible (because there was so little), took all the man's time. While the woman, busy counting pennies, seeing to the meals, cleaning up the kids, scrubbing the floors, always *alone* (even when her husband, stiff with fatigue, was lying by her side), could hardly imagine any way out of her misery other than a long, hard road of relentless, *individual* labor, beset with uncertainties and threatened time after time by illness or unemployment. A tenacious labor which all the same represented a will to live and prosper, but which did not count on any help from others. A solitary labor which often consisted of going around in circles through the daily chores: washing, cooking, cleaning. . . . Which also often became perverted, and degenerated into avarice, selfishness, narrow-mindedness, and a hardening of the heart.

The misery created by the system pushed my parents into marriage after a brief acquaintance. This misery did not disappear by virtue of the sacrament. It remained unchanged, heavy, demanding. It separated husband and wife, enclosing them in two different universes. The system shut my father up in the shop and my mother in cramped lodgings. At the shop my father had the fraternity of men working together; the work was hard, but there were many of them doing it, and they all wanted to free themselves from it. At home, on the contrary, my mother was alone with the children, and she was always faced with the same drudgery; she was forbidden by tradition from trying to "escape her duty" as a Christian-mother-submissive-to-the-will-of-the-Good-Lord.

If love was there in the beginning, a host of factors very soon forced it out of this world monopolized by the million little worries that poverty engenders. And this was not an exceptional "case." Only priests imagine that love can adapt itself to misery, to a stupefying daily routine, to crass ignorance of the laws and beauties of sexuality, to Jansenism and the dictatorship of capitalism. Only priests can see a kind of paradise in the proletarian hell; and how useful they are then, without knowing it, to capitalism! When a woman makes love out of a sense of sacred duty and submits to her husband's passion the way a prisoner submits to torture by the military police, how can joy dwell in her? When a man abandons the control of his own destiny to his wife—to please her, or prevent her from making a scene—how can joy dwell in him? And when children grow up in an atmosphere of constant frustration, how can joy reach them?

Sometimes it seemed to me that my father was ashamed of himself, and that my mother was afraid of her own desperate eagerness to preserve present security and ensure it in the future. The more I became aware of this spiritual poverty that went around in a vacuum, the more I said to myself that to accept this state of things was a crime against oneself and against others, and that one had to do *everything* to break the vicious circle of misery. In the beginning, the absolute evil, the foundation of this absurdity, seemed to me to be the family. Later, I came to understand that the family—more precisely, the working-class family—was only a product of the condition of the working class, which was itself the product of centuries of exploitation of man by man.

The terrible thing about the working-class family is the function, imposed on it by the present system, of renewing and perpetuating the supply of slaves, of niggers, of cheap labor to be exploited, alienated, and oppressed. And the inhuman thing about a working-class childhood is the child's powerlessness to resist the conditioning not only of the system itself but of all the frustrations of the life around him, frustrations that are generated by the capitalist organization of society and that contaminate him even before he becomes aware of their existence. The children of the bourgeoisie are frustrated too, but not in the same way. The bourgeois child, when he becomes aware of reality, revolts against his parents and only rarely against his milieu or his class, *which is in power.* The proletarian child too revolts against his parents, but very early his revolt turns against the condition of his class and those who are responsible for that condition. The revolt of the bourgeois child and adolescent usually remains an individual affair. The revolt of the working-class child and adolescent is, from the outset, a larger problem: first, the son of a proletarian is ashamed of his humiliated class and wants to get out of it; opposed to his entire milieu, he often seeks, through individual success, to be admitted to the middle class even at the risk of betraying his own. But the bourgeoisie can admit to its ranks only a tiny number of "parvenus," for otherwise it might lose control over the exploitation of the working masses. That is why, in the majority of cases, the revolt of the worker's son changes into class consciousness and an increasingly resolute will to work toward overthrowing the system. Of course the system crushes a great number of them, for it has many methods of oppression, psychological as well as economic; but in the long run the revolt spreads, grows deeper and more lasting, and it is then that the union of all these workers, who are profoundly frustrated but increasingly *conscious*, begins to make the ruling class feel that its days are numbered.

It is therefore very difficult for a member of the working class to "make it" on his own. In order to liberate themselves, the workers must unite to tear down the old order and the old values and to build on their ruins a new order and new values, which will make new men, create a new society, and constitute a true humanism, for the first time in history.

Notwithstanding the fact that it remains a social monstrosity, as is clearly expressed in the literature of the nineteenth and twentieth centuries in capitalist countries, the bourgeois family nevertheless retains an economic base that enables even "its" rebels to prosper, to achieve fame and fortune. Gide, Mauriac, and Sartre remain bourgeois and privileged members of the system in their very revolt. Even their blasphemy is profitable[2] and can earn them a Nobel Prize! In Quebec the same remark holds good for the Maheus, Chamberlands, Préfontaines, *et al.*, who while cursing their families and their class make enormous profits from so doing.

The worker's son, with rare exceptions, makes no money and achieves no honor or renown by revolting—for the simple economic reason that he does not have the financial means to publicize his revolt and to buy literary prizes, fellowships from the Conseil des Arts, and finally a chair at the University. The bourgeois manufacture "shocking" and even pornographic novels for the same reasons that they periodically invent "quiet revolutions": to give themselves progressive airs, to salve their consciences and to create a little "change" from time to time. For even the bourgeois are *bored*, as contemporary novelists bear witness.

If the bourgeois family is a social monstrosity, as is scientifically demonstrated by psychoanalysis, psychology, pedagogy, and contemporary sociology, what term shall we use to characterize the working-class family, which capitalist religion, capitalist education, capitalist ideology (the state), and capitalist economy have constructed on the model of the bourgeois family, while at the same time—by exploiting the labor of the "head of the family" and often of the mother and children—they deprive it of the economic base of the bourgeoisie? It is an understatement to say that the working-class family is a double or quadruple monstrosity. This "possessing unit"—as Engels calls it—is a hell, a room with no exit,° in which the self-destruction of human beings is accomplished mechanically, like an automatic extension of the exploitation of the worker by his boss, of the farmer by the food trusts, the student by the university of the bankers and pharmacists, the consumer by the department stores and finance companies, the believer by his curé, the patient by his doctor, the accused by his lawyer (the attorney for the "defense"), the journalist by high finance and politics, the entire people by the state, capitalism, and imperialism.

When you are only a "kid," what can you do to escape from the room with no exit, the hell of the frustrating conditioning that seeks to demolish you before you have even become a man? And when, as an adolescent, you stand up, with your back already bent by too much effort, are you in any better position to win out?

And when you are a man, how much energy it takes just to *try* to "reverse engines," as the saying goes. How many sacrifices and how much willpower, how many painful years to reach the point where there is nothing left in you of that childhood and adolescence, nothing left of . . . the nigger, of . . . the man who was born defeated. And in spite of everything, some part of it always remains, not only in your memory but in your flesh and bones.

In the account that follows, I judge not my parents but society. I describe the life of niggers that we led as I lived it. And at first glance it might seem that I am judging men. But that would be a false impression. I have never judged those of my class. But neither have I ever been complaisant toward them. I refuse to pity them, the way one refuses to humiliate someone. I am not the boss of a French-Canadian manufacturing concern!

° This is an allusion to Sartre's well-known play *No Exit*, in which the action takes place in a room in hell. (Trans.)

Pity is a crime against man. Man has a right to the truth, even if it is hard as granite. For a human world can only be built, develop, and endure on a foundation of truth.

My only regret is that it took me so long to understand many things, that I was a cruel adolescent and that, among other things, I discovered my father's mixture of kindliness and sorrow only when he was no longer good for anything but to die of generalized cancer (what an atrocity!) at the age of fifty-three, after twenty years of "loyal service" to the Angus Shops of the CPR! My father still lives among his comrades at Angus Shops. But what is that survival compared to his life? My father "never missed a day of work." When he left Angus, it was to die of exhaustion: what glory!

They say that one must love the living and forget the dead. But I love this dead man who gave me life and with it gave me the visceral need to change our inhuman society. I learned more from this dead man, from his life and the life of his family and friends, than from all the theoreticians of socialism. Another man, who may also be dead, seems to me to have incarnated one of the great dreams that my father transmitted to me as my only inheritance: Ernesto "Che" Guevara.

But right now I am talking about my father and my class as I see them *today*. I did not always think of them in this way. If as a child I was unhappy but integrated with my milieu, as an adolescent I was in continual revolt against my class and also against the bourgeoisie, the entire society and its mythology: God, religion, Evil, Good, etc. But as will be seen later, I was struggling in ignorance and more than once came close to being swallowed up by the things I hated, just as my father had been defeated by his wife's insecurity—an insecurity which nevertheless inspired in him a revolt sympathetic to Communism.

His revolt was gradually drained of its force and meaning and buried in the depths of my parents' life together, a life that steadily shrank into a pitiful existence. But my revolt, confused and demanding, full of love for mankind and rage against injustice, steadily grew.

My story is going to seem brutal to certain members of my family, especially to my mother, if she deigns to read these pages written by her son who, she must still be saying to herself, will "drive her to the grave."

But I believe the time is over in Quebec when you "washed your dirty laundry in private" and thereby escaped your social responsibilities. So much the worse for the laggards, the fearful—or the cowards—who will some day reap the benefits of our hard-won freedom, the bloodsuckers!

2

Sometimes one imagines that his past has disappeared leaving no memory, like a cloud that has drifted apart in the sky. But that is an illusion. One has only to be immobilized for a few weeks (in prison, for example) to find his past again and relive it in its smallest details. Then not only does one rediscover what one thought was forgotten or lost, but in the light of the present and looking back on the route one has traveled since childhood, one understands the meaning of his destiny, its significance. And believe me, there is nothing metaphysical about that significance. It is enough for it to be human.

For the first seven years of my life, I lived in the "East End" of the city, more precisely in the quarter that was at the time (1938–1945) called "Frontenac Park." It was bordered on the west by Logan Street, on the north by Sherbrooke Street, on the east by the railway tracks of the CPR which ran from Angus Shops to the port of Montreal, and on the south by the waterfront. It was a "tough" neighborhood full of rival gangs. Burglaries were common. Every day there were family brawls conducted with iron bars, chains, chairs, or baseball bats. There were days when Harbour Alley, to the east of Frontenac Street, was turned into a veritable arena. It was the poorest alley in the quarter, and my parents forbade my brother and me to venture into it because there were frequent rifle shots, murders and, as *monsieur le curé* used to say, "vulgar spectacles" that did irreparable harm to the youth of the parish.[3]

My favorite occupations were, in summer, wagon races with the kind of carts the newsboys use, and in winter, tobogganing down "Sherbrooke hill." Sherbrooke hill lay to the north of our area, running east and west. We played as freely in the streets as in the fields. Even in summer we would sometimes coast down "the hill" on wagons, which was extremely dangerous because when we got to Hochelaga Street it was very hard to stop. I had some disagreeable accidents that way. But each time I played it tough, because it was the rule of the neighborhood never to bawl. Once a milkman's truck ran over my foot. I was in great pain, but I told the milkman that it didn't hurt at all. When I tried to get back up on the sidewalk, I was unable to move, and the milkman had to take me by force and carry me up, protesting, to my parents' flat.

At that time we were living in a third floor flat (on the corner of Hochelaga and Gascon) and my brother André, who was a few years younger than I, was getting into the habit of rolling down the stairs, at the risk every time of cracking his skull on the sidewalk. My mother was at her wits' end. She couldn't lock us up in our little flat, because we always managed to escape. And once outside, we had no thought but for dangerous games. We associated with shady individuals whom my mother hated and feared. On rainy days, when we were forced to stay home, we made such a racket that despite her fears, she could not help wanting us to go out as soon as possible, to "cool off" a little, as she used to say. As for Raymond, my other brother, he was not yet walking and my mother had no problem with him.

I hung around the sheds of the quarter. The sheds were the headquarters of the gangs. At the age of five, I already belonged to a gang that specialized in turning in false alarms, setting fires at the back of courtyards, and running after girls (with a view to terrorizing them in various ways). I was too young to take a real part in the plots hatched in the sheds, but there were days when I witnessed spontaneous acts of barbarism so cruel that even today they fill me with revulsion. Thus, one of my playmates, Ti-Rouge (or "Carrot"), was a great girl-chaser. He always had a kind of vengeance to work out against someone. I did not know why this boy had so much hate inside him. I only knew that he belonged to a very large family and that his father did not often work. Near his home there lived a couple who were known as "snobs" because they had forbidden their two children (a boy and a girl) to play with the "common people." Ti-Rouge hated this couple. Their boy often escaped to join us, but the little girl told her parents and our friend took a beating. Ti-Rouge had promised himself to teach the "tattle-tale" a good lesson. One day the little girl was walking alone on the sidewalk. She was coming back from the corner restaurant, where her mother had probably sent her to get some candy. As soon as he saw her, Ti-Rouge made a rush, caught her by the hair and with one jerk tore out a braid. Blood began to pour out and the little girl uttered terrible screams. I had witnessed the whole scene. When the little girl began to scream and the blood started to flow, I ran away. When I got home I told my mother about it. And I never saw Ti-Rouge again.

In this violent universe, in which children dreamed about gigantic conflagrations, terrible murderers of women and kidnappers of babies, going to school was, to say the least, a boring diversion. My companions and I were all completely disgusted with it. We constantly made fun of the teacher, whom we found as ugly and amusing as an old wax statue melting in a damp museum (the school). My mother had taught me to read and write two years before I was admitted into the school, so I never knew what to do with my body and my mind in class. As I was then too young to play with my you-know-what, I made paper airplanes and launched them right and left, or else, with the help of a pea-shooter, I bombarded the teacher with spitballs. That was lots of fun . . . until the "old fool" sent me to meditate in the hall. Alone in the corridor, I would think about the conspiracies of the sheds. I said to myself that one day I too would have my own gang . . . and that this school would be razed to the ground! But meantime there was not much I could do, and I would ask the hands of the clock to turn faster, because I was tired and my stomach was empty.

I was seven years old on February 22, 1945. I was in first grade. Only one event impressed me that year: the announcement of V-E Day on May 8, 1945. All the church bells began to ring at the same time. Automobile horns and factory whistles joined in the concert. There was general euphoria. *The war was over.* At least, in Europe. It remained to settle the fate of Japan. A few months later, we heard on the radio that the atomic bomb had just put a definite end to the Second World War and thrown humanity into a new state of suspense: Would the Russians succeed in manufacturing the Bomb? And if so, would it not soon be the end of the world?

When my parents decided to "emigrate" to the other side of the river, the Cold War had come to the rescue of capitalism by preventing the war factories from grinding to a halt.

3

One of the most critical problems of the postwar period was housing. The poor French quarters of Montreal were overcrowded. Rents were going up while wages remained "stable." Many working-class families of the metropolis began to move to the suburbs: Montréal-Nord, Sainte-Rose, Sainte-Thérèse, Ville Saint-Michel, Pointe-aux-Trembles, L'Assomption, and that vast territory on the south bank of the St. Lawrence which was to become Ville Jacques-Cartier.

At Angus Shops, as in many other plants, the workers talked all day long about their housing problems. It was there that my father learned that at Longueuil-Annexe one could get a plot of land and even a house for a reasonable price. There was neither an aqueduct nor a sewage system, but that was only a question of time. A transportation company had bought a few buses and organized a regular service between Montreal and the South Shore. A few families from Montreal had already established themselves there and the children, it seemed, were blooming in the fresh air.

One weekend I went with my father to Longueuil-Annexe. For me it was a big adventure. We had to take the bus at the entrance to the Jacques-Cartier Bridge. We waited a long time before an old gray bus arrived. My father asked the driver if he knew Briggs and Saint-Thomas streets. The driver nodded and told my father he would let him know when we got there. "It's at the end of the line," he said.

The bus gradually filled with passengers and drove onto the bridge. I opened my eyes wide to stare at the river, the boats, St. Helen's Island. Then the bus reached the opposite bank. My father and I had never been on that side of the river. We were in completely strange territory. The bus continued straight down Sainte-Hélène Street, then turned left on the Coteau-Rouge road. This was a real country road. Narrow, zigzag, bumpy, it crossed vast fields in which a few small houses of wood or sheet-metal appeared here and there. For quite a long time we saw only empty fields. Then we saw a farm with a poultry yard and a few cows by the roadside. Finally the bus entered a kind of village and a thick cloud of dust began to vibrate in the air. As most of the windows on the bus were open, we absorbed this dust, which smelled of dry earth, crumbled stone, and drought, through our noses, ears, eyes, and mouths. Turning toward my father, the driver shouted: "We're almost there!" The bus turned left and started down Briggs Street. The cloud of dust hid the houses and made the street disappear behind us as we advanced.

"Saint-Thomas!"

We got up. The bus stopped and the driver wished us luck the way a friend shakes your hand and says something encouraging when he thinks the adventure you are about to embark upon is sheer madness. We got off the bus, awkwardly; we were nervous, like travelers setting out into unknown territory.

Was it possible that freedom lay in this little village with dirt roads and scattered, dilapidated little houses, that it was to be found in this out-of-the-way place full of dust and dirty children?

There were only about ten houses on Saint-Thomas Street. On either side of the street and around each plot ran ditches filled with black, stagnant water that gave off a strong smell. "Tainted water," my father said to me. It was thick, sticky, covered with a cloud of flies and buzzing insects. We swallowed the dust that had stuck in our throats.

We walked for a while without hurrying. Then my father stopped in front of a little red and white house. "Eleven ninety-seven," he murmured. "This is it." A man came out of the house to meet us. He had the broad, toothy smile of a vegetable dealer who is about to cheat you. I didn't like his looks, but my father seemed to get on easily with him. The man said banal things to me: "How's it going, my little man? You go to school? You like the country?" etc. I did not answer. No, decidedly I did not like that man. But the impressions one has at the age of seven may not mean much.

I did not like the man, or his wife either, for that matter; she looked even more like a storekeeper than her husband. I saw that they wanted to sell their house and that they were only interested in us two as possible buyers of that house. I have never liked trade or tradesmen. For trade divides men into antagonistic groups, stimulates the exploitation of the weak and naive (the "pure," the simple), by the strong and "smart," constantly enriches some and constantly impoverishes others.

Nevertheless, I was happy to be in the country, and the smell rising from the ditches was less disgusting to me than the forced smiles of the man and woman. I stayed outside, gazing at the landscape (a grand word for such a shabby reality), while my father followed the couple into the house.

On the other side of the street there were only three houses, separated by fields. A little farther off were some woods. I imagined them full of Indians and wild animals. I began to hope my father would buy the house. I couldn't have cared less what the house would be like to live in. It was the woods and fields I was suddenly interested in. They would be much better than the sheds in the city.

When my father came out of the little red and white house, he seemed pleased.

"You know," said the owner, "there are no taxes to pay here. There's no mayor, no city hall, and nobody who gets political patronage. It's all bound to come some day, but in the meantime they leave you alone."

My father asked him why he had put his house up for sale.

"I've just built a bigger house on the Coteau-Rouge. I have five children now, you know. And then, I want to start a business around there, a grocery. The population is going to grow fast. Some plots have already been sold. They're talking about opening up several new streets next spring. I've always dreamed of working for myself. Sooner or later you've got to make up your mind to take a risk, no? Otherwise, you're just marking time. . . . Right now I'm a longshoreman. It's irregular. In the winter there's no work. I'm fed up with that life. It's slavery, and I've put up with it for too long. And then, I want to send my children to the best *collèges*. I don't want them to have to do the same as me. I want them to have good jobs and an easy life. . . . Anyway, if I don't make it, we won't be any worse off than we are now."

My father listened to the man, devouring him with his eyes.

How long would *he* remain a slave of the CPR?

My father, who was then thirty-three, had been working since the age of fourteen. He had had to leave school in the fourth grade because his father, paralyzed by a serious illness, could no longer earn enough for his wife and fourteen children. "The oldest ones," and my father in particular, had had to resign themselves to taking over responsibility for the "Vallières tribe."

It was a few years before the crash of 1929. When the Great Depression came, the whole "tribe" had had to struggle in abject poverty, like most of the working-class families of Montreal. A few years later, the war and the draft were to increase their many difficulties by adding the fear of dying on a battlefield for a cause that was of no concern to the working class.

My father sometimes talked to me about those years of black misery. And from the things he told me, I have the impression that at that time the relations between one man and another, one beggar and another, were enveloped and steeped in a silent despair . . . silent because it was too profound for men to believe in the efficacy of cries and tears. Until the day when the anti-conscription movement reawakened the old revolt and set off the riots of 1917. But until the war, a despair like that of men condemned to death was the daily bread of the workers of Quebec.

My mother's family, like my father's, went through the black misery of the 1930's. My mother's father also fell sick during the Depression, and my mother had to abandon her studies and go to work. When she became a "secretary" in some office, she had just finished her ninth year with the Soeurs de Notre-Dame. These aristocrats of the Catholic world of Quebec had taught her, among other things, to despise her class ("the common people") and had given her a taste for bourgeois "good manners." My grandfather's illness suddenly put an end to my mother's ambitions, and she tried to turn her disappointment into Christian obedience to the will of God. Like most of the Québécois women of that time, she began to amass credits for entrance into Heaven, although unlike other Christian women, she did not feel obliged to go to church every morning. Her bitterness was her form of prayer, and her daily toil was her liturgy. She detested the pious women (praying machines) just as much as she did the local gossips. She prayed, hated, tormented herself, suffered in her heart, for herself.

My father and mother were both twenty-five when they were married, two years before the Second World War. My grandfathers had died almost at the same time, six months earlier, after very long illnesses. My parents had met in Lafontaine Park. They had decided almost at once to get married. They betook themselves to the church as soon as they had saved enough money to buy the essential furniture. There was no banquet on their wedding day and no honeymoon. They immediately installed themselves in a little house on Gilford Street. It was there that I was born in February 1938. A few months later, my father had managed to find a job at Angus Shops and we moved to Frontenac Park. And it was in that quarter, one of the many French-Canadian ghettos which the merchants call the

"French East End," that our little family lived through the war and all the problems it created.

At this time the Communists were very active at Angus Shops, and my father, while outwardly practicing "his" religion, agreed with the ideas of these men who wanted to give power to those who worked and wealth to those who produced it, who wanted to give the government and the factories to the workers. To a large extent the Communists ran the union of the Angus employees, but unfortunately their work was sabotaged by the Stalinist bureaucracy, which was as active in Quebec as in France, Italy, Spain. All the strikes they organized in Quebec in the thirties and forties only served in the end to put pseudo-Leftists in power (in the Canadian and American unions), men who soon made way for the capitalists and the gangsters of big-business-style unionism. The handful of revolutionaries who managed to retain their positions were reduced to impotence and used by the Big Labor Bosses to give reactionary unionism a progressive appearance. Capitalism has always tolerated a small minority of dissenters —of men who "talk" revolution—as a clever subterfuge to make people believe in the existence of democracy, freedom of speech, and freedom of thought (without freedom of action!). Business unionism, which is an institution of the capitalist system, applies the same strategy to maintain the illusion of democracy among the working class. But strikers have only to reject the betrayals of the leaders they are supposed to have elected themselves (in their own interest) for "democratic" unionism to call out the cops with their nightsticks and the goons of the underworld. And while the most courageous of the strikers take their way to prison like common criminals, the bigshots, in the name of the working class, sit down with the bosses to a good steak!

In 1938, '39, and '40, my father firmly believed that once the war was over, the unions would transform the life of the workers in Quebec. The American union movement was dynamic then, and the Québécois-Catholic-and-French unions were slowly beginning, with some hesitation and confusion, to reject the corporatism of the encyclicals.°

° Corporatism was a notion picked up from European fascist ideology in the thirties by the Québécois élite of the classical *collèges*. In essence, it stated that every sector of society should be represented in the state by its representative association. (Trans.)

At this time my father would doubtless have been active in a political party had it not been for the stubborn opposition of my mother, for whom "getting involved in politics" was "a waste of time and a way of letting yourself be exploited by unscrupulous people."

"Rest a bit," my mother would often say to my father when he began to talk politics or union affairs. "When you get sick, *they* won't be the ones to take care of you."

Later, my father thought about participating in various social activities. He wanted to join the others in Ville Jacques-Cartier who were trying to find a way to give themselves, to give the whole population, *dignity*, so that they would not be treated in the newspapers like the human refuse of the neighboring metropolis. But there too, my mother used her veto. (Very early in life I promised myself that nobody was going to get *me* with vetos, with "you'll-only-wear-yourself-out-you'll-only-let-them-put-one-over-on-you-you'll-only-get-yourself-killed-for-nothing.")

It was not that my mother, like Duplessis, saw the red devil (Communism) in all forms of social activity. No. For she was hardly more "faithful" than my father to the teachings of the Mother of mothers, the Church. In her it was irrational. Her stubborn opposition to all social and political activity was a kind of neurosis and, as such, was obscurely rooted in the unconscious, probably in the congenital insecurity of the working class. For my mother was not an exception. Capitalism and religion have mass-produced mothers like mine . . . and rare are the Québécois—at least in the working class—who, at a certain period of their lives, have not been suffocated by the love (?) of a possessive mother.

I have already said that my parents were not particularly pious. Like all the troubled and the anxious, they attended Sunday Mass, and from time to time they went to confession. They were not the sort who collected sacred pictures and went in for pilgrimages. They practiced their religion partly out of tradition and partly out of fear of hell. They obeyed the law. Their love of God did not go beyond the minimal observance of the commandments. They did not seek the company of priests or members of religious orders. They detested the "sisters" because they saw them as nothing more than avaricious businesswomen who were hostile to the poor, especially in the hospitals. My father, even more than my mother, was a Catholic in spite of

himself, a Catholic who—like many another in this country—did not
dare to declare publicly his indifference to religion.

4

On the way back from Longueuil-Annexe, my father was not
thinking either about God or politicians. He was dreaming of the
house he would build out of this shack he had decided to buy. It remained only to convince my mother of the advantages of exile to the
suburbs.

"If only Madeleine can agree to it," he said to himself. He was
marshaling his arguments and silently preparing his case. "We'll be
at peace. The children will have all the room they need to play. We'll
be masters in our own house. There will be no more stairs to go up
and down. André won't kill himself rolling downstairs. Pierre won't
hang around the alleys and sheds any more. . . ." My father tried to
visualize the future: "The area is going to develop. The owner said
so; the men at the shop say so too. There will be schools, stores, all
the conveniences of the city. The slums will gradually disappear.
They're going to install an aqueduct and a sewage system. They're
going to pave the streets with asphalt and make sidewalks. They're
going to plant trees. The government has already promised a hospital
for the South Shore. . . ."

The owner was prepared to stretch the payments out over many
years. . . . The union would soon obtain raises. . . . Life would become easier. . . . He would enlarge the house. A few years from
now, Madeleine and the "little ones" would have peace and comfort.
He could save a little money, and when the children grew up he
would be able to allow himself to do a bit of traveling with Madeleine, a Madeleine relaxed, reassured, happy—they would take a
vacation in the north country, see the Gaspé and the sea, and—who
knows?—some day they might go to Vancouver, see the Rockies, the
Pacific. . . .

My father was building the future in his mind, trying to imagine
his domain, which he would build patiently when he got home from
the shop, on weekends, and during his annual two weeks' vacation.
He would draw up the plan himself. He would do everything himself.
Others were doing it, why not he? . . .

The bus, now on the bridge, had just passed St. Helen's Island.

While I looked at the boats riding at anchor, I asked my father if we would be able to go hunting in the woods across the way, which I had spent part of the afternoon gazing at. He only replied: "First we have to persuade your mother."

For eight years my father had been dreaming of some day owning his own home. Of course, the shack was no castle, but it was still better than spending the rest of your life as a tenant in the damp apartments of the Royal Trust. "At least in Longueuil-Annexe," he said to himself, "there aren't any rats, or soot, or smoke. . . . You've got fresh air." (He was forgetting the polluted water, the dust, the queer smells.)

And then, what did he know about people's habits, about their mentality?

When we got home at supper time, my father realized that he had forgotten to ask the owner of the shack if there were a few stores around, a doctor, a church, a school, etc.

All he knew was that there was regular bus service between Longueuil-Annexe and Montreal.[4]

5

Madeleine said yes. And a month later we moved to Longueuil-Annexe.

The shack was made of wood covered with *"papier brique,"* a kind of tarpaper designed to look like brick. In the center front was a little white porch. Inside, only three rooms: in the middle a kitchen, which also served as dining room, living room, bathroom, etc.; to the left, a large bedroom which my parents shared with Raymond (who was not yet walking); lastly, to the right, a tiny room with a double-decker bed and a chest of drawers: this was the room of the "two oldest," André and me. The rooms were separated by walls of *"donnacona,"* a kind of hard, thick cardboard which could be bought quite cheaply from any dealer in building materials. Manufactured by Domtar in the Portneuf region (I think), *donnacona* was easy to cut up, install, and paint, and it was usually sold in panels four feet by eight. Many of the shacks that went up in Ville Jacques-Cartier in the years following our arrival were built entirely out of two-by-fours and broad panels of this economical cardboard, which was then covered with tarpaper. It was not exactly warm in winter, but it didn't cost much, and with this miraculous material you could build a little house in two days!

Our shack seemed almost luxurious compared to most of the hovels in Longueuil-Annexe, which were covered with black tarpaper and looked like sinister old shanties abandoned in a swamp. On rainy days especially, Longueuil-Annexe looked like a burnt-out shantytown. The only trouble with this shantytown was that it was inhabited, to adopt a phrase from the Québécois poet Roland Giguère.[5]

As can be seen, paper played an important role in the construction of the houses, which were also called "shit-houses." *Papier brique*, tarpaper, *donnacona* . . . From the surplus wood and paper they did not export back home, the Americans made cheap building materials to be sold to the cheap labor of Quebec to make them masters in their own houses!

Unlike most of the houses, our shack was located not at the back of the lot but at the front. There was a little hay growing around, which we were going to try to make into a lawn! To the right, between the street and the house, there was a cement well where you pumped water by hand. My father was supposed to install an electric pump soon, and he was already thinking about building on another room. He was forever making plans, while my mother scrubbed the floors and my brother and I went looking for Indians in the woods across the way.

In 1945 Longueuil-Annexe had a population of perhaps one or two thousand. There was no administration, and you had to go to Longueuil to obtain a building permit or any other such paper. But at that time Longueuil-Annexe was only the largest of an infinite number of little islands of houses springing up here, there, and everywhere out of the immense fields which in the space of a few years were to be transformed into a vast mushroom-city. These blocks of houses had not yet been named, and life there was, as my father said, "rather primitive." Longueuil-Annexe, a better-organized shantytown—it had four "main" streets and four cross streets, a grocery, a post office, bus stops, and even a little school run by nuns—was in the enviable position of having a chapel that served the surrounding area. Every Sunday a priest from Longueuil came to say Mass in the little wooden chapel at the corner of the Chambly and Coteau-Rouge roads. The bishop had promised the local "petty bourgeoisie" (the two old maids who ran the post office and the proprietors of the grocery store) that he would soon appoint a curé and grant Longueuil-Annexe the status of a parish. As soon as this news began to circulate, people said that soon they would have to pay for the construction of a luxurious presbytery (a curé is a personage who does not live any old place), when they themselves had to go into debt to pay for the cardboard to cover their houses. No one concealed his annoyance, but neither did anyone dare oppose the decision of the Bishop of Saint-Jean, who was the boss of the diocese. People said to themselves that the arrival of a curé heralded the arrival of the tax collectors. For the curé would surely create a cooperative savings bank and would want the assistance of a mayor to administer this new parish where there were no services of any kind. The administration would need revenues to pay a chief of police, a few firemen, a secretary, etc. Which meant that it would soon be necessary to pay higher and higher taxes. Most people did not suspect the scale of the coming invasion. They thought they were isolated, safe from outside interference, left in peace. They did not know that the owners of the abandoned fields were selling dozens of lots every month to workers who were only waiting to save up a few hundred dollars to move their wives, children, and furniture to the other side of the river.

The impending arrival of a curé disturbed them because most of the adult couples lived together without being married and practiced no religion; very often their children were not baptized. Furthermore, some of them dealt in petty crime and did not care to have a curé inquire into their affairs. A few families were like ours: good family, "hard-working" father, possessive mother, children clean though poorly dressed. My father was very surprised to learn that most of these "good neighbors" were, like himself, employees of the CPR.

I mentioned a local "petty bourgeoisie." I did not mean it as a joke. For in this wretched little village there already existed irreconcilable antagonisms. Even in the beginning, the few "snobs" in the neighborhood formed a separate world. They all lived on the same street: the Chambly road. They all had money and were the only ones who had big houses. The proprietors of the grocery store were the richest. Since they had no competition, they had a monopoly on the trade in foodstuffs and made large profits. Rationing had not yet been abolished. Wages remained very low. But the cost of food was constantly going up. The grocer and his wife extended credit to "the poor," but only so as to justify the robbery they committed daily. "What can we do, madame? With all these unpaid accounts, we'd go bankrupt if we sold things for less!" Of course the accounts were always paid, for the grocer had a lawyer-friend in Longueuil who knew how to force "the poor" (who had suddenly become "drunkards" to the grocer) to pay what they owed. Everyone hated these tradesmen, but no one could afford the luxury of going to Longueuil to do his shopping. In this matter as in others, since you had no money you had to consent to being fleeced.

The great friends of the grocer and his wife were the two old maids who ran the post office. They had also founded a private school for very small children. In the beginning they had only a half dozen pupils to whom they mainly taught the catechism. Having inherited their mother's fortune, they gave themselves the airs of provincial countesses. As soon as the curé arrived in the parish, they became his most assiduous courtiers. They soon founded the sisterhood of the Dames de Sainte-Anne, while the grocer tried, unsuccessfully, to form a Ligue du Sacré-Coeur. The "petty-bourgeois" circle expanded a little with the arrival of a barber and a few small tradesmen who sold clothing, shoes, hardware, etc. But it was at least ten years before this petty bourgeoisie, having profited abundantly from political patronage (the county was "blue"), was in a position to play a role in politics. For the expansion and fusion of the nameless blocks of houses very quickly turned Longueuil-Annexe into just another "quarter" among a score of others and made its inhabitants a minority overwhelmed by the influx of thousands of new "poor." Ville Jacques-Cartier, whose population was still 98 percent working class, was to be surrendered to the looting, corruption, and violence of the big-time gangsters . . . under the benevolent eye of the man who is known today as His Honor, Judge Redmond Roche, and who is said to be very hard on anyone who steals a loaf of bread or a sausage.[6]

6

In September of 1945 my mother sent me to the little local school run by three nuns from Longueuil. The faculty was lay and consisted entirely of old maids who lived in Longueuil or Montreal. They acted like missionaries. We were the savages of Peru whom the White Men from the big city had come to *enlighten*. We had everything to receive, nothing to give. We had to say: *"Merci, mademoiselle," "merci, ma soeur," "merci, monsieur l'inspecteur," "merci, monsieur l'abbé," merci, merci, MERCI!*

If I had known English, there were days when I would have shouted at them: "Mercy! For Chrissake leave us alone!"

Their condescension underdeveloped us, humiliated us, made us constantly restrain our spontaneity . . . for we were afraid of seeming too wild. Ah! cursed school that constipated us and paralyzed us! Prison where, day after day, *they* bored us to death with their disgusting, maternal stupidity! School of childish despair, which gradually turns into a monstrosity daily endured! Incomprehensible punishment . . .

We were happy in the fields, for there at least we did not feel the unbearable humiliation of being regarded and taught as children of "the poor" and not as "normal" human beings.

The sisters and *monsieur l'abbé*—who often kept for themselves the classes in the catechism—were perfectly acquainted with all the tactics of dictatorship and the degradation of minds through humiliation.

The "world of good" was constantly opposed to the "world of evil," saintly women to great sinners, the Salazars to the Stalins, the men respected by "public opinion" (Duplessis, *et al.*) to the union leaders, industrious tradesmen to the "lazy" unemployed. . . . And the meaning of all that was: the bourgeois, who are "good" Christians, are coming to help you, "poor" little things, so that you may learn to work and love God . . . as do Duplessis and Salazar and the successful tradesmen and the sisters who go out as missionaries.

Longueuil-Annexe, mission country. . . .

We had been so happy living as pagans! Why were we going to school? To learn how wretched it was to be far from God, wealth, and success? To learn to be ashamed of the paganism of the poor and to hate each other, so as to put into practice the evangelical teachings of the nuns and abbé of the Longueuil bourgeoisie?

The only thing I remember having learned in school was to be ashamed of my—of our—condition.

A number of parents understood instinctively how pernicious was the official, clerical education. They refused to send their children to school, and the nuns declared that those parents were degenerates who would burn in hell throughout eternity. My mother thought as the nuns did. She despised these "ignorant" people. For my part, I did not agree with her in the least. I knew several boys who did not go to school (lucky devils!). They were my best friends. Their parents were poor and bitter, but they were *independent*. They did not easily accept the lessons and commandments of the bourgeois catechism. They knew too well the daily exploitation that was practiced in the name of Love, Obedience, and Virtue. They did not want to be virtuous: sheep among the wolves, humiliated creatures among the rich, sinners among the pure . . . and "the cursed poor" to be assisted. They needed neither help nor advice. They wanted to be left in peace in *their own* houses.

I agreed with that kind of revolt. But at this time I was still too little to defend myself against my mother's will. So I went to school, the way one goes to a funeral parlor, walking slowly and in silence.

During recess, since there was no organized masculine sport (how could you expect old maids to organize baseball or hockey teams?), we would lean against the gloomy school wall while the girls, who were deliberately separated from us, chatted or sang hymns with the teachers.

A real paradise, in short!

We learned about boredom listening to the song of the angels!

Then we would go back to class, like prisoners returning to their cells. To pass the time, I would draw faces on my desk or make the others laugh, right in the middle of a lecture on religion or grammar, by letting out a fart as loud as a firecracker. I would pretend to be "embarrassed," while the others doubled up with laughter and the teacher or nun waved her witch's wand over our heads.

"*Will* you be still, you wicked children? I am going to speak to the Inspector about that. . . . And you, Vallières, if you're sick, go see a doctor."

"There's no doctor around here . . ."

"Then restrain yourself! Do you understand?"

"What?"

"Do you understand?" (She was as red as a tomato.)

"Me no understand . . ." (I was imitating the way the Iroquois talked.)

The whole class broke out laughing again.

"Vallières, go stand in the hall!"

"THANKS!"

Then I would feel relieved of a part of my revolt, less unhappy than when I had been sitting motionless in the midst of the class, with *other people's* lessons buzzing in my ears. In the hall I could at least stand up, and my thoughts were not disturbed by the disdainful remarks of the teacher or nun on the wretched condition of people who had no manners or religion. I was proud of myself, and having that little two-bit pride made me happier than sitting stiffly in class with my mouth shut, learning that God loved me in-fi-nite-ly. . . .

At four in the afternoon, liberated from school, I would go home with an immense feeling of joy. On the way, I had as much fun as possible with my companions. And very often I would arrive home covered with mud, my clothes torn and my schoolbag broken.

The joy of being delivered from the monsters who were called my teachers helped me bear my mother's remonstrances or cuffs.

Then, after a quick wash, I would mechanically eat the meatball, the two or three pieces of potato, the two slices of bread, the pickle, and the three cookies set out for me. I would hurry through my homework and, while I waited for Grignon's *Un Homme et son péché* to come on the radio, I would leaf through *La Presse* or play with my brothers. Our favorite game was to pretend we were crazy. We would shout, weep, laugh like madmen. That was our way of protesting my mother's refusal to let us play outdoors after supper. My mother would try to make us keep quiet, but there was nothing she could do.

"I'm going to tell your father all about it tomorrow," she would say.

My father worked from four in the afternoon to five in the morning, and on week nights he was never home. When Raymond learned to walk and started imitating André and me, my mother began to wonder what was the good of bringing children into the world.

"They have no gratitude, no respect," she would sometimes say. "They won't understand until I'm dead. It's no life trying to bring up children like that. . . ."

We had only a few toys and quickly tired of them. What we liked was the freedom of the streets and fields, the freedom to run where we pleased, to play with the girls and boys we liked, without anyone to tell us which road to take, which companions to choose, which games to play. Didn't we know better than anybody what made us happy? But my mother did not feel we had been brought into the world in order to be happy.

So we roared out our discontent like caged lions. We were not aware of everything that was going on inside us and around us. It was only life—life that had been given to us by chance (but given to us all the same)—asking to live. Was it not natural?

But to my mother, as to the teachers, the nuns, and the abbé, we were grieving the Good Lord, we were committing sins, we were constantly guilty of disobedience. I envied those of my friends whose parents were less Christian than mine and more given to drink: they, at least, were free; they were not continually prevented from being themselves by the necessity of being Good.

I suffered increasingly from my father's absence. On weekends I could talk with him a little, but he was in such a hurry to enlarge and improve his shack that he thought about nothing else. I contented myself with sharing his plans for the future, playing the favorite game of the workers in our shantytown: building castles in Spain. Every weekend my father spent long hours talking with the neighbors about a hypothetical happiness. I would have liked him to give me the certainty that in this world we would not always be *losers*. But my father had no certainty. He had faith, the obscure belief of the poor in some sort of justice. Not one of us ever dreamed of *making* that justice. We were all waiting for it to be given to us, as a reward. We all believed in Santa Claus.

Some nights I went to bed not to sleep but to think. I was not yet ten, but I thought a great deal. I questioned everything I saw: things and men. (The philosophers call that "calling things into question.") Sometimes I felt sad and lonely. At other times, especially on days when school had been more trying than usual, I would clench my childish fists and dream of insulting my teachers in public, of humiliating *them* for a change, of throwing mud at them and shouting: "Hey! you, daughters of God, and you, *messieurs les abbés*, why don't you go do a little work building houses for 'your' poor that wouldn't be so cold and cramped, instead of teaching them to repent their sins. . . . Besides, if 'your' poor didn't sin, you'd be out of a job. What have you got to give us in exchange for everything you want to take away from us? Why don't you leave us our freedom, our sins, our filth, and our peace! Take your catechism, your good manners, and your holy water back to Longueuil! Isn't the important thing to be happy? And (except for a few 'converts') we're happy to remain savages and not have you trying to civilize us."

Of course I didn't say these things to myself in that style. My thoughts were not so well expressed. But I nonetheless felt a kind of wound inside me that penetrated the deepest recesses of my anguished mind.

Their ready contempt seared me; *their* habit of humiliating the "ill-dressed," "unkempt," "snot-nosed" children . . . the dirty children of the common people!

Oh! cursed masters of sacred *cleanliness!* Imbeciles with immaculate hands, projecting ears, pointed noses, disdainful mouths, glassy eyes, and sandpaper faces! Empty heads. . . . Deep inside, with all my heart, with all my intelligence, with all the hardness of a *degenerate* child, I proudly told you to go to the devil! If hell existed, it was your appointed residence. Imbeciles, you had everything it took to make "devilish" fine candidates for damnation! What did you expect out of this life? Why did you exist? Why were you our teachers?

In third and fourth grades, my hatred for school increased; for my mother forced me to continue my education with the nuns in Longueuil.

Bus service had just been inaugurated between Longueuil and Longueuil-Annexe, but it was very irregular. Often (especially in winter) I had to walk to school; it was hard going but "healthy exercise."

In Longueuil I made a few friends but I felt myself an outsider among these children who were "well dressed," "neatly combed," "cared for." Comparing myself with them, I became more and more ashamed of my milieu. I was alone, incapable of communicating what I felt. And the nuns who took pity on me made my existence even more painful.

Two years later, my mother went to see the Brothers of Christian Schools, who ran a big *collège* in Longueuil. This time, terror seized me. On registration day, completely ignoring the arrangements my mother had made, I went to the wretched hovel on Briggs Street which had just been converted into a temporary schoolhouse: for two years families had been arriving by the hundreds in the still nameless town, and the government was in no hurry to build schools. Throughout the whole area shacks were being turned into schools overnight and muddy lots into "recreation grounds." But there, at least, I felt *at home*, with my own kind.

When I went back to school for the fifth time in my life, I had determined that henceforth it would be *I*, and not my mother, who would decide what school I went to. My mother resigned herself to my stubbornness, only muttering under her breath: "Damn pigheaded child! You'll regret it plenty later on."

For the first time, a man stood in front of the class and wrote on the blackboard the list of subjects to be studied at home. I mean just that: to be studied at home. For this teacher taught us nothing. He would tell stories, comment on current sports events and, between classes, take the most depraved of his pupils and teach them to refine their vices, distributing obscene photographs and selling them "good marks" in exchange for certain little services. This bastard, who had been a guard at the Saint-Vincent-de-Paul Penitentiary, not only taught fifth grade but was in charge of discipline for all the grades (five or six) that had been housed in two adjacent buildings. He had no diploma whatever, no training whatever.

Sick of being subjected to his stupidity and assaults, the boys decided one fine day to go on strike. A number of mothers joined us, and *monsieur le professeur* was expelled from the parish. He was replaced by a pretentious hypocrite who was an excellent professor of sacred history but just as depraved as a Brother of Christian Schools. We put up with him without too much protest. We were getting blasé! And basically, it was all more comic than tragic. Didn't we go off with the girls after school to do those "dirty little things" that *monsieur le curé* called "sins against purity"? We were not Dominic Savios or Maria Gorettis.° Far from it. We just didn't like having the adults meddle in our affairs. Particularly since we had already known

---

° Dominic Savio and Maria Goretti are modern Italian models of youthful purity (both have been canonized), cited by the Catholic Church as examples to young people. (Trans.)

"the facts of life" for a long time! Indeed, that was about all we did know of life, except work, poverty, and humiliation.

Ever since we had moved to Longueuil-Annexe I had had a "girl friend." She was sort of my "mistress"(!). Of course I couldn't make a baby for her, but we often amused ourselves playing with our . . . We would laugh like crazy, hidden under a gallery, or in the woods, or in a shed. Sometimes she would cry out when I bit her new little breasts a little too hard. She was older than I (by three years, I think). She was gentle, independent, and proud, in spite of the fact that her family was extremely poor. I had met her the day we arrived and she had immediately become my best friend. She was only ten years old then. When she was fourteen and I was eleven, we talked about getting married and going to live in Ontario, around Timmins, where she was born. She wanted to go even farther north if possible. She was like an Indian: she needed to live in the midst of forests, near lakes, under a sky that was clear and always young. When she was fifteen, more than one lad wanted to sleep with her. She was not the sort of girl who looked down on making love with different boys. She felt as if she were doing them a service. She told me about everything she did and *taught* me. I was twelve. I loved her very much and she loved me very much too. At least, I had the firm impression that she did. One day I learned that Lise F. had gone away and was never coming back. Had she returned to Ontario? Neither her parents nor her brothers and sisters would answer my questions. They all seemed to have accepted her leaving home as a normal and even ordinary event. As for me, I experienced my first true sorrow, and I finished out the school year without enthusiasm. Lise had disappeared around May 15. The weather was beautiful. The trees were budding and here and there wild flowers scattered a little color and beauty in the dust that dried up everything, that would also dry up the flowers.

7

In the meantime, Longueuil-Annexe had ceased to be Longueuil-Annexe. Our quarter was part of a big city which the government had decided to name Jacques-Cartier. The first mayor and a few aldermen had been elected, all of them ignorant men of good will. It would not be long before they were eliminated or assimilated by the underworld. The deputy from the constituency kept making promises, but the government didn't do much. Every spring, as soon as the snow had melted, an army of bulldozers would lay out dirt roads between the houses. The shacks would be moved about, some backward, some forward, in a laughable attempt at town planning.

Everywhere, for miles around, mud streets full of puddles. When it didn't rain too often, the sun managed to dry up the puddles and the mud. Trucks came and poured tons of gravel on the streets. Bulldozers hastily spread the gravel out. The next time it rained the gravel sank into the mud, the puddles reappeared, and everything had to be started over again.

On dry days, in July and August, dust filled the air whenever automobiles and trucks went by. Some families bought a few gallons of oil to spread on the streets and prevent the dust from poisoning the atmosphere. But that, too, often had to be done over. And even without dust, the smells that rose from the ditches and privies (commonly called *"bécosses"*) were still as tenacious as poverty.*

When there was no oil on the streets and the dust hovered constantly in the air, the spaces between the black or multicolored shacks would turn yellow or gray, depending on whether the sky above was blue or dark with clouds.

On days when it rained hard, everything turned black. The houses, flattened and ashamed, took on a sinister, tormented look. The people picked their way through streets transformed into rivers of mud. The few puny trees, which each family had tried to preserve on its lot, bent their branches toward the wet earth. It was as if they wept at being powerless and ridiculous witnesses to all the misery that was obstinately trying to persuade itself the future would be better.[7]

On these rainy days, if I wasn't sleeping in class, I would stand for hours at a time on the front porch of our shack watching the water trace figures on the windowpanes. The neighboring houses, the streets, the sickly trees would seem to be transformed into a storybook landscape, and between reality and myself I would try to interpose one of the dreams my father sometimes talked to me about on weekends, his gentle eyes fixed on the yellow, limitless horizon beyond which there seemed to lie other worlds, less cruel than this one for men, for workers.

But the older I grew (for poor children grow old faster than they

---

* The word *"bécosse"* is a Canadian-French corruption of the English "backhouse." (Trans.)

grow up), the more my dreams came to resemble those of a man condemned to death who cannot drive hope from his mind.

8

While my father was expanding the house, to make it more live-
able, my mother hardly dared invite "the relatives" to visit us. She
was so ashamed of "the surroundings," as she said. In spite of the
misery that encircled and penetrated his domain, my father was
happy to have something to build . . . even if it was only an extension to this jerry-built shack. But my mother dreaded letting others—
city people—see our poverty.

It was as if our entire existence was nothing but a daily obscenity.
We had to hide *that* from the people of the big city.

But the people of the big city and the rest of the province soon
learned the truth . . . from the newspaper headlines in capital letters
reading: "THE WHOLE TRUTH ABOUT VILLE JACQUES-CARTIER" —
"BABIES DYING OF COLD IN COTEAU-ROUGE" — "TERRIBLE POVERTY
ACROSS THE BRIDGE" — "A CITY OF SHEET-METAL" — etc. We would
read these reports with rage in our hearts. What were we *guilty* of?
Of having wanted freedom? We had never had it. Painfully, we were
trying to achieve it. Why did these newspapers talk about us as if we
were barbarians spewed out by Montreal, like bile spewed out by an
unhealthy liver?

For some newspapers, which I need not name, we were not men
but "the dirty masses" of Ville Jacques-Cartier, the human "scrap"
of the biggest garbage dump in the metropolitan area.

After the stories in the newspapers came the "collections," the dis-
tributions of food and whatnot, the *charity* of all the people who had
guilty consciences or who simply adored helping the poor. Fortunately, we were not armed; otherwise the Church would have acquired a few more martyrs and the statue manufacturers would have
made money.

Everything was increasing: the population, the slums, the publicity, the taxes, the number of unemployed, of sick or crippled children and of unwed mothers, the churches, the thugs, the grocers, the
thieves, the murderers, the drunks, the wretched . . .

Angus Shops, Vickers, Canada Cement, Canadair, etc., were
laying off hundreds of workers every week. And each time the unions
said it would only be temporary.

Some families converted their sheds into lodgings, moved into them, and rented out their shacks . . . so as to be able to buy enough "baloney" and Weston bread to feed the "little ones." Others sold their houses—because of the taxes—and went off to build others in Saint-Amable or Sainte-Julie, beyond Boucherville.

More than one mother tore her hair in despair, and more than one man thought of stealing, killing, or committing suicide. Some set fire to their houses in order to collect the insurance and try to start over again somewhere else. The Established Order declared that henceforth laziness and slovenliness would be forbidden in Ville Jacques-Cartier, that norms would be established, that those who did not meet them would be expelled and that taxes would be raised in order to force the "lazy" (that is, the unemployed) to leave the city. The underworld, which with the support of Duplessis controlled the city, tried to put up a respectable front and held numerous press conferences announcing reforms such as Quebec had never known. They began to build schools and distribute little gifts to their friends. Overnight, grocers, wrestlers, bandits became "entrepreneurs" and contractors for primary schools, churches, and administrative buildings. All this was financed with government subsidies or "Sunday collections"—in other words, with money stolen from the people, with the broad, hypocritical smile of a gentleman-thief. The purpose of building schools was not to educate children, but to grant "paying" contracts to supporters of the regime. So it was that Duplessis, financed by his friends on Wall Street, created his own class of petty bourgeois out of the very misery of the workers and farmers of Quebec who, taken in by a cunningly organized system of patronage, voted for him *en masse*—*against* their true interests and without quite realizing what was going on.

Around 1950, a vast, slow construction project was undertaken to provide a complete system of aqueducts and sewers for the "dirty masses" of Ville Jacques-Cartier. The underworld rubbed its hands at the thought of the enormous profits it would reap from this very humanitarian enterprise. They began by raising taxes. One after another, all the streets of the city were transformed into long trenches eight feet deep, with heaps of earth on either side about six feet high. Paths were improvised between the houses, piles of earth, trenches, sewer pipes, dynamite, steam shovels, etc. The daily dynamiting cracked the walls of the shacks and ruined the wells, which ran dry or filled with muddy water. A few public drinking fountains were installed here and there, on the privileged streets, which were served by the aqueduct from the first year on. But after a lightning beginning, the work slowed down. Everywhere there were trenches, unusable wells, and mud . . . mountains of mud. And the work did not progress: lack of funds, people said. But Quebec had put millions into the project. Where had the money gone? The people asked questions while the months and years passed. The work advanced at a snail's pace, a little here, a little there. In winter all the machines fell silent. The long trenches filled up with snow.

Most families had to collect rain water in huge barrels or buy water by the pail every day from a tradesman to whom the city authorities had granted a monopoly on the sale of water. Water cost five cents a pail. Many families, including mine, had to tighten their belts to buy water for cooking, bathing, doing laundry, etc.

That lasted for years, years during which Duplessis was letting the Americans loot the rich iron deposits of northern Quebec.

The Americans were making billions off *our* iron, Duplessis was making millions off the Americans, the political machine of the National Union Party was distributing its millions to the supporters and thugs of the regime . . . and we, poor starving wretches, we had to buy water!

As this situation went on and on, people tried to find ways of getting free water. Some of them walked a mile or two every day to fill a few pails at the fountain on one or another of the privileged streets, the streets that *had* water. But that was not always possible, either because the weather was bad or because the trips were too tiring.

My family lived about two thousand feet from the new Longueuil, where modern cottages were being built for the petty-bourgeois families who wanted to live in the suburbs. Together with our neighbors, we tried to get *permission* from these richer suburbanites to take the water we needed from the fountains in their quarter, whose streets were already paved with asphalt. They treated us with unbelievable contempt (and yet they were not English). A few weeks after they had spat in our faces, the petty bourgeois of new Longueuil built a high wooden fence so they would not have to meet the thirsty eyes of the "dirty people" every day. All the streets which up until then had crossed Longueuil, new Longueuil, and Ville Jacques-Cartier were blocked off at the border of Ville Jacques-Cartier and new Longueuil. (With the exception, however, of Saint-Alexandre Street and the Chambly road.)

If a revolutionary party had existed in Quebec at that time, it would have found thousands of workers, women, and young people ready to take up arms in Ville Jacques-Cartier. Some people thought about that possibility, but without acting on it. There were many street fights with picks and shovels, but nothing lasting. Only, the consumption of beer rose steadily.

Senseless crimes were reported daily. My mother dreamed of leaving this accursed city. But where was the money to come from? In this atmosphere of desolation, increased by the vast, unfinished construction works and the water shortage, to try to sell the shack would have been to fly in the face of common sense. *We waited*, we survived everything, like thousands of other men, women, and children who did not have the means to escape from their absurd condition. We waited for it to be over . . . the way, in 1940, people had waited for the war to be over so they could learn how to live once more.

Weariness, bitterness, and resignation again followed upon disappointed hopes and took possession of the manipulated, despised, worn out, powerless, demoralized people.

9

For the last several years a dedicated man, silent and shy, had been ceaselessly working in their midst. An unpretentious doctor who spared no pains to serve these people whom he loved and who loved him.

Jacques Ferron was not the sort of man who took advantage of his privileged situation to exploit the "ignorant." I do not know what motivated him to establish himself in Ville Jacques-Cartier. But he certainly did not come in order to make political capital for himself! Although he was a candidate of the NDP and the RIN,° Jacques Fer-

---

° The NDP (New Democratic Party) is social democratic and a member of the Socialist International. The RIN (Rassemblement pour l'indépendance nationale) was a center party and is now merged into the Parti québécois. (Trans.)

ron went into politics in order to *serve* his friends in the socialist and independence movements who needed a good candidate, and not in order to build himself a personal reputation. For him, people were always—and always will be—more important than parties, and human fraternity more important than politics. In fact, I believe that for Ferron that is all that counts: fraternity. The bourgeois of the literary salons are going to be very surprised to read that. Because to them, Ferron is the brilliant, ironical writer, the artful storyteller. And he is also the founder of the Rhinoceros Party.

In short, he is an "eccentric."

To the citizens of Jacques-Cartier also, Dr. Ferron is an eccentric, in the sense that, unlike the other doctors they have known, he very often refuses or "forgets" to collect a fee.

I was not ten years old when Dr. Ferron came to our house for the first time. We were very much struck with his shyness and kindness, especially as he left the house refusing to accept payment. Could this man be a qualified doctor and at the same time refuse payment? We did not know whether to be glad or suspicious.

Before his arrival, the local gossips of Longueuil-Annexe had gone in for much knowing speculation.

"He must be really brilliant, this guy, to come and bury himself out here!"

"He must be an old army doctor, an old monkey with no brains and no heart," replied another.

"Unless he's very young, just hatched out of the university—and poor as Job?"

"In any case, he needn't expect to make a buck off us!"

"The curé says he's an ex-Communist."

"Communist? What's that?"

The doctor installed himself in the basement of a two-story building whose first floor was occupied by a pharmacy.

Distrustful at first, the people soon discovered that in spite of his diplomas, *he* had not come to despise them. He was a very different sort of man from the curés and politicians. He was *with* them. He did not judge them. On the contrary. He listened to them, treated them, served them in a thousand ways, living among them as among friends, recognizing their freedom, accepting even the baseness and narrow-mindedness that are generated by too long and painful an experience of poverty, never preaching to them, accepting, despite his own political convictions, the fact that they were disgusted with politics and on election days voted against his own political commitment. He had not come to preach or command, but to help; he was conscious of the fact that he owed "his" scientific knowledge, "his" profession, "his" social position to the silent labor of the poor, to the daily exploitation of those whom nowadays we call the "economically weak."

A Communist? Yes, a *real* one. Consequently, one who remained outside the Party, detesting all the sacristans of the pro-Soviet chapels, all the second-hand theologians who knew so much more about Garaudy and Stalin's encyclicals than about the people in whose name they spoke . . . among themselves.

An apostle? No. He loathed pity. For pity is the opposite of fraternity.

That is why the curé of our parish feared him so much, for in contrast to the ideology of the Church hierarchy, Jacques Ferron offered a fraternity he really lived, creating the need for fraternity around him and thereby isolating the curé in his presbytery. Like many others, I heard the calumnies that the curé invented to drive the people away from Ferron. But the minister of God was wasting his breath. People saw what Ferron did. They compared him to the curé, who was always preaching without ever practicing what he preached, who only seemed interested in taking up the Sunday collection. People could not help being on Ferron's side.

Ferron's office was near my home, and I often went to him for treatment. It was always for the terrible boils that worry and nervousness brought out on my neck. I never went home without a few newspapers the doctor had given me: *France-Observateur* or *L'Express*, which in the fifties were militant weeklies. But we never talked politics. It was just that Ferron had realized that while I waited my turn in the hall, I would devour these papers, which were placed among others on a little table. . . . He had understood that I was hungry for *that*.

I was very withdrawn at the time, and I never dared tell the doctor what was on my mind. Later, when I was cured of my timidity, I saw him only rarely—usually at some literary event where neither

Ferron nor I felt really free to talk about "the people across the bridge." There are things which cannot be said just anywhere.

I hope to see this great man again some day—he is still practicing in Ville Jacques-Cartier, without growing rich, simply for the love of men. Meantime, in these pages written hurriedly in prison, I wanted to tell Jacques Ferron that he is not unrelated—far from it—to my present political engagement.

As an individual, Jacques Ferron has the right to prefer people to parties (the present parties, in any case). But his whole daily activity —which goes beyond the mere practice of medicine—must in the end lead to politics. Otherwise, fraternity itself may take men down a blind alley. The fraternity that does not lead into a popular revolution is a dangerous fraternity. For sooner or later it becomes a "religion" or an "ethic"; in the end it makes no change in the *material* condition of men, in the division of society into classes, in the exploitation of man by man. Men of quality may love those whom the majority of bourgeois despise and exploit. But only a revolution will change their lives. I think Ferron understands that. And that is why I think he has long since oiled his rifle!

He himself does not organize men into an effective political force. But by fraternizing with the workers, by helping them and trusting them, he gradually forces more than one man who is bitter or resigned to choose hope, which represents his better self, and finally, to choose the struggle against capitalism. For the personal engagement of each worker is as important as his rifle.

This type of revolutionary action is, after all, not very widespread at the present time. There are not many who take it on as a daily *responsibility*. Thank you, Jacques Ferron.

10

It was as if the more people there were in Ville Jacques-Cartier and the more complicated everyone's problems became, joining and intertwining to form huge, hard knots, the more difficult it was for men and women who had been aged by the Depression and the war to believe that freedom, peace, and prosperity were not just words, not just a deputy's promises. They were weary, but they had not lost all hope; for in a universe like this, filled with noisome smells, what was it, after all, that still made it possible for men to breathe and to go on in spite of everything, if it was not the hope they bore within them?

Even when they wish they were dead, men never *will* to die. Especially when they know that their dying will not make history condemn their life of slavery, that their death will be as anonymous, useless, and absurd as their present condition. To give a meaning to death one must begin by giving a meaning to life. And even then . . .

Not everyone dies who wants to.

Despite all the shit, in the midst of all the shit, hope took all sorts of forms.

For instance, not far from where we lived was a little restaurant run by a man from the Gaspé who had been mutilated in the last war. Right leg amputated, father of twelve children. Living on his veteran's pension. How had he managed to make the journey with his family from Matane to Jacques-Cartier, rent a little house, and open a restaurant? The oldest of his children was not thirteen. His wife did not work away from home. Six or seven of his children were in school.

This man was extraordinarily gentle. Notwithstanding his crutches, he had the bearing of a general or a lord. The bearing of a nobleman without arrogance, a nobleman who knew too much of life and men to *judge* and *dominate*. An odd sort of restauranteur, who gave credit to everyone without calculating and let himself be exploited by the very ones he did the most for. It was almost as if he were an accomplice of the army of debtors who unscrupulously took advantage of his kindness. And I believe he really was their accomplice. He borrowed money from the finance companies so as to be able to sell bread, "baloney," and candy for the children on credit.

One day he put his store up for sale to pay off his debts. His feelings toward others did not change. He had wanted to make a go of it. He had wanted the others to make a go of it too. But the others hadn't wanted to . . . or hadn't been able to. Nor had he been able to—or wanted to—without them. How can you understand it? How explain it?

This story, out of which Camus could have made a magnificent tale of the absurd, was not just the experience of one citizen of Ville Jacques-Cartier. And perhaps in the last analysis that is why nothing happened in this town. Fundamentally, every man was alone. People came and went too fast; they did not have time to get to know each other. Hopes were built up hurriedly, at random, and crumbled a little later amid general indifference. It takes many years of struggle, of victories and defeats, many fresh starts and hopes lived through in common to make a true human fraternity. But in Ville Jacques-Cartier, a totally new town made up of shacks and exiles, there were still only individuals. All the Jacques Ferrons were isolated from one another and alone in the midst of the anxious, sometimes panic-stricken mass. Even if they forced the humiliated, the disappointed, the utterly disheartened more and more to choose hope, they remained powerless, unable to organize that hope, to arm it with anything more tangible and effective than kindness, etc. Nonetheless, from the seeds that rotted in that wretched ground there would one day spring up something stronger than humiliation. No doubt some seeds must rot so that others may germinate. But how many? How many?

My father, like the others, felt weariness overcoming him. The Angus union had betrayed the men by making compromises with the government and the management of the CPR. The fervor aroused by the heroic strike of the miners in Asbestos died down and went out in discouragement.

And the town, turned upside down by gigantic construction works that made no progress, taught the men who had expected so much from their new postwar freedom how hard it is to find peace without fighting for it.

If you would have peace, prepare for war.

The new citizens of Jacques-Cartier had not yet fully understood that. But the idea was making headway all the same. And out of this ruined garbage dump there would at last spring a hard and enduring fraternity. More enduring than the brief uprising in Asbestos.

Notes

1. In *Bonheur d'occasion* (translated by Hannah Josephson under the title *The Tin Flute*), Gabrielle Roy has quite accurately described this climate of misery, of small, gray moments of happiness enlivened with a little

hope, although the book does not give a complete idea of the conflicts affecting the working class at the time. Her novel remains more a study of "character" than a description of a social milieu. Her characters belong to the working class, that is all.

2. Profitable for them, for their publishers, for the wholesale book dealers, the book stores, the film companies, the owners of movie houses, the collectors of "indirect taxes," the state and, finally, the bourgeois class itself.

3. It is from this universe that Marcel Dubé has taken the subject of *Zone*, his most celebrated play; and André Major uses it for the little masterpiece called *La Chair de poule* (Gooseflesh).

4. This service was provided at the time by the Laval Transport Company, whose president was to become one of the first mayors of Ville Jacques-Cartier.

5. An allusion to the title of a collection of poems by Giguère: *Le défaut des ruines est d'avoir des habitants* (The trouble with ruins is that they are inhabited).

6. Judge Redmond Roche is a former National Union deputy from the county of Chambly. The government made him a judge even though he had been implicated in an abortive attempt—abortive, thanks to the action of the citizens—at embezzlement (of funds amounting to something like a million dollars, if I remember correctly) in Ville Jacques-Cartier. The government "subsidies" to the town were supposed to have been transferred in large part to certain persons whom ordinary people, like you and me, call crooks.

7. In the study entitled *La troisième solitude*, made by the Montreal Labor Council and published just recently, Ville Jacques-Cartier and its environs (Laflèche, Notre-Dame-du-Sacré-Coeur, etc.) still appear in the category of the most disadvantaged areas of the metropolitan region.

3
The Great Darkness

Spring 1951. I was soon going to leave primary school for good. To go where? To the long, dank rooms of the Raymond canneries, to hull strawberries all day long? To the city streets, to work as a drawer of water . . . or be one of the unemployed? To the *collège* in Longueuil, to study for a job as an office clerk—"bilingual," if possible?

I was thirteen. For the first time in my life I had to make a choice. Over the last few months I had hungered and thirsted for knowledge. I had read biographies of some contemporary scientists in magazines and had been much impressed by their will to understand and transform the world. The biography of the Curies had made a particular impression on me. But could a worker's son aspire to the scientific knowledge of the Curies or of an Einstein? Poverty in childhood had not prevented certain scientists from realizing their ambitions. It had been very hard for them to get started, but their determination had overcome all obstacles, one after another. Would I have the strength to do that? I looked at myself. It was perhaps the first time I had ever looked at *myself:* I was small, puny, poor, ill-dressed, crude, ignorant . . .

I reread the biography of Madame Curie, studying especially the way she had behaved as an émigrée in Paris—poor, but proud and tenacious. To pursue my studies, to go to the university some day, seemed to me like going into exile, emigrating to a foreign country, breaking with everything that had hitherto constituted my life, "my world." My anxiety was as terrible as my hope was profound. I was afraid. But at the same time, my determination was growing stronger.

I knew very well that my mother would oppose my ambitions in the name of the religion of the "half a loaf." She would tell me one had to learn to be content with what one had. To be content—what exactly did that mean? To sacrifice oneself? I had no desire to sacrifice myself. I felt, more than understood, that that kind of sacrifice was the worst mistake a man could make. It was not the life of Donalda, Alexis, and Co. that I wanted but the life of the Curies. I wanted to *do* something, to become someone, to get out of this shit, this glue that we were stuck in and that only filled my mother with contempt for everything. Did I feel *responsible?* I do not know. At least I wanted to *live.* I knew I was responsible for *my* life. Perhaps you have to begin by assuming that responsibility before you can join with others to assume a greater one.

The closer we came to summer, the more determined I was to become a scientist. To whom should I turn? And where was I to find the necessary money?

I was obsessed by this question of money.

Money had turned all of us into perpetual rebels who rebelled in vain. Protesting victims, how could we seriously believe in our freedom when we knew that freedom was based on money? And how could we not protest, when we knew that that money was being stolen from us every day? But our protest changed absolutely nothing. It was a small thing compared to the capitalist system, compared to the economic, political, and social organization of exploitation of the masses by a minority. We had to act, not protest. And in order to act effectively, we had to unite, to confront the systematic organization of exploitation with an even stronger organization. But can oppressed people, even millions of them, really constitute a force when they are opposed by . . . It was the time of the Korean War. Another war. So it would never be over! I was tormented by the immensity of the tasks to be accomplished and by the kind of collective self-destruction that the depressed working class was engaged in. Resistance to oppression was no longer anything but a concept. It seemed to me that everyone had abdicated. I could not count on others to help me. At the time, I did not clearly understand what I am now trying to describe, but I knew that *in the beginning* I would have to count only on myself.

After a few months of hesitation, torment, and insomnia, I resolved to take the plunge. "Come what may," I said to myself, "I have nothing to lose and everything to gain."

1

At thirteen it is hard to be confronted with such choices without having anyone to turn to for support or understanding. The grief I had known when Lise F. had suddenly disappeared was nothing compared to the anxiety which now took hold of me. I slept badly. I ate little. On the way home from school I would take long detours so as to give myself time to think in peace before going home. My friends wondered about my prolonged reveries in class. My mother watched me out of the corner of her eye. As for my father, he was still working from 4:00 in the afternoon until 5:00 in the morning. I almost never saw him any more, for on weekends I would often "go into exile" in Longueuil. I would sit down at the foot of the Quai Saint-Alexandre and plunge my dreams into the depths of the river. I would stay there hours at a time, alone, lost in silent meditation. When I came home, I would feel stronger and more optimistic. The peace of the river did me a world of good. But it was not long before the stifling atmosphere of the house would exasperate me. And I had to start all over again.

It was at this time that I began to think about breaking with my family, *for good.*

2

In June I left primary school like someone coming out of prison. "At last," I said to myself, "I am going to be able to study seriously and learn something."

The year before, the Franciscans had started to build a classical *collège* on the Chambly road, five minutes' walk from my home. I did not know what a classical *collège* was. Shortly before leaving school, I had asked the director to explain to me what a classical *collège* was all about. The *"dic"* told me that this new *collège* was a day school and that its purpose was not to turn out priests but to prepare young people for university studies.

"Ah!" said I, gaping. "And does it cost a lot of money?"

"I don't know. But I—don't think so. Anyway, there's the Oeuvre des Vocations . . ." °

"The Oeuvre des Vocations? You said it wasn't a seminary."

"Yes, I know. But there's always a way to work it out. The director and founder of the school isn't a bad fellow. He quite understands the problems of the people around here. He's sure to help you if you go to see him. He looks after the parish of Saint-Jean-Vianney. He even started a class in Latin Fundamentals this year in the parochial school. There are thirty pupils. All boys from around here. It's the Oeuvre des Vocations that pays for all thirty of them."

"Ah!"

"All that Father Vary is going to ask you is if you are opposed to the 'vocation' in principle . . ."

"What?"

"If you are opposed to letting yourself be 'influenced' by the Holy Ghost. All you have to do is say 'No,' and the whole business is settled. You can see there's nothing very tricky about it. I'm going to write you a letter of recommendation, and I'll ask the curé to give you one too. Come back and see me the day after tomorrow."

The *"dic"* began to laugh, clapped me on the back, and wished me luck.

I was skeptical, suspicious, worried. In July I made an appointment with Father Vary. Everything was settled inside of ten minutes. All that remained was to convince my mother. Father Vary told me he would take care of that. He invited my mother to come and see him and probably asked her not to oppose the "will of God." My mother resigned herself, but this time with ill humor. I didn't say a word. Secretly I was triumphant. I would have laughed in my beard if I had had one. But I was trying not to further irritate my mother who, quite correctly, did not believe a word of this business of a "vocation" that the Father had talked to her about. As I was only thirteen, she told herself that I was still too young to work. On the other hand, she would have preferred to have me go to the *collège* of the Brothers of Christian Schools, where I would learn more useful things than Latin—English and math—so that at sixteen I could find a job in a bank!

° The Oeuvre des Vocations was a fund for the assistance of future priests. (Trans.)

3

My first year at the *collège*, financed entirely by the Oeuvre des Vocations, was completely taken up with the small concerns of a diligent pupil. It was no effort for me to study, and the first thing I learned was to free myself from the thoughts that tormented me by reading or sports. To tell the truth, the haunting fear that I would never be able to finish these studies never left me. I tried every possible way to put it aside. But I did not succeed. Still, outwardly I was the merriest, most carefree student in the *collège*.

At that time the Franciscans' classical day school was only a vast, half-finished structure in which some sixty pupils had been installed with great difficulty. There were two classes: Latin Fundamentals and Syntax. Syntax was made up of graduates from the parish of Saint-Jean-Vianney; Latin Fundamentals of newcomers. With few exceptions, we were all sons of workingmen. The majority of us came right from Ville Jacques-Cartier. We formed a strange group of students. For most of us, the usefulness of the education we were receiving was completely incomprehensible. We were there without exactly knowing why. It was a little like primary school. Only the subjects had changed. There was little difference between the dilapidated buildings where we had gone to school on Briggs Street and this *collège* that was still in process of construction, half-unfinished and filled with the deafening noise of drills, etc. Every two weeks we changed rooms or floors, according to a plan drawn up in advance by the plasterers, carpenters, painters, and so on. Some days the *collège* was full of thick, white dust and we could hardly breathe. The desks, the blackboards, the books, the classrooms were all temporary. The new equipment would not be installed until the building was finished. That would take two years. In the meantime, we had to "do the best we could."

In this half-built *collège* we felt more like juvenile delinquents than students. We spent more time playing gangsters in the chapel and the auditorium than studying Latin. Behind the *collège* there was a vast field: in former days we had gone there to pick strawberries; now we had secret rendezvous there with the girls from Ville Jacques-Cartier.

The courses given us by *two* Franciscans were absolutely worthless. We memorized Latin conjugations, rules of grammar, definitions from the catechism, a few historical dates; then, periodically, we recited what we had memorized. Our two professors were perfect ignoramuses who had been sent by their Order "for the time being," until more competent personnel could be found. Like the desks, they were "temporary." Neither one of them dared preach morality to us. Having always lived in monasteries closed to the world, they were out of their element. It shocked them to hear us swear and tell "dirty" stories. But like prison chaplains, they contented themselves with praying for us, without making comments. As for the director, Father Vary, he left us completely free to do as we pleased. (He was to die three years later. People said then that in reality his kindness had only been weariness. They reproached him with having been too "understanding." But Father Vary, like Ferron, *saw clearly,* too clearly to impose on us the Truth and the Good as envisioned in the manuals of the Département de l'Instruction Publique. He was not a superintendent of souls and minds. He did not insist that we should be Perfect or that we should learn the Truth by heart, but only that we should have "the right to make mistakes," in other words, *freedom.* He had founded this *collège* in the desolate landscape of our town in order to give each of us his chance, his life. Unfortunately, he died too soon. The superintendents appointed by God and the DIP lost no time in imposing their Order, their values, and their secret ambitions on the bunch of idiots that we were in their eyes. For how could anything good come out of Ville Jacques-Cartier?)

Personally, I was less interested in the required lessons and exercises than in this freedom which made me feel I was entering upon a new life. I read all the books I could find and understand. When I got home in the evening, I would eat in silence, trying to talk as little as possible about what I was discovering day by day: freedom, which made me secretly despise everything our family had always known. Now I demanded a great deal from life. Never would I be content with half a loaf. If my mother did not want to give meaning to her life, that was her problem, not mine.

The year passed like a dream. First in my class in spite of myself, I had received excellent grades on the June examinations. The authorities of the *collège* thereupon decided to have me skip Syntax, so as not to waste my time. The Oeuvre des Vocations renewed its "subsidy," and I was able to find work in July and August. The money I earned as a laborer on a construction job enabled me, for the first time in my life, to buy a real jacket, some new pants, white shirts, a tie, and a few books.

In Method, my classmates were older than I, but I got on better with them than with the boys of my own age. There were now four classes: Method, Syntax, Latin Fundamentals A, and Latin Fundamentals B. The building was not yet finished, but the faculty was of better quality than the year before. The Method teacher, Father Charles, was an exceptional man. But we were too young and too unstable to realize it. He often became discouraged, but he stuck it out. Just imagine Malraux explaining the greatness of Egyptian art to five-year-olds who have never known anything but a world of rusty sheet-metal! But he did manage to make us understand that the content of great works of literature and art was much more important than their form, that form served content and not the other way around. Which was enough to make us prefer Shakespeare to Sully Prud'homme.

Father Charles was a nonconformist who detested narrow-mindedness, especially in religion. Like all of us, he hated the new rector (who was soon to supplant Father Vary as the real director of the *collège*). This rector, who also taught religion and history, was the very incarnation of narrow-minded piety. He had close connections with the profiteers of the DIP and was always preaching charity, so that people would not judge his little "deals" and, particularly, would not criticize them publicly. Once a week he went to Quebec to pay court to Duplessis and his chief assistants. It was common knowledge that Father Charles and the rector were not on the best of terms.

One day the rector called me in for a talk about my "vocation." I understood at once that my interests lay in pretending to be undecided.

"You know," the rector said to me, "you must be *frank* with us. The Oeuvre des Vocations is poor. We must think first of *our* priests. If you do not feel 'called,' you must be frank enough to tell me, my boy."

He stared at me with an icy, insistent look, while I remained motionless.

"Always remember, Vallières," he continued, "that this money *is not yours* and that sooner or later you will have to pay it back. It is money that belongs to the Oeuvre des Vocations . . ."

He went on talking for a solid hour, but I was no longer listening. I was furious and humiliated. I would have liked to blow his brains out and shout: "But dear poor servant of the Lord Jesus, who is it that finances your damned Oeuvre des Vocations? Your friend Duplessis or the workers you exploit in the name of the Father, the Son, the Holy Ghost, the Virgin of Fatima, and Saint Anthony of Padua?"

"The old fart," I said to myself as I left him.

It was around the same time that Father Charles asked his pupils to write a little story. We were free to choose the subject and the form. I decided to express the thing I was most troubled about (the question of my future) in the form of a soliloquy. However, in the story it would not be myself speaking but my father on his way home from the factory, as he sat uncomfortably on the bus that brought him back every day to his family problems.

I had my father say what I was feeling and ask himself all the questions I was facing. I had him admit that he was powerless but that, at the same time, he hoped I would succeed a little better in life than he had.

I did not expect anything to come of this story. I had written it spontaneously; it was an easy subject for me to develop! Father Charles, who was first of all a man, did not correct my paper; he read it aloud in class . . . the way one reads a document or an eye-witness report. He did not reveal my name, but since I was visibly moved by what "Charlie" said about my little story, the whole class guessed what was going on inside me. I was profoundly shaken by this first "literary" experience. I suddenly understood that through writing I could communicate to others what I was too paralyzed by shyness, fear, or shame to express in speech. And I decided that some day I would write a book about my family, my social milieu, my hunger for freedom and justice.

All my classmates were my friends, but there were a few who understood better than the rest what I hoped to get out of these years at the *collège:* a better knowledge of myself, of others, and of the world. I wanted to give meaning to my life, the life of a frustrated but impassioned French Canadian.

Among these friends there was Ti-Guy, a shy lad from Longueuil with a heart as big as the class. After "Charlie" read my little story aloud, Ti-Guy began to lend me books I had never heard of: *Wind, Sand, and Stars, Swann's Way, The Conquerors*. I marveled at these books. Was it possible to transform all human experience into such masterpieces? I wondered. Could a French Canadian ever write like these great men? I spent more and more time dreaming, indifferent to the courses, which did not answer my questions. Henceforth, I would not go to the *collège* to listen patiently to stupidities but to exchange books and ideas with Ti-Guy and a few others.

June came all too quickly.

4

The summer of 1953 was a veritable hell for me.

Every day, every week, a word, a gesture, or a quarrel clarified the outlines of the crisis that was brewing. Like the inevitable, logical outcome of a long cold war (between my mother and myself, in particular), the decisive confrontation took shape, becoming a direct threat to "family harmony" and to my reputation as a "good-student-destined-for a-great-future."

Determined that I should study English and mathematics, my mother nagged me continually: "You've got to leave this day school! When you're through studying there, where will you be able to work, especially if you can't speak English? You needn't expect that we're going to pay to send you to the University. You're not the only one around here. Your brothers, your father and me, *we've got a right to live too*, to live better than now, to buy a better house. If you went to work, instead of reading all those useless clever books, we could move . . ."

How could I answer her? I knew that I was condemned to say no or rot. For reasons which I did not clearly perceive, my mother wanted to force me back into the passivity, docility, resignation, and humiliation which were precisely what I wanted to escape from once and for all. What is the good of having realized that you exist only to be exploited, if you then refuse to rise up against this fundamentally unjust state of things? I was surprised to have to argue that with my mother. Had she not already gone through enough to *understand*? I thought about my father. His life no longer had the slightest meaning. All his acts were nothing but habits. His life: a routine. His body: a worn-out machine, reduced to skin and bones, nerves and tendons. His mind: a lamp with run-down batteries. His dreams were steadily shrinking. His strength was abandoning him. In a few years he would die of exhaustion. Why would he die? Why would he have lived? For nothing. To serve as cheap labor for the CPR. Yes, for nothing.

My mother had said to me once: "Fortunately, your father doesn't think he's as important as you think *you* are."

"Fortunately, you say? Fortunately? No, unfortunately, you should say. Yes, I think *I'm* important. I don't intend to be defeated before I've even fought. You can stay in all this shit, if that's what you want. I say, no thanks! Call it pride—I don't give a damn. Me, I call it dignity, a *minimum* of dignity. And I mean to say so, whether you like it or not!"

"Where do you come from, for God's sake, to be so pig-headed?"

"From this shit, from this filth, from this misery—from Ville Jacques-Cartier. You know all that a lot better than I do . . . What do you want me to do in a bank? Let myself be exploited in a *clean* way? Be a slave in a white shirt . . . making twenty bucks a week lining up figures? No, never. I'd rather starve . . ."

"It's Father Vary who's taught you all these fine things?"

"Leave Father Vary out of this. I can think and decide for myself. And if that doesn't suit you . . ."

"Shut up, you heartless wretch!"

These quarrels exhausted me. In August they occurred almost daily. If I had had any money I would surely have left home. But I could find almost no work that summer, and I returned to the *collège* in September poorer and more unhappy than ever.

In another six months I would be sixteen. My mother had decided that I would not go back to the day school after my year of Versification unless I really wanted to become a priest. I told her that the priesthood had nothing to do with it and that I would pursue my studies to the end.

"Are you afraid of working?" she asked.

" . . ."

"You know, your father, he's been working since he was fourteen and he hasn't died of it!"

"I'm not my father!"

"Or the rest of us either, we haven't died of it."

"No, you're not dead, but you're not much better off than if you were. *I* wasn't born to be a slave! I mean to be free."

"Why you . . ."

"Wake up, for Chrissake! For centuries we've been letting ourselves be ground down while we blessed the Lord! Don't you think it's time we wised up a little?"

"You despise us, damn you! Ever since you've been going to the day school . . ."

"Just try to understand a little. I don't despise anybody. I'm trying to wake you up."

"That's right, we're only a pack of idiots, while you, you're the one with the education! You spend your days reading. *The rest of us, we work*. We don't read. Don't have the time, and besides, we're not educated. We can't all afford the luxury of being smart and shitting on our parents, the way you do!"

"Just try to understand . . ."

"You'll drive me to the grave! I assure you that your *brothers* won't go to your precious day school. One lunatic in the family is enough."

"I'm not the one who's so damn pig-headed, it's you!"

"Shut . . ."

"You don't have to shout. I'm going out. What a hell-hole!"

I would go out and not come back until as late at night as possible.

At the day school I was no longer quite the same. Everywhere I went I was in a sort of daze produced by insomnia and worry, which were becoming habitual. In October, however, I found a degree of peace: I had suddenly fallen in love with M., and with her I escaped into a fanciful future. We both liked going to the movies and taking long walks at night. M. was a very simple girl who had had little education but who was "open" to all questions. She was affectionate without being maternal. She did not let herself be caressed like a passive doll, but was as "active," as wild, as I. She too liked to have long periods of rest after times of ardent frenzy. She was sixteen and her breasts were firm. Her skin was soft, and when I caressed her I had the feeling that I became better, more tender, more human. For the continual scenes with my mother were hardening my heart. M. was the medicine I needed.

Her family was like mine, except that her mother was less old-fashioned and authoritarian.

When we went to the movies, it was to lose ourselves in imagination with people who were able to impose their dreams on the world, to transform it, or at least to transform themselves. As in the movies, nothing seemed impossible to us then, and we would caress each other in the dark as if to persuade ourselves that our hopes were tangible.

Soon we talked about getting married, and I decided that I would abandon my studies in June in order to write and work toward the realization of our dreams. I understood then that I was going to the *collège* only to escape the morbid atmosphere that reigned at home; for when all was said and done, what had I to learn from my so-called teachers? The writers I was beginning to discover taught me infinitely more. Father Charles, who had grown peevish from fatigue and illness, had become unapproachable. The other teachers, except for the one who taught mathematics (a layman) were simply fools. Perhaps I had been wrong to quarrel with my mother so often . . . In any event, I would not be a bank clerk . . . And besides, I would be leaving home at last.

My "fiancée's" mother thought we were too young and would not listen to anything we said. For my part, I had decided not to alert the family until everything was settled. M. did not dare go against her mother's wishes and told me it would be best for us to continue as before.

"Maybe you're wrong to despise your teachers and the classical course. How do you know that next year you won't really learn something?"

"Maybe I'm wrong? Maybe you're right? Maybe. Sooner or later you have to know where you're going!"

We went on as before . . . but with a little less enthusiasm.

Sometimes I would take M. to the *collège* for a dance. But most of the time we went to the movies, unbeknownst to the others. We were very guarded about our privacy.

Then, with the approach of the Christmas holidays, I was seized with the desire to give her a magnificent present. To collect the necessary money, I increased my pilfering here and there. To pay for the movies, I had already more than once stolen quarters from my mother.

One fine day my mother discovered the source of my finances and got together with M.'s mother to stop us from seeing each other. My mother knew nothing about our love; she thought we were just friends. M.'s mother, however, was better informed; but she quickly came to an understanding with my mother. Why? I never found out exactly, but I think she suddenly saw me as a thief. Her own father was a thief and had been in prison for years. M. wrote me a short letter begging me not to try to see her again for two months. She wanted to think things over. I replied at once that I was not at all happy with the pact concluded by our pious mothers, but that I would respect her wishes. At Christmas I received a little card with just her name written on it. I wrote her several letters. No reply. I dared not believe that her love for me had evaporated. Was M. only a little fool who had let herself be frightened by her mother's stories about thieves, abandoned wives, jailed husbands, and starving children? I wrote her one last time to arrange a meeting. I begged her to come and talk things over with me. She did not keep the appointment.

This love story, which trailed off into nothing, made me even more unstable and tormented than before. I no longer quarrelled with my mother; I had simply ceased to speak to her. Nor did I speak to my younger brothers, who followed this drama (or melodrama) in bewilderment. My father remained the Absent One, the man who worked at night. I had given up the idea of talking to him; I thought about it as little as possible. It was as if he were dead. But stuck in the damp and soot of the factory, he was doubtless trying to understand what was going on at home, in his absence. At least, that is what I want to believe.

Never did my father speak to me about my studies. Occasionally he would discuss union affairs with me, during those rare moments when we had an opportunity to exchange a few ideas. He was increasingly disillusioned and refused to take sides, letting events follow their course. He no longer believed in anything or anyone. *He worked.* He had no energy left for anything else. When he came home, he was drained. To discuss, to dream . . . he had lost all interest in that.

It pained me to think of the dreams of the old days, which had crumbled into dust under the terrible alienation my father experienced in the only life he had ever known: poverty, work, and oppression.

He was so completely crushed that there was no room left for revolt or hatred. In those eyes as deep as mine shafts there arose from time to time only a faint rush of tenderness that could twist your guts with pain.

In this town haunted by the impotence of the exploited, the humiliated, the weak, the utterly disheartened, there were others in whom the same experience had produced a savage hatred of the world, and of themselves. Deep inside, a fierce need to kill gnawed at their shame and humiliation. Sometimes they could not resist: they killed, carrying out blind vengeance at random . . . in order to feel that they were men. And as if by a kind of diabolical coincidence, it sometimes happened that these men became auxiliaries of the underworld and, by their wild freedom, helped to augment the degradation, weakness, dejection, and impotence of their class, to increase everything they had such a horror of. But one could hardly expect their revolt to lead them into the ranks of revolutionaries who could give them an ideal and the means to achieve it! There were no revolutionaries.

The months went by and I felt more and more alone. Ti-Guy generously loaned me books, and I tried to set my thoughts in order and at the same time suppress a host of feelings; which was not very good for my physical and mental health. Once in a while I would venture to confide in one or another of my teachers, who would suddenly change into my "spiritual adviser" for the occasion. He would listen to me absent-mindedly. And noticing, after fifteen minutes of monologue, that the monk didn't give a damn about what I was saying, I would feel like bashing in his skull with a chair.

By the time school ended in June, I had completely lost my bearings.

5

I looked for a job, as in previous summers, and spent hours filling out forms in various placement offices. The first job I was offered ("helper" in a small factory on Lagauchetière Street, in Montreal) was not exactly well paid: $15 a week. I took it anyway. A few weeks later I received a letter from the Banque Provinciale du Canada: they were offering me a job in a branch office that had recently been opened in Ville Jacques-Cartier. The next day I presented my resignation to the boss of the dump on Lagauchetière Street. I was not particularly enthusiastic about becoming a bank clerk, but since it was only for the summer . . . And besides, the bank was near home.

I gave half my wages to my parents and with the other half I bought books, especially novels: Gide, Malraux, Sartre, Camus, Proust, Mauriac, Dostoyevsky. In the evening I would read for five or six hours, then, before going to bed, I would practice writing. I was thinking of doing a kind of fictionalized essay in which I would protest as energetically as possible against the Québécois' traditional capacity for resignation and try to persuade them to choose freedom, to break away from the old values and to undertake a struggle to the finish with obscurantism and exploitation. But like all the other Québécois, I too was imprisoned in the land of winter and the great darkness. The pessimism of the great contemporary writers made me increasingly doubtful that the mass of men was capable of awareness, freedom and courage. Nietzsche stunned me with his ferocious logic, and I began to have a cold contempt for my class. How can you base new values on such a brutish mass, I said to myself. But at the same time I was thinking: if this mass, composed of alienated men, is incapable of total revolution, what good does it do *me* to base new values on nothingness, in solitude and oblivion? Where there is no solidarity, does man really exist . . . ?

I was sixteen. What could I do in this world? And did this world need me? If men were really powerless, inevitably and eternally defeated . . . If life could not become better . . . If wars and massacres must go on forever . . . If none of it could be changed . . . then, yes, decidedly, as Sartre said, I was superfluous.

"If humanity is to be buried in 'great cemeteries under the moon,'" I thought, "well, let the evil genius who threw us into this world make haste to exterminate us and let's say no more about it.° Above all, let's say no more about it! If man's fate is only plague,

---

° *Les Grands Cimetières sous la lune* is the title of an anti-fascist, anti-clerical book by Georges Bernanos (1938) dealing with the purge of Majorca during the Spanish Civil War. It has been translated into English by Pamela Morris under the title *A Diary of My Times*. (Trans.)

nausea, or remembrance of things past, why bother about it? Has existence nothing to offer men but pain . . . and, in the end, death?" I wracked my brains for an answer but felt I was struggling in vain, like a cat that is carried around in a sack of flour until it suffocates.

What's the use? What's the use? Those three words hammered in my brain like a leitmotiv.

In September, to my mother's amazement, I decided to go on working at the bank, reading, writing and . . . surviving. I did not go back to the *collège*.

Ville Jacques-Cartier was still one vast construction site. Men were no happier, but there were more speculators and big-time crooks. Everywhere were huge blotches of black misery. There are certain individuals who love a social milieu precisely because they have great *pity* for it. And so they go from one poor shantytown to the next, arms outstretched, embracing the people with their ardent pity. But their hands are empty, even if their pity gives them a clear conscience.

My hands too were empty. But I was not full of pity. I was full of fear—fear that the people would die suffocated in poverty and passivity . . . It was not pity they needed but a kick in the ass!

I did not want to judge, for to judge is to not understand. But neither did I want to be duped by an understanding that was "soft" and ineffectual. I tried to see things clearly . . . At sixteen one never sees things clearly. Also, despite my good intentions, one feeling gradually came to dominate all others: exasperation. A painful exasperation, aroused, sustained, and nourished by the daily spectacle of the silent servitude of those around me. An exasperation that asked nothing better than to change into active fraternity. But can one build fraternity with thousands of living dead?

Like my father when he was at work, I had nothing to keep my will alive but nervous energy. At that time I weighed no more than 110 pounds. They called me a "bag of bones." A bag of bones with a restless mind, I read, I wrote, and I searched; with passionate impatience and a confused, dread feeling of urgency, I searched . . . for the right direction. I had the distinct impression that I was going around in circles or, worse, that I was running like a squirrel in a cage. The cylinder turned, turned, but the breathless squirrel always stayed in the same place. It was certainly not I, a lone adolescent, who was going to influence anyone or change . . . No, I could do nothing. I was so tormented by the absurdity of this universe seething with daily tyrannies, tears, illnesses, and insecurities, that I was reduced to a feverish desire for a better world and, at the same time, to a restless impotence, a will groping in the uncertain dark ("You're pretty mixed-up," my mother would say), a freedom appalled by the immensity of the changes that had to be made and by the almost infinite capacity of men—the men of Quebec, at any rate—to accept defeat, to drug themselves with the opium of Christian resignation. I exerted all my nervous energy and all my intelligence in an attempt to find an explanation and do something, but the harder I thought, the more confused I became and the less I wanted to act. My ideas, my desires, my feelings all seemed to partake of a strange madness. No one here understood what I was saying, what I wanted. No one wanted to become aware and take action. Everyone seemed to have definitively chosen defeat. What a fate!

One day I said to my mother (questioning, through her, the entire population): "For God's sake, why do you go on existing?"

". . ."

"You're not living any more . . . you're just running on the last momentum of . . . I don't really know what. You're going to die of old age the way a watch wears out in the end, inevitably. Why don't you even protest? Why?"

"We don't have the means to protest. And besides, even if we did . . ."

". . ."

"We don't have the money, we don't have the education, we don't have any experience in all those things that you call politics. What do you want us to do? With whom? We don't even know each other in this damn town . . ."

"If you went out more . . ."

"Went out? To meet who? Ignorant women and sluts!"

"You desp——"

"Don't you talk about 'despising'! You're a fine one to lecture me about that!"

"I . . ."

"For Chrissake, we don't even know each other in this house! You know that as well as I do, YOU, WITH THE EDUCATION!"

"I . . ."

"There's nothing we can do about it. When you're born . . ."

"For half a loaf . . ."

"You have to learn to be satisfied with it, that's all!"

She went back to her chores sadly, that day. It was the only time my mother seemed to me to be made of the same stuff as my father. Certainly, her despair went very deep. For the first time I was *touched* by her suffering. For the first time I saw her as something more than just a stunted mechanism exclusively engaged in the routine occupations of a housewife. For the first—and last—time.

My mother never talked to me about these things again, as if that time I had awakened an old—and unavailing—sorrow . . . one it would be better to deaden and extract, like a decayed tooth.

That was precisely what depressed me most.

This tenacious refusal, as tenacious as poverty. This hardness.

And I thought: you have only one life, *one* life.

"Why don't men want to unite? Happiness—like love, or friendship—cannot be achieved individually. Men must unite . . ."

But these men, who did not really have either love or friendship, were not seeking happiness. *They were working.* Subsisting. And . . . *they had no choice!*

I wanted to talk to them about *dignity.* But there is no dignity for those who work all day long, without knowing *for what* . . . but knowing all the same that *others* profit from their work. A nigger's life is not a life. And all the Québécois were (and are) niggers.

I wanted to preach to them. But it was not a moral problem. That's what I didn't understand. Or rather, no. I knew it was necessary to act, but I did not know it was necessary to organize. I expected the workers to unite the way one expects a good speech to produce a spontaneous revolution. How can I put it?

I was completely ignorant of the practical aspects of revolution. I had only ideas and words. Nobody was interested in *them.* Even the fact that . . . I had guts. Because what's the use of having guts if it doesn't change the conditions of your life? But the others, the others, what did *they* have, for God's sake, what did *they* have inside them?

I suffered a great deal, because all my thoughts were asking to live. But life is not to be had for the asking, it seems.

What was I to do with my life, if the others didn't . . . . What are you to do when you are the *only* one who wants to live? No, other people were not hell but rather a desert, indifference, death almost.°
The earth was shrouded in the disillusionment of men who had been crushed. Would they ever be healed of their wounds?

"Unless it's me . . . ? Maybe my thoughts are really only a sickness (even worse than the disillusionment of the others): a sickness of the mind, a high-grade form of decay! Ugh! Like the obstinate, blind contemplation of a God who does not exist . . ."

What was I to do with my ideas, my hopes, my life, if freedom—like God—did not really exist? No one could give me an answer. I had to formulate one myself, alone. At least, that is what I was beginning to believe. For at this time, the more I wanted to choose action, the more I chose anguished reflection—that terrible literary and philosophical exercise of the "existentialist" thinkers— the more I experienced, in the words of Kierkegaard, "fear and trembling" . . . and the more mystical I became!

I was in real trouble.

On the one hand, I could not really live on ideas that were not translated into acts. On the other hand, I felt powerless to perform those acts, because I was alone and also because I was so young.

My solitude burned inside me. Why was I alone? Was I not one of them, I who from the day I was born had had both feet planted in shit? I who had the same problems, the same resentments, and the same enemies as they? What was it that *separated* me from them? My awareness? Were not they too aware? Their daily experience . . .

It was as if the more my understanding of our common condition of slavery deepened, the more I separated myself from them. And yet, by deepening my understanding I was only trying to bind myself more closely to them. But apparently it was not a question of binding myself to them, since my fate had been bound up with theirs from birth. It was a question of something else: of transforming our condition, transforming it materially. To do that, there had to be *many* of

---

° This is another allusion to Sartre's *No Exit*, in which one of the characters (Garcin, Scene 5) says "There's no need for red-hot pokers. Hell is—other people!" (Stuart Gilbert's translation). (Trans.)

us. And I was alone. And I was confused about all that and misunderstood it, because I was profoundly ignorant of the forces that govern human history.

And then there was the influence of existentialist literature, which instilled in the individual Pierre Vallières the idea that he should live his own life and define himself on his own without concerning himself with revolution . . . for as Sartre told me in one of his works, "Hell is other people."

Existentialism was a great temptation to me. I succumbed to it all the more readily because everything around me seemed as lifeless as a vast cemetery of soldiers who had fought, for no reason, in a war engineered by other people.

The great darkness of the Duplessis era seemed to be a vindication of existentialism, and *Nausea* became my bedside book.

At the end of February 1955, completely disgusted with my job at the bank, I decided to go back to the *collège* . . . not so much to pursue my studies as to see my friends again. For seven months I had not talked to anyone.

The day-school authorities permitted me to take "my" place in Belles-Lettres as though I had registered in September and been absent since then "on account of illness." A few weeks later, Father Vary died. The school really began to change into a classical *collège*. Everything became formalistic and disciplined, in the old-fashioned way. The instruction was worthless, especially in universal history and the history of Quebec. Duplessis and Salazar, standing on either side of a Pius XII as cold as a block of ice, infused their orthodoxy into the teaching of the imbeciles who had the presumption to bring us Truth as a gift, the way missionaries bring Baptism to the natives (who, fortunately, are not taken in, and let themselves be baptized in the hope of obtaining a bit of the capitalist wealth that the Church takes with it everywhere). We put up with the Truth in the hope of some day enjoying the material privileges attached to it! We all lived in a state of forced hypocrisy. For to be frank and honest immediately meant "the door," that is, the end of our studies—and a life sentence of poverty.

We were all Catholics, perforce. But very few of us really believed in God. We went to Mass every Friday in order to qualify for the as-

sistance of the beautiful Oeuvre des Vocations! But that did not stop
us from occasionally partaking of a few "sacrilegious" communions.
I remember that during Mass I used to read Baudelaire while the
monks took note of the edifying spectacle of my piety!

I kept up the pretense until December 1955. I was then in Rhetoric. First in my class, I had an unstable temperament but was an intelligent pupil who, they said, "showed great promise." (I wonder
what my Alma Mater thinks of me today!) I had no choice but to play
the "vocation" game, because if I didn't, I would go back to the bank
and lose my few friends. Among ourselves, my friends and I often
discussed this demeaning hypocrisy.

We would say to each other: "It's not our fault, after all, if in our
milieu the only way to get yourself a minimum of education and a
ticket to the university—that is, a B.A.—is to take advantage of the
Propagation of the Faith and the Oeuvre des Vocations . . . Faith
doesn't give a damn about Justice! Why should *we* be afraid to not
give a damn about Faith and to take advantage of it! Charity doesn't
give a damn about low wages and unemployment! Why should *we* be
embarrassed to exploit Charity? It certainly isn't our fault if the
Church and High Finance imprison us in an empire (their empire) in
which men have to alienate themselves, prostitute themselves . . . if
they don't want to die like rats."

The Church, religion—was it anything more, after all, than rites
and collections? Rites that justified the collections. Collections that
financed the teaching of the catechism. Teaching of the catechism
that justified poverty and exploitation, that "sanctified" slavery.

One day I couldn't take it any longer, and I began to publicly ridicule this masquerade, this monumental farce. Around that time, the
Abbé Pierre gave a famous speech in Montreal, a speech which
greatly provoked His Majesty Cardinal Paul-Emile Léger, known as
"Kid Kodak." ° Abbé Pierre had to leave the country.

I asked the best of the priests who taught us whether they sided
with Abbé Pierre or with the Cardinal. They all took refuge in *neutrality*, like the rest of the clergy; which just suited Paul-Emile.

One day I told one of them that they were all a bunch of whores

---

° The Cardinal was given this nickname because of the frequency with which his
photograph appeared in the newspapers. (Trans.)

and the worst enemies of the people of Quebec. He replied that "morally" he supported Abbé Pierre, the worker-priests, etc. But that he didn't want to get involved in politics or fall into "extremism."

I asked him: "What do you expect the people to do with your *moral* support?"

" . . ."

"You are *all* accomplices in exploitation, obscurantism, and injustice as long as you do not perform ACTS. ACTS, not sermons!"

"You are hard . . ."

"I'm not hard enough. Listen, I'm going to tell you something that some day I will say in public. To me *all* priests will be profiteers and cowards so long as I don't see them *helping* the workers, the farmers, and the students of Quebec to burn their churches, their seminaries, their presbyteries, their Cadillacs and the rest! It's all very fine, my dear Father, to be honest and virtuous in one's heart, but that doesn't do much for the people who are oppressed every day by the regime. You have hands like every other man, use them!"

The good monk was thunderstruck and only said in a faint voice: "And I who believed that you . . . were . . . the *model* of your class! What has come over you?"

"Nothing at all. Or rather, yes. It has come over me . . . that I'm fed up with play-acting with you pack of idiots!"

From that day on, my hatred for *their* Authority and *their* Truth prevented me from studying. My friends and I began to frequent the taverns of Longueuil.[1] There we would read Rimbaud's *A Season in Hell*, which had quickly become our Bible. We did so many eccentric things and created so many scandals that at one time the authorities of the *collège* thought of expelling the lot of us. We were becoming a "public danger" for the new generation of students, whom we supplied with the banned books that were the *bêtes noires* of the professors.

In June I took the examinations with an indifference from which I could be roused only by beer consumed at the tavern. I then resolved never to set foot in the day school again and to devote myself entirely to the novels I had started to outline.

6

During the summer of 1956, thanks to one of my comrades at the day school, I found a job . . . on the Rue Saint-Jacques. I went to work for the biggest French-Canadian brokerage house of the time, L. G. Beaubien and Co., which is now the property of Jean-Louis Lévesque. I was to remain a clerk there (assigned to the payment of dividends) until the summer of 1958.

I began to live among shadows, among men who had been annihilated by the incessant, deafening, monotonous sound of IBM machines and by a routine of the same insignificant motions, the same checkings and re-checkings, the same initials scratched on thousands of little sheets of paper that were all alike. A place of scribblings, figures, additions and subtractions, speculations, hypotheses, false rumors, lies, and profits, where the Sisters of Wisdom strutted about with those whom Caouette has so aptly called the "sharks of finance." The brain and soul of capitalist society. A dreary and stupid universe!

The great majority of my co-workers were poor men and women whose wages ranged from $25 to $60 a week. Some of them had been working for the Beaubien family for more than twenty years. Those were the most exploited, the most underpaid, and the most alienated of all. They justified their slavery by a very simple story: they had lived through the Depression of the thirties; at that time most workers were unemployed; the Beaubiens could have thrown them out into the street because business was bad; but the Beaubiens had kept them on just the same; ever since they had felt obliged to be eternally grateful to the Beaubiens, and accepted as a *gift* their small wages of $50 or $60 a week—after twenty, twenty-five, or sometimes even thirty years of "loyal service"!

It was in these surroundings that I came to understand that white-collar workers also belonged to the Québécois nation of "cheap labor" and that they were even more alienated than the factory workers and the farmers. During the two years I worked among them, I did everything to start a revolt inside the tidy, well-lit offices where exploitation had clean hands and a respectable face. I could never get anything more than vague sighs. A few women seemed to be the only ones in that gray hell who had the courage of their opinions and of the revolt they felt. But they were rare, very rare.

At New Year's Madame de Gaspé-Beaubien, spouse of the deceased founder of the enterprise, would come in her wheelchair to offer us chocolates and her sanctimonious old smile! She was president of the Hôpital Sainte-Justine (Justine was her first name), and all the nurses in the hospital detested her. The brokerage house L. G. Beaubien looked after the investments of the nuns, and the Cardinal-of-the-Poor presented the Pontifical Cross to the great Christian lady whose fortune had been made out of the exploitation and alienation of the people.° Ah! the remains of our "national" bourgeoisie! To be incinerated, comrades, to be incinerated!

After we had swallowed Madame's chocolate and her ghastly smile, the "big party" would begin. This was our annual bonus: as much Scotch, whiskey, gin, and beer as we wanted, and a few ten-dollar bills. After this evening of grotesque, paternalistic debauchery, the routine would bring us back to our basic dependence, to the daily reality of our servitude—and of our growing frustrations; for the bosses made no secret of the fact that one electronic computer was worth more than 10,000 men. The threat of unemployment haunted us from morning till night. All the more so because there were (and still are) no unions on the Rue Saint-Jacques. We earned starvation wages, we had no security; laborers and journalists were treated better than we, but were we going to soil our hands by forming a union as the workers did? Here, to be a "worker" meant to be low, ignorant, etc. If they formed a union, would not the white-collar employees make pariahs of themselves? They thought they were *educated!* And they were so proud of being able to read the financial pages of *Le Devoir* and *La Presse* that they forgot that they themselves were exploited, that they were "cheap labor" in well-pressed ties and skirts, "cheap labor" wearing glasses (the men) and careful make-up (the women). Did not the *clean* "cheap labor" of the Rue Saint-Jacques and the other offices of private enterprise and government belong to the vast lunch-box family which has never yet eaten its fill, materially and intellectually speaking? How many illusions can be built on the simple fact that one holds a pen in clean hands and can initial forms, tons of forms! What a sorry affirmation of one's self! And yet even today, despite the unionization of the government employees, who are of their own kind, how many white-collar workers still have the illusion that they belong to a "superior" world—be-

° The "Cardinal-of-the-Poor" is another reference to Paul-Emile Léger and to the publicity surrounding him. (Trans.)

cause they scribble notes and sort papers instead of screwing bolts in a factory!

The absurdity of this artificial feeling of superiority, together with the hypocritical, profit-making paternalism of my bosses, made me sick. I kept the job, in spite of the disgust I had for it, because it demanded very little of me and left me plenty of free time for reading, writing—and subversion!

When I was home, in Ville Jacques-Cartier, I lived only for "my" work! Every evening, every night, I spent long hours writing—or rather, describing myself. During these hours of silence and solitude I lived out my narcissism to the full. Perhaps at that time it was the only way I could escape from the intellectual conformity, banality, darkness, and nothingness of the "nation." Who knows?

Writing thus, day after day, revealed me to myself and made me exist. I was laboriously working my way out of collective anonymity, like the earthworms that crawl over rich people's lawns on rainy days. A few friends consented to read what I wrote, and for them I began to exist "in my true light." They listened to me, they understood me. For the first time in my life people thought I had something to *say* and to *give*. At last I was no longer struggling alone. People knew . . . that I could do something, become someone . . . I was flattered and at the same time terribly anxious: supposing, I wondered sometimes, it was all only an illusion? Naturally my friends wanted to please me, to see the pained expression I always wore disappear from my face. But did they really believe in my worth as a person? If my mother had not been able to discover . . . how could they . . . ?

"And I," I wondered when I awoke from my long narcissistic meditations, "and I, what do I think of *them*? Am I capable of recognizing their worth . . . and of loving them for what they are?"

Since my abortive adventure with M., I had become a little like an oyster, and I had hardened myself outwardly in order to avoid being wounded or humiliated. With my friends I would talk about literature, painting, and philosophy, but I avoided talking about myself or listening to what they said about themselves. When I had them read a chapter of the novel I was working on, I would try to discuss only the style, the impressions I had splashed on paper like paint on canvas, the construction of the paragraphs, the "metaphysical" (*sic*) ideas mingled with the poetic images, and so on. The question I was most afraid of was: "This guy is you, eh?" I didn't want to answer— but the description was all too exact.

My friends went to the *collège*. They were now in Philosophy and were dying of boredom. Occasionally I would "call in sick" at the office while they did the same at the *collège*. We would meet in some tavern, and there, over large quantities of beer, we would discuss the absurdity of human existence. The events in the Suez and in Hungary had deepened our pessimism. The launching of the first Russian Sputnik, in 1957, filled us more with disgust than enthusiasm. Was it in order to send their Sputniks up higher that the Russians had crushed the revolt of the Hungarian students and workers?

We talked more about Rimbaud, Léo Ferré, and Dostoyevsky than about international politics.° We made regular visits to the Montreal art galleries, discovering Pellan, Borduas, Bellefleur, de Tonnancourt, Dallaire, Mousseau, Riopelle . . . who were trying to put a little color into the grayness of Québécois existence. We read an issue of the "Communist" review *Cité libre* from time to time and went to the Théâtre du Nouveau Monde. Two or three times a year we could see a good French film, and that was quite an event!

We were bored with Montreal. We dreamed of Paris and New York. I went with two friends to spend a few days in New York. Our stay consisted of spending the whole day gazing at the paintings and sculptures of the great masters. Then in the evening we went to the movies to see one or another of the films that were banned by the censorship in Quebec. In New York, for the first time in my life, I felt truly free, and it was not without a certain rage in my heart that I came back to Montreal, the city of boredom and stupidity, a city that Mayor Jean Drapeau was clothing in the purity and morality of a dried-up, ugly old maid.

Ti-Guy, Johnny, Yvon, Raymond, a few others and I dreamed of escaping to Mexico or France, of leaving Quebec forever. This country had nothing to offer us.

But while I waited to *leave*, I continued to write. I covered hun-

---

° Léo Ferré is one of the leading writers and singers of French popular songs. His lyrics are often revolutionary in content, but as Vallières implies, he is popular mainly with intellectuals in Quebec. (Trans.)

dreds of pages with my disgust, revolt, and violence mingled, despite everything, with hope. What I called my "work" was a mixture of moralism à la Camus and obscenity American-style. I took pleasure in it but was not attached to it. And that is why, in 1958, I had no difficulty destroying the whole thing in less than an hour.

Once in a while I went back to the *collège* to see how things and men were evolving there. The day school now presented a "respectable" appearance. The registration and tuition fees were very high. The Oeuvre des Vocations, I believe, had been abolished. There were more petty bourgeois than workers' sons. The place looked more presentable in general, and there was talk of competing some day with the Jesuits of the Collège Sainte-Marie. A very liberal spirit reigned at the *collège*, but unfortunately, in order to enjoy the privilege of sharing in that liberalism one now had to have a fair amount of money. The boys from the surrounding area, the boys from Ville Jacques-Cartier, did not have that money. They became laborers like their fathers, passing the classical day school of the rich, morning and evening, with their lunch boxes under their arms. The streets of Ville Jacques-Cartier were now paved with asphalt, but the poverty was as great as ever.

More than once I wanted to pack my bags and leave Ville Jacques-Cartier to live alone and free in Montreal. Each time my father, who only spoke to me on these occasions, managed to persuade me to remain with them. My father had built me a little room where I could write in peace, night or day. I stayed, but as a "stranger," a "boarder," never talking with my mother or my brothers, who understood nothing of what I was doing and thought I was crazy.

I felt cut off from the people around me—and guilty of a crime difficult to describe and define. It was as if my "education," as they said, was a shameful blot that humiliated *them* and made me ill at ease, guilty, troubled.

Instead of discussing it with them, I took refuge in a steely silence . . . when my heart was mush! I could not speak a word to my mother, for it seemed to me that she had lost all understanding of the things I would have liked to talk to her about. As for my father, he was becoming a veritable ruin of a man. I loved him very much, but crushed by work he had turned into a creature whose energies were totally absorbed by a single preoccupation: to survive, not to fall sick, not to die . . . And as for my brothers, they were too young to have the least idea of the drama that was being played out.

In the morning, when I was going to my job along with all the other workers, or in the evening on the way home, it would wring my heart to meet old classmates from my first years at the *collège*. The great majority of them had had to leave the day school in the middle of Syntax, Method, or Versification, for lack of money. Now they were day laborers, but day laborers who went to night school.

"Do you think," one of them would sometimes ask me, "do you think it's worth while going to night school?"

All the hope and suffering contained in that question would make me want to bellow like a calf.

Night school . . . Another racket! How could you escape exploitation, dear God, how could you escape it?

I did not know what to answer my companion. To tell him the truth, to tell him those schools were organized by thieves, would be to demolish his last remaining hope. And I had *nothing else* to suggest. It was that that hurt me: nothing to suggest, nothing . . .

"I don't know," I would say at last. "You can try. You'll find out . . . You . . ." My voice would choke on the lie: "You can try." What a farce!

7

Nowhere did I feel at home. In Ville Jacques-Cartier I lived like a stranger, instead of being in the midst of the others, instead of *serving* like Jacques Ferron. I was only interested in my "work," in myself. In the art galleries, the "beatnik" restaurants in the West End of Montreal or at the Ecole des Beaux-Arts (where I had a few friends), I never felt I was with "my own kind." As the people of my milieu say, I looked like a lost penguin. I was more at ease and had more *joie de vivre* with my old comrades from the *collège*, but there was also something that separated me from them: they were content to talk, to discuss; they never had anything to offer, to exchange. So I felt very much alone, until the day I met Gaston Miron and Maurice.[2]

I met Gaston Miron in 1956, when he was sales manager at Beauchemin's. It was Claude Fournier, one of the first Québécois poets published by Miron, who had advised me[3] to make his acquaintance.

Every Friday (pay day), I would go to Beauchemin's, buy a pile of books, then have supper at the Restaurant Saint-Louis (near the square of the same name) with Miron. We would stay for hours at the restaurant on Saint-Denis Street, mostly discussing poetry and decolonization. It is thanks to Miron that I came to know and love contemporary poetry, as well as the literature of the colonized peoples (Aimé Césaire, the Algerian poets, Pablo Neruda, and so on). I became profoundly attached to René Char, Paul Eluard, Aragon, and the Welsh poet Dylan Thomas. But above all, many a time I had the privilege of listening for hours to Miron himself reciting his *Marche à l'amour* and recounting his *Vie agonique*. No Québécois poet, in my opinion, has expressed *us* with so much authenticity, not even Grandbois, Hébert, Gíguère, Pilon, or Préfontaine. Isolated as I am today in my steel cage, how I would love to read and reread those poems, that long, sorrowful song of our alienation and our will to live in spite of the winter that Vigneault speaks of! At that time Miron was only the penniless publisher of the Editions de l'Hexagone, the man who "launched" two or three new poets every year, the man whose poetry only evoked cynical, amused smiles. I have heard respectable, sophisticated poets say that Miron did not know how to write and that his romanticism dated from the nineteenth century. But he is the only one of our poets the Quebec workers understand, when on May Day he *tells* them with his whole being about his love and his revolt. Except for the *chansonniers,* Miron is our only popular poet . . . and he doesn't write in *Joual.*°

At the Restaurant Saint-Louis we sometimes met a dry man with the piercing eyes of an eagle. Miron called him "the gray eminence." It was Claude Ryan. He spoke little, answered our questions vaguely, scrutinized us the way an entomologist scrutinizes insects.

Fortunately, Gaston knew a great many people who were more

° *Joual* is the name given to the language of Quebec, a French that retains some holdovers from the seventeenth century and is heavily corrupted by English. The term was popularized by Desbiens (in *Les Insolences du frère Untel*), who said that his Québécois students so pronounced the word *cheval.* The radical *joualistes* (André Major, for example, who is mentioned in the notes at the end of the preceding chapter) write in *Joual,* claiming for it the status of a separate language. Vallières opposes this position. His own work, while it is sprinkled with English words ("les businessmen," "l'Establishment," "un racket," "cheap labor," "le Big Boss," "le fun," etc.) and contains a number of peculiarly Québécois expressions, is written in standard French. (Trans.)

likable than the future director-dictator of *Le Devoir*. First there was Miche, who was wonderfully beautiful and intelligent; then Yves Préfontaine, Jean-Guy Pilon, Hénault, Ouellet and Portugais (the future founders of the review *Liberté*); Roland Giguère, who was soon to go into exile in France and whose poems I devoured—poems which scarcely two or three hundred persons were reading at the time; Michel Van Schendel, Adèle Lauzon, Rina Lasnier, Alain Grandbois, Anne Hébert; persons who are now famous and respected but who, in the fifties, were all hesitating between exile and "belonging to the country." Quebec was not Algeria; it was not even Martinique.

What was one to do in this country whose inhabitants rejected all passion? Some had a go at social democracy. And Miron, like Ferron, became (in 1957, I think) a candidate of the NDP. But he dreamed— we all dreamed—of France, the incarnation of the Nation and Intelligence, the country that spoke to the world in language adapted to its needs and aspirations. We were all obsessed by the desire to *leave*. To leave, to leave, to leave . . .

I thought about it every day. But when would it cease to be a dream? I did not earn much at Beaubien, and I spent almost all my wages on books. I drowned my impatience in beer or in writing.

I wrote like a madman, for hours on end, and sometimes for entire nights. Miron was worried about my *fervor* and often suggested that I go to the country for a while. I did not take his advice and later I was to regret it bitterly.

At that time at least (1956–1958), Gaston Miron was not one to impose his ideas on others, but he had great insight into people and was master of the art of bringing out the truth and freedom that were in them. I think he knew me better than I knew myself, and it is thanks to him that I read the authors whose thought or passion responded to my own. Unfortunately, I was too withdrawn to give Miron what he may have expected from me. I took everything; I gave nothing. But it is also possible that Miron expected nothing of me. I knew (and anyway, it cries out in all his poetry) that he had already been profoundly disappointed and that many of his wounds were not yet healed. Miron was a wild, loving sorrow that roamed the streets of Montreal, arms outstretched to embrace men and, at the same time, to take them with him, to awaken and stir them. Those who know him know that Gaston Miron has remained the same and that the "quiet revolution" has not changed him; it has revealed him, it has shown him to the blind men who thought themselves geniuses and copied René Char while Miron lived and created his poetry . . . without knowing that he was expressing *us* with the profound genius of a François Villon, despising publicity and renown, seeking only one thing: love. Like all of us. A hard thing to find in Quebec. A thing he is no doubt still seeking. Like most of us.

Some people will be surprised that I give so much importance to Gaston Miron. They will think I am exaggerating. In reality I am not even doing justice to this great living poet who (despite his youth) is the spiritual father of the FLQ, of *Parti pris*, *Révolution québécoise*, *Liberté*, and many other political or literary movements. So far as I personally am concerned, Miron is the one who developed my political consciousness and turned the course of my philosophico-literary search to practical political engagement. It was he who gave me the idea of writing my first "engaged" articles for *Le Devoir* in 1957, and who made me understand the importance and political significance of the Murdochville strike. But my articles published in *Le Devoir* were far from reflecting coherent political thought. They were a mixture of half-digested ideas—spaghetti with existentialist sauce! Still, it was the first time in Quebec that a young man (I was seventeen) had dared to tell the old men that they were on the point of collapse, and the intellectuals of the time that they were useless manufacturers of third-rate novels or skillful editorialists incapable of assuming their responsibilities and acting when social justice demanded it. At that time the only people I admired were René Lévesque, Judith Jasmin, Gérard Pelletier, Pierre Trudeau, Gérard Filion, Jean-Louis Gagnon, André Langevin, and Jacques Hébert. Of those, all but Judith Jasmin, André Langevin, and Jacques Hébert are now more or less whores!

The first article I wrote, in 1957, was entitled "The Fear of Living" and was an attack on the slave's "philosophy" that was hidden behind the title of a novel by Jean Filiatrault, *Le Refuge impossible*. The search for a "refuge" had gone on long enough, I wrote. It was time to learn how to *live*.

But perhaps at bottom it was myself I was trying to persuade, for in reality I was not living. I was consuming myself, I was "burning the candle at both ends," as the saying goes. And all my activity was primarily cerebral. Miron was increasingly worried, and he had good reason to be.

8

Maurice was a very different sort from Miron (whose "eccentricity" he did not think much of, by the way). He was an artist, a Christian thinker, a happy (?) husband, an excellent father. I met him early in 1957, at the Musée des Beaux-Arts, where he was having a show.

We got into the habit of meeting regularly, at his place or at l'Echourie on the Avenue des Pins. He was the first, along with Ti-Guy, to read my novel *Noces obscures (Dark Wedding)*, destroyed in 1958, in which I told about my confusion, dryly, in the manner of Camus or Sagan. It is thanks to Maurice that I acquired that minimum of self-esteem and self-confidence that every man must possess to be able to create something. *Noces obscures* was a book filled with my narcissism. Maurice taught me to take responsibility for that narcissism without being ashamed of it. He urged me to submit my manuscript to the Cercle du Livre de France, which refused to publish it because of the ending, which was too fiercely immoral. In the meantime, I wrote a second novel, *Les Démons*, which was very bad and which I destroyed a few weeks after finishing it. Only Maurice read this unsuccessful novel, while *Noces obscures* was read by most of my friends (whose number was steadily growing).

Maurice was first of all a "Christian personalist." A personal friend of Albert Béguin, whom he had met in Paris, he lived by the thinking of such men as Mounier, Ramuz, Unamuno, Bernanos, Kierkegaard, Pierre Emmanuel, Domenach, Berdiaeff, and Teilhard de Chardin— all that group of thinkers who were trying to reconcile ideal justice with practical political engagement, necessarily "biased," and whose lives were a perpetual yearning for an unattainable purity. Maurice was aware, by the way, that what was called "personalism" was a *select form of alienation*, but he could not rid himself of it. And I, whose knowledge was rather sketchy, and who lived primarily with my instincts and my inner monsters (even if I did so in a style that was outwardly cerebral and cold), was incapable of understanding this alienation clearly and analyzing it rationally. At that time I was an agnostic, that is, fundamentally an individualist and an anarchist, ready for all intellectual adventures, all the "inner experiments" of the kind that Georges Bataille was promoting. I was happy to write engaged articles in *Le Devoir*; I believed in the social responsibility that Miron talked to me about; but I believed in it after the fashion of Sartre, as the Grand Panjandrum of Existentialism had defined it in *What Is Literature?* A responsibility that engages one's conscience more than one's life. Besides, this existentialism was only an atheistic personalism, an individualism decked out in false "Marxist" garb. It is not for nothing that Mauriac, Mounier, and the Abbé Moeller tried to "baptize" Sartre, Simone de Beauvoir, and Camus—something they never tried to do with Marx and Engels!

"Lucidity" became the big thing! And as each man was to determine his conduct and morality on the basis of *his* conscience and *his* freedom, that is, in the last analysis, on the basis of his personal interests, "lucidity" varied from one individual to another and everything became "ambiguous" and consequently "gratuitous." Sartrian responsibility, like Christian responsibility, was only an ideology that served as a façade, an ideology required by the daily spectacle of millions of innocent people throughout the world being massacred by the imperialist West. "Lucidity," verbal protests, petitions, scathing essays, denunciations that earn you the Nobel Prize, etc.—"refined" and artful ways of washing one's hands! And to think that after twenty years, in the era of the atomic bomb, the war in Vietnam, famine in India, and the bloody repression of the revolutions in Santo Domingo, the Congo, and Watts, this "respectable" comedy still goes on in Saint-Germain-des-Prés and elsewhere.

The high treason of the pure and of the right-thinking who disdainfully judge Lyndon B. Johnson but who will never perform the smallest concrete act to overthrow him! The clear conscience of those who weep over the assassination of Kennedy and the much more terrible assassination of the Vietnamese people, but who will never dare to compromise themselves by joining with the "disruptive youth" who get clubbed down in the streets of the "free world"!

Nothing is so disgusting to me as the lucidity of the members of this new Establishment. And I don't care whether they refuse Nobel Prizes or not. That kind of honesty makes me want to vomit. The pharisaism of the rebels in dinner jackets and satin slippers is an admirable complement to the neo-pharaohism of the Soviets who condemn the war in Vietnam and at the same time collaborate with the Americans. What do we care—we, the hewers of wood, the drawers of water, the cutters of sugar cane, all the niggers of the entire world —what do we care about intellectual and moral "trials"? What do you expect us to do with all these piles of papers that "judge" but *do not change anything?* We need hands, brains, and weapons . . . not bourgeois literature-with-a-bad-conscience-but-a-fine-lucidity!

"Worse than de Gaulle," François Maspero correctly wrote in regard to the "French Left," the old and the new. "Worse than the Christians," one might write in regard to these existentialists who *exist* so vigorously only in their books and who *are nothing* to the workers and the colonized peoples of the whole world.

Pharisees, impotent men, who unconsciously exploit our oppression and enslavement, who profit from the disarmed and thousand-times-repressed revolt of the niggers! You remind me of the journalists who make their fortune out of the easy "scoops" abundantly provided by the misery of those who do not know how to write—of those who feel betrayed, robbed, raped, and despised every time they read what "objective" pity is pleased to tell about their hopeless existence. I am thinking of certain journalists, *certain* intellectuals, whose "prestige" (alas!) eclipses all others. I am thinking of those brilliant minds in love with justice, purity, and integrity, who end up in the Academy or in Parliament! High-class rabble!

Yes, high-class rabble! The young fascists of Greenwich Village who draw swastikas on the walls of their theaters and cabarets are also fervent readers of Sartre, Genêt, and Gide! A coincidence? An accident?

Existentialism is a Nietzschean individualism that has borrowed from Marxism a vocabulary capable of expressing the revolt and boredom of a decomposing bourgeoisie in words comprehensible to the masses. That is why it had so great a vogue. But the results of this "fashion," in Europe as in the United States, are, among other things, the rebirth of Nazism and the resurgence of nihilism. Is not Heidegger the father of Sartre? And is not Heidegger, even today, a defender of Nazism? I know that Sartre has written prefaces to Fanon and Nizan. He has also praised Gide, Genêt, Montaigne, and Descartes with equal fervor. Is Sartre also going to write a preface to the complete plays of Brasillach and say of Céline that he saved the "soul" of anguished France under the occupation?

"Personalism" grapples with the same contradictions. Thus Bernanos, who supported Maurras, deplores the Spanish Civil War and, like Unamuno, refuses to take sides in the name of justice . . . as if justice could be on both sides at the same time. To condemn bishops who are politicians and chiefs of state in no way changes the social, or rather anti-social, function of the institution called the Church. And to claim that one belongs to the "mystical body" of the Church does not justify apoliticalism. For apoliticalism is always, always, the politics of the strongest, the fiercest, the politics of the vulture.

It is in vain that Unamuno, from his university chair, curses the Franco officer who shouts: "Shoot them! Long live death!" Unamuno's last-minute cry will never make us forget that by his refusal to fight side by side with the Republicans, the workers, the women and children of Spain, by his very abstention and his purity, he worked *concretely* for the coming of fascism and the crushing of his people. If he had not died "of a broken heart," it would have been necessary to shoot him!

(If there is a heaven for the Miguel de Unamunos, the Pius XIIs, the Claudels and all the clear consciences of the world bourgeoisie, I prefer the worst of hells to that heaven, to the selfish happiness of the Pilates and the cowardly aristocrats. For if Heaven is theirs, God, if he exists, is surely not "on our side," on the side of the majority of the human race; he is surely not on the side of the people . . . but rather in the very midst of the napalm the Americans are showering down upon innocent, "free" Vietnam . . . Let us not forget that God is an invention of the dynasties, of the aristocrats of the five continents. This invention began to haunt the minds of men from the moment there appeared on earth the first tribal chief who needed to create a "divine right" in order to preserve his rank, privileges, and power. How many men have been massacred, how many peoples crushed, in the name of the Lord God of the Christians, the Moslems, the Hindus, and the Buddhists! As you read these lines, the God of Paul VI and Lyndon B. Johnson is flying over Asia, Africa, Europe, and the two Americas in a B-52. God of the atomic age, God who fights relentlessly to vanquish Communism on earth, with his apostles, the

Marines! It is no longer as it was in the time of Jesus Christ, when the first disciples gave their goods to the poor and Christ himself drove out the exploiters with a whip!)

Mounier himself, who has nevertheless fought more than the other "personalists" and who even "offered his hand" to the Communists, participated in that vast enterprise for hoodwinking the masses which is Catholicism by remaining *faithful* and publicly defending a religion and ideology which, as he very well knew, served the interests of capitalism and fascism.

Living with such profound contradictions, how can one help living and dying with anguish in the very marrow of one's bones? One cannot reconcile the irreconcilable, and each man, within his own class, must take a clear position for or against the established Order, against the essentially economic organization of present society on which political life, religious life, intellectual life, and even artistic life depend. Because they have refused to see what the daily activity of men and peoples teaches, what history teaches of its own accord—for history is "objective," it serves no interest, it is not politics but a science—the personalists, like the existentialists, are trapped in the status quo. (Except, of course, in certain exceptional circumstances that are transitory and concern only one aspect of society—like the Algerian war—when even the Church, the democrats, and the conservatives take sides.) Furthermore, not only are they trapped in the status quo but they defend it, if only by their mystical, disillusioned, or "charitable" passivity. For there is only one way to oppose the status quo, the reign of organized exploitation, institutionalized injustice, and oppression baptized with the blood of Christ, and that is to organize everywhere the revolt of the exploited, of the vast majority of mankind, against the established Order—established, but unstable and vulnerable. But the personalists and the existentialists think only in terms of metaphysics, of being and essence, of being "in itself" and being "for itself." "To be or not to be, that is the question"! I am in complete agreement with Shakespeare. "To be or not to be" is not, as is believed by the inventors of various metaphysical systems (one more absurd than the next), a philosophical problem but a practical problem, a problem of action. And unfortunately for tender hearts, noble minds, and sensitive souls, action can only be conceived and resolved in terms of action. "To be or not to be," in our "civilized" world, in our asphalt jungle, means simply: "To be or to die."

I have nothing against those who believe in God. But I do have something against those who believe they are exempt from opposing injustice and taking practical action against it, those who believe they are justified in remaining neutral by virtue of imaginary divine commandments, revelations, or teachings. Such men, in my opinion, deserve neither respect nor "understanding." The starving and the humiliated have no use for the moral scruples of well-fed bourgeois who are honored by their class, which is in power.

That is what I reproach Maurice (and a number of his friends) for today: for not having wanted to understand, and still not wanting to understand even now, that the most elementary rights of men demand total revolution, a revolution not in people's minds, in their "mentality," but in the social relations, the relations of production, on which every "mentality" is founded, built, and developed.

Today I reproach him for his absenteeism, and in spite of my friendship for him and my gratitude for all the services he has done me, I am tempted to call him a coward. But in those black years 1957 and 1958, I too, like nearly everyone else, was hooked by the "depths of existence"![4] I lived more and more on myths that contradicted each other and mingled to form an agnosticism with a thousand facets, none of which had a precise meaning—a fact that spared many men from having to make a direct and necessarily costly commitment. I consoled myself for my impotence or fear by repeating to myself that I was "a child of the Absurd," begotten by the War and infected with the sickness of mind that had been caused by the shocks of the thirties and forties. I was a victim, a creature shattered from birth, sitting on a heap of ruins and trying to reconcile Rouault, Cézanne, Malraux, Dostoyevsky, Camus, Lenin, Picasso, Sartre, *France-Observateur*, Eluard, Césaire, etc., with a meaningless universe.[5] I saw man's fate through the war in Algeria, the way Malraux had analyzed it through the beginnings of the Chinese Revolution and the Spanish Civil War. But Algeria was far away. And I was living in Quebec in the great darkness of Duplessis, in a desert where men ate, worked, and begot children out of habit and *without enjoyment*, with a boredom as profound as the country was broad and the horizon distant. Duplessis seemed as invulnerable as God, and no one disputed his dictatorship. Asbestos, Murdochville, the students' sit-in at the doors of Parliament . . . they were the pathetic endeavors of a freedom that did not believe in its own strength or even in its own legitimacy. Most people were not taking any risks, not even the tiny core of "Leftists" who were trying, without much enthusiasm, to politicize the Murdochville strike and to publicize the tame socialism of the PSD.° [6] The newspaper *Vrai* was finding it very hard to interest the people in truths that were nevertheless under their very noses, and *"cité libre"* looked like a pious hope. Besides, it often boiled down to the demand that laymen have the right to speak out on the affairs of the "nation" and the Church, which were inseparable (a real revolution). It was simply an attempt to resuscitate Clovis in backward Quebec and see if he could not once again accomplish the deeds that had made him famous! Scarcely ten years ago, any Catholic layman who professed his religion openly and took the liberty of quoting a piece of scripture himself, without permission, was considered a rebel fomenting a *coup d'état* to overthrow the hierarchy! Gérard Pelletier led this little vestry revolution, while Trudeau, who was more pragmatic, was laying the foundations of his *"politique fonctionnelle"*—opportunistic and *liberal* politics, as the word was understood in the days of John Stuart Mill—which in 1965 were to make him parliamentary secretary to Lester B. Pearson, the most insignificant prime minister Canada has had in all its hundred years of Confederation. As for the *jéciste* rebel Gérard Pelletier,† he has become one of the many silent members of the Ottawa Parliament who always vote with the government. But when you can sell your freedom and principles for a *good* price, right? Why have scruples about it? After all, Quebec and its little population of starvelings are such small things!

But in the fifties, these veterans (who are now living on pensions from a government that stinks with corruption) were heroes to me, or at least Québécois Voltaires. They incarnated a freedom that was narrow and arduous but a freedom all the same. And under Du-

---

° The Parti social-démocrate (PSD) was the Quebec branch of the Cooperative Commonwealth Federation. (Trans.)

† *Jéciste* is the popular term for a member of the Jeunesse étudiante catholique (JEC), a Catholic Action youth group. (Trans.)

plessis, any freedom was a scarce commodity . . . which, as such, cost dear.

Following the example of Miron, I tried to participate somehow in political life. I met some of the leaders of the PSD and the FTQ,° but among these defenders of the people, who lived in Outremont and were led by Madame Casgrain, I felt rather like an awkward, crude delinquent who had been adopted, because he had a kind heart, by a very rich, paternalistic family whose daily concerns were not on the level of the working class but of the bourgeoisie. I should have liked very much to know Michel Chartrand who, with his wife, was giving the curés and the businessmen some good kicks in the ass . . . on state television. But I never had the opportunity of meeting him.

Since, except for the PSD, there were only the old traditional parties, I said to myself that Quebec politics were not worth devoting one's time to, even so much as an hour a week. I dabbled in municipal politics in Ville Jacques-Cartier, but without enthusiasm. It was very hard to tell the "good" underworld from the bad, and I was soon fed up with that world of more or less shady "deals."

All this made me susceptible to the arguments of Maurice, to whom the essential thing was *to be* a man, in the metaphysical sense of the words *to be*. To be a man who was true to himself in purity and to others in friendship. Why cling to political ideologies? The only thing that counted was the inner adventure, which a man undertook alone or with a few others. The hermitage or the little circle of friends. The mass, the crowd, the noise, sweating humanity— that was only the blind herd, a pointless destiny, or rather the absence of a destiny. Politics soiled what was best in man: his silence, his gaze fixed on the *fundamental*, on Being and Essence. One had to live in being for being's sake, as one lives in art for art's sake, to discipline one's mind in accordance with an exclusive search for the essential, for the basis of human existence. To spend hours contemplating Cézanne's onions and more hours meditating on a maxim of St. John of the Cross or Ramuz. Was not the universe of the artists and

---

° The Fédération des travailleurs du Québec (FTQ), or Quebec Federation of Labor, is the Quebec branch of the Canadian Labour Congress (CLC). The CLC has branches throughout Canada and has close ties to the AFL-CIO in the United States. (Trans.)

mystics the only one in which man could find his worth? Lavelle complemented Ramuz. And Mounier's political writings disappeared under thick volumes devoted to Being. In Maurice's living room, stuffed with paintings, books, and art objects, one would have thought the humiliation of the workers had lost its revolting reality. It was reabsorbed into Cézanne's onions, which Maurice gazed upon the way believers worship the Host, seeing God in it.

Maurice believed that true engagement, for each man, consisted in gaining access through art and prayer to his original purity and drawing from it a kind of grace that would wash away the stains of humanity, a light that would reveal to mankind the heart of the world. Maurice was also a fervent disciple of the German theologian Hans Urs von Balthasar, who thought he saw this "heart of the world" in Christ. Teilhard de Chardin, for his part, talked about the "divine milieu." Heidegger was obsessed with Being and Time, and with the essence of human freedom. St. John of the Cross described "the dark night" of the union with God.

Teilhard, Heidegger, St. John of the Cross—a fine lot for whom *renunciation of the world* was the Way, the Truth, and the Life! Heidegger's being-unto-death was the sinner described by St. John of the Cross who had to let himself be consumed by Love through self-renunciation. Besides, one could only know Love through death, and Love was Being . . .

Since Quebec could not change, since everyone was certain that Duplessis would not stumble, that he would continue in power for years and that the great darkness was not coming to an end, mystical theology became a logical occupation and the exploitation of men gradually ceased to be a moving spectacle. People in ordinary life were dying of boredom and servitude. Perhaps renouncing life would bring artists and saints happiness, the beatific vision, communion with Being, the only true life? Did not the greatest happiness lie at the end of that long inner tunnel which the artist and the saint "knew" they were called upon to traverse in pain and darkness?

One had to engage not just a small part of oneself but one's whole being, one's entire life, one's body and mind, one's past, present, and future, everything, absolutely everything . . . and wait in tears and torment for the contact with Being, the Divine, Love—in order to learn at last what one was, and what purpose one served!

But perhaps at bottom we expected God to make *men* of us . . . as if we were only sub-men or monkeys seeking intelligence? I don't really know. The more I thought I knew Maurice, and the more discussions I had with him, the more I let myself sink into a kind of dream that was half rationalized, half purposely mad.

What did Maurice talk about, then, when he was alone with his wife? She seemed so uncomplicated and so far removed from our search! Could they understand each other without speaking the same language? She never participated in our long "philosophical" conversations. She would prepare the meals, wash the children, put away the books that were lying around, and serve us coffee with a gentleness that made her more beautiful than Modigliani's women. And every time I looked at her, I would silently recite a poem by Eluard or Aragon. (I would have liked her to be capable of adultery, even if Maurice was my friend.) Then, after this period of relaxation that should never have come to an end, we would return to our effort, our need (?) to discover, at all costs, and to know, once for all, in precisely what domain lay the fundamentals we were seeking—the way other, simpler men patiently do crossword puzzles. But for us there was never any answer, and in the end we were not sure of anything, except that this search was making us increasingly weary of Quebec, of the Québécois, and of ourselves.

We discovered with amazement that there was a vast emptiness in our lives. I was seventeen or eighteen. He was twenty-four. I was a bachelor. He was married and the father of three children. But our emptiness was the same. When we looked into ourselves, we experienced the same dizziness: a Québécois had nothing to *live through* . . . not even a war, like the Algerian who, in the depths of his little village, still felt that he had freedom, dignity, and concrete worth. *We* had to find our worth in something that perhaps did not exist: in Being, which was always ready to take, in our imagination, the form that our preoccupations or feelings of the moment lent it. And it never answered back, any more than Cézanne's onions dared contradict all the things that Maurice made them say.

I became addicted to this strange mysticism the way one becomes addicted to opium. I acquired a taste for intoxication, for mythomania. I invented a universe for myself in order to deny the life and the country I despised. It was necessary that nothing else should exist, in order for Being to appear and devour me; for in my heart of hearts I was asking to die . . . For years on end, ever since I had been a child, I had applied all the intelligence of a humiliated creature to finding a way out, then to justifying the despair of the poor, then again to seeking a way to awaken those around me . . . In vain. "Nothing was going to change," as Maria Chapdelaine had said. Nothing was going to change . . . Then why was I not like the others, resigned or benumbed, crushed or asleep? Why had I learned to read and write, if it was only to feel more uncomfortable in my skin than most men?

I began to write a third novel, which I called *Les Porteurs d'eau* (*The Drawers of Water*). I stopped sending articles to *Le Devoir*. The Murdochville strike had come to an end amid almost general indifference. Duplessis, having once more won a brilliant victory, was completing the sale of Quebec to the Americans. In this country as still and silent as a great, pale corpse, living men were suddenly questioning themselves as if they were in peril of death; they were not wrong.

Poems filled with violence were published here and there, announcing the coming thaw and the first hope of Quebec since 1837.

Maurice watched events unfold with a detachment mingled with disdain. Miron lost none of his faith and his madness. As for me, I was exhausted, torn between Miron's hope and Maurice's detachment. In order to escape this torture, I spent months freeing myself from my monsters by letting them howl, kill, rape, pray, weep, love, and murder in this formless novel that had nothing in common with what I had written before.

The characters of Faulkner (*Absalom! Absalom!*, *The Sound and the Fury*) and of Joyce, Molly Bloom in particular, my heroes, prisoners of the great darkness—how they struggled in a violence of words that was both terrifying and terrified, in which uncontrollable fits of laughter were desperate sobs, and cries of despair were shouts of laughter that would split your face with anger!

And all of it amid the unchanged landscape of Ville Jacques-Cartier: blackened hovels, dusty streets, naked, grimy children, men who got drunk, women who cursed, and curés who clamored loudly every Sunday because the collection wasn't bringing in enough!

9

In the meantime, I had met Michèle,[7] at a party given by the Editions de l'Hexagone to launch Alain Grandbois' *L'Etoile pourpre*. After exchanging a few words with Grandbois and Anne Hébert, I had retired to a corner of the room in the Ecole des Beaux-Arts where the party was taking place. I was sipping a glass of cider and observing this sophisticated society with contempt.

A young woman with very black hair and green eyes, wearing a red wool dress that accentuated the beauty and firmness of her breasts, offered me a little cake, saying: "How scornful you look! This crowd is like a circus, isn't it?"

"Oh you know, people . . . They are what they are . . ."

She smiled with her whole sensual mouth, with her large, luminous eyes, with her long hair falling on her bare shoulders—which I already wanted to caress.

"What are you reading?" she asked, noticing the slim volume protruding from the left pocket of my jacket. "Poetry?"

"Yes. Dylan Thomas."

"Oh! Who's that?"

I told her the story of Dylan Thomas's life, and during this recital I spoke more and more about myself, about that search for the absolute of which I have spoken above.

She listened to me without saying a word. Never had I seen such intense curiosity in a woman's look. She pressed her knees against mine, placed her hands on my thighs and, still silent, brought her mouth so close to mine that it made me dizzy. Then she withdrew her hands, preparing to rise.

"Pierre," said she, "you want to come to my place on Sunday? Robert . . . in short, my husband will not be there. You must tell me more about Dylan Thomas. It's as if his drinking . . ."

She did not finish, quickly wrote her name, address, and telephone number on one of the pages of the book, just above that long poem the title of which I have forgotten but which recounts, with nostalgia and a profound need to love and be loved, the childhood of this alcoholic Welsh genius.

"Till Sunday!" she said.

"Till Sunday!"

And she disappeared into the literary circus.

For a while I stood rooted to the spot. Then I left the room quietly and returned to Ville Jacques-Cartier, interrogating the smiling image of Michèle.

A dream?

I saw less and less of Maurice, Miron, and most of my other friends, devoting my weekends to discovering and possessing Michèle, and letting myself be explored and bewitched by her. Our relations were sensual and tormented, like the soliloquies that the drawers of water invented with a liberating complaisance for immorality.

Robert continued to be her husband and they continued to sleep together, except during those weekends when his job as a journalist obliged him to be away covering some congress or convention.

I was jealous and I admitted it to Michèle, one Sunday when it seemed as if her caresses would never let go of my fevered flesh. I began to speak, and bitterness sprang from my mouth like an insect repulsive to women. She broke off her caresses as one breaks up a dream and told me that I was only a friend, while *he* (who was at least fifteen years older than she) was really her man. With me, as with others, she had amused herself playing bedtime games between two sad songs by Léo Ferré, with a glass of whiskey within reach . . . And I, who thought I possessed her and was penetrating her completely when with all my strength I pressed her on my body strained to the cracking point, I was ejaculating my virility into a silken doll. I might as well have masturbated with an expensive handkerchief!

I withdrew from her body with a raging pain in my belly. I wanted to slap her, to break a record over her head, to drown her in her bath. But my only thought was to caress her again. My hands wandered over her magnificent body. Humiliated and half mad, I asked her to explain. She smiled, as on the evening we had met, as if to say: "My poor friend, you ask too much. Why isn't it enough for you to have a good time, like the others? There's nothing extraordinary about sleeping with someone, it doesn't commit you any more than an evening at the theater. A game, a game, Pierre! Stop looking for the Absolute in everything. After all, to make love is not to find . . . God, or even to find oneself."

Suddenly words of great gentleness fell upon me: "You know,

Pierre, too many things, memories, habits bind me to *him* now. We are not married, legally speaking, but we are too united to part from each other. We have a good time with other people, as opportunities and individuals present themselves, but we only really make love *together*. I don't know if you can understand . . . We have 'betrayed' each other hundreds of times, and each time it was an occasion for reconciliation between us—as if, each time, we made love *anew*, differently. You are not the first man who wanted to beat me. And I suppose there are many women who dream of killing Robert, because he's a pure-bred Don Juan . . ."

I felt I was being tortured, as if her nails wanted to tear off a piece of my flesh. Maybe she wanted some for lunch.

I sank down on her bed like one of Picasso's clowns interrogating Fate. I was not a Don Juan.

10

I saw Michèle again a few times; for one does not easily forget a skin like hers. But jealousy almost made me impotent. Only to think that we were playing a game made me want to throw her in a corner like a child's doll that cannot communicate with its owner. I was dreaming of "Elsa," and all I had in my arms was a bundle of sensations.° I was discovering that sexuality in no way engaged *being* (which I had discussed at such length with Maurice) and that it was only a physical exercise more subtle and spellbinding than the rest. It was not love. But did love exist? Perhaps "Elsa," after all, was only a poem?

I gradually returned to my philosophical meditations without telling Maurice what I had just lived through, talking about essence and existence and at the same time devouring his wife with my eyes.

From time to time I went to Miron's, on Saint-André Street, to listen to the sorrow recited by that man who so greatly loved women and his country and who felt free only to suffer out loud. I understood better the *"marche à l'amour"* and the advantage that prostitutes have over the beautiful "free-love" women: the gift of themselves. And Saint-Denis Street was our domain, for it was the street

---

° This is an allusion to the "Elsa" often celebrated in the poems of Louis Aragon. In reality, she was Aragon's wife, Elsa Triolet, a prize-winning novelist in her own right and, like her husband, a prominent member of the French Communist Party. (Trans.)

of brothels, cheap restaurants, and raw truth. Here women and men did not play the game of false emancipation and amoral egotism (amoral like money) but lived simply, exchanging ordinary, necessary, consoling *services*. Blessed debauchery that never humiliates the poor, the deformed, the tormented, the worker, or the beggar . . . and that so often, so often, saves a man from the throes of death or from suicide!

11

All these experiences formed the living, almost volcanic material of *Les Porteurs d'eau*. The novel cast a spell over me. It was as if I was injecting myself with a drug of my own invention, a drug which at certain privileged times could transform into vivid colors—red, yellow, green—the great darkness of life in Quebec, a darkness unknown to the outside world.

This drug could alternately produce euphoria, despair, mysticism, the taste for death, or the need for a god. But it could not change the daily servitude, the stale, morose boredom of my life as an office clerk. And when I was not working at L. G. Beaubien, Brokers, writing, discussion, or friendship were merely distractions (in the Pascalian sense of the word "distraction," as Maurice would say) from my profound disgust for life, which was only the perpetual torment of an unconscious and tenacious guilt.

I felt guilty of high treason to my class, to my own people. *They* were not existentialists but practicing Catholics; *they* were not writers and "geniuses" but "cheap workers" without a voice, without an education; *they* were not waiting for the revelation of Being, of Meaning . . . but only—even in the depths of their resignation, or rather of their total defeat—for the *practical organization* of their limitless potential, of their immense, unemployed, throttled, alienated strength. And perhaps that is why one spring day (in April 1958, I think), I suddenly cast in my lot with the alienated and gave to the garbage collectors who were running behind an incinerator truck on my street, the thick, nearly completed manuscript entitled *Les Porteurs d'eau*.

That same evening I bought some flowers to give to my mother for Easter. Unfortunately, she found my gesture as pointless as sending a conventional Christmas card.

I went for walks beside the river. I liked to interrogate existence through that mass of water which for thousands of years had been ceaselessly flowing down to the ocean, with a regularity, a calm, that only men could disturb with their inventions: their freighters, liners, and seaplanes. I would have liked to slip into that water, to belong to the vegetable kingdom, to become a peaceful seaweed in the depths of the water, a thing that did not ask itself questions, a being that did not need Being in order *to be*.

I had lost the taste for action, the need *to do*. What was the use of being a man?

I had given flowers to my mother. What was the use?

I had destroyed my literary drugs. What was the use?

I had loved Michèle. What was the use?

I was the son of a worker. What was the use?

Miron, Maurice, Raymond, Ti-Guy, Johnny, Yvon . . . heaps of friends. What was the use?

With all my heart I was with the Algerian and Cuban partisans. What was the use? *Here* in this accursed country, I was nothing!

But I had a confused sense of guilt . . . or responsibility. I didn't know any more.

I was eighteen years old.

Notes

1. Taverns were "forbidden" in Ville Jacques-Cartier, headquarters of the underworld! The curés had no doubt obtained that from the underworld in exchange for something else.

2. Maurice is a pseudonym for one of my best friends, who might be embarrassed by my remarks on his conception of life if his name were known.

3. At that time Claude Fournier's *Le Ciel fermé* had just been published by Editions de l'Hexagone, which was run by Miron. I had liked this collection of poems very much and had written to Fournier asking to meet him. He had replied at once. He was my first "contact" (anglicism) in the "literary" milieu of Montreal.

4. An allusion to an article I wrote for *Cité libre* early in 1962 entitled: "Nous éveiller à la profondeur de notre existence" ("To Awake to the Depth of Our Existence").

5. Paul Van den Bosch has described this state of mind well in a little essay, *Les Enfants de l'absurde*, published by La Table Ronde (Paris) around 1957.

6. The former name of the Québécois section of the CCF-NDP.
7. Michèle is a pseudonym for the woman I have loved the most and who has made me suffer most. Since I have been in prison I think of her so often that sometimes I cannot resist the need to speak to her by means of a poem or letter that I hide under my pillow. It is terrible how sentimental prison life makes you!

4
Freedom Lying Fallow

After I had burned my last handwritten notes (all that remained of so many years of agonizing—and useless—struggle), I felt liberated from everything, released from the heavy burden of giving a meaning to my destiny as a philosopher-proletarian, absolved, by Him who had permitted me to exist, from the obligation of choosing "my future" myself. I began to dream about God and to feel a kind of happiness in abandoning my fate to him. Something profound and indefinable welled up inside me. Insane thoughts came to me: "Death is just as good as life. Everything is vain. Perhaps beyond death there even lies the beginning of life . . ." Later, on a bridge over the Seine in Paris, I was to feel the same thing, along with an almost uncontrollable urge to plunge into the blackness of the river.

But in the autumn of 1958 it was "the religious life" into which I plunged, with my eyes closed, the way one commits suicide. A few months before, disillusioned and weary to the bone, I had had a "revelation" while reading Teilhard de Chardin's *The Divine Milieu*, and like Charles de Foucauld, I had suddenly been "converted."

Like a madman, half poet, half philosopher, I attempted to unite myself through God with a universe I did not understand. I "took a chance on" the *inner adventure* called for by Maurice's conception of human existence, and I tried to push it to its utmost limits.

1

The year of my novitiate unfolded in that peace which accompanies the madness of the mentally ill who are in a state of euphoria.

169

No fits of rage. No pounding on the walls. Nothing but blissful in-difference to the world.

How could I really believe in God? In the God I had only heard about from imbeciles who called the drying up of the mind and body "chastity," stupidity "humility," and fear of living "obedience"?

Besides, my "spirituality" was something rather unique. It drew its inspiration as much from Martin Heidegger's "essence of freedom," Georges Bernanos' "why freedom?" Kierkegaard's "anxiety," and the search for Kafka's "castle," as from the mystical writings of St. John of the Cross and the Gospel according to St. John, the only two Christian works I knew that seemed "solid." When I got sick of waiting for "contact" with the Heart of God, in my desert full of the silence of men who had renounced the world, I did a little philosophizing and said to myself: "Old friend, the more profound the inner search is, or tries to be, the more likely it is to provide a haven and justification for anguish, despair, lying, cowardice, hypocrisy, and plain stupidity . . ."

Why, indeed, was I *there*? In the midst of these easy-going Franciscans who seemed so little touched by ordinary life, with all its suffering?

Because of Saint Francis? What did I know about that holy man who had dared to brave the material power of the papacy and who fasted in the caves of Italy to expiate his sins?

Really, I am unable, even today, to explain exactly what happened. A woman psychoanalyst once told me that unconsciously I had wanted to reconcile myself with my family, my milieu, and the traditional values of that milieu, because at that time my revolt had not reached a high enough level of consciousness to be free of a profound feeling of guilt. Guilt that was kept alive by "the morbid universe of Sin" in which Quebec developed during the first three centuries of its history, under the influence of the Vaticanists who (up until very recent years) organized the real inner structure of Quebec society: the Catholic Church, which was able to combine its hierarchical system of classes and functions with the equality of all men—before God—in *original sin*! A pretty arbitrary equality, but one which, implanted in our minds from childhood, accomplished the rather fantastic *tour de force* of making us for centuries *equal* in guilt, in shame, in the constant impression that we were defeated, and in the feeling, which still runs very deep in Quebec, that when all is said and done, life is not worth living. The Church—with the help of the conditions of our existence as exploited, colonized, "ignorant" men—has turned us into a population of citizens who are ashamed of themselves, guilty before they have even had a chance to perform free acts, who are disgusted with life and seek refuge in the promise of an eternal celestial happiness. The "quiet revolution" has begun to break down this alienating, dehumanizing "routine," but there is still a long road to travel before all the rebels of Quebec are really liberated from guilt and are able to determine their own destiny without reference to what they have been taught, to the religion of the enslaved and the oppressed.

During my novitiate I tried to understand the "equal and fundamental original sin" which the Protestant Kierkegaard speaks of in several of his works. I tried to make a connection between this postulate and the second statement that many are called but few are *chosen* . . . and that even the "chosen" would not be equal in paradise: on the celestial dais where God on his throne spends his eternity being worshipped and served, they would not all have as good seats as the angels and saints.

We were equal in sin, but not in redemption!

Furthermore, equality in sin was rather difficult to perceive concretely. For certain sinners wore crowns or tiaras on their heads, others had golden insignia on their chests, some were wealthy businessmen and exploiters of the people, others were heads of state who were anti-worker, colonialist, and militaristic. But the vast majority of men, it is true, were equal in poverty and insecurity. It was said that they would be first in Heaven. But how could you give "first" place to so many people? Especially when *few* would be chosen?

I sought answers to these questions in the Bible, but the books of the Bible often contradict each other, and even the parables of the gospels and the teachings of Christ are full of contradictions.

Did not this "dialectic" that fascinated Kierkegaard play into the hands of the capitalists by remaining on the level of inner conflicts between the flesh and the spirit, and by transforming itself into individual mystical activity that was inoffensive (because it was committed in advance to nonviolence and the "expiation" of sins) rather than into collective social activity that was practical . . . and necessarily violent?

Kierkegaard, like all the curés, said one should make "the leap" into Faith, into nothingness, into belief in the Unbelievable, the Unintelligible, the God of Abraham, Isaac, and Jacob.

I had made "the leap" . . . and I found myself the same as before. All questions remained open. But while *before* the leap into Faith I was allowed everything, now everything was forbidden. And it was in contempt for myself and the world that I was being taught to find Love, the Way, Truth, Life, Being. I found nothing at all, unless it was a certain bodily discipline that greatly improved my health and made me less nervous. Just as the organism is rested by a long vacation in the country.

Deep inside, I despised this life in which individual personal wills were equal to the extent that those wills *wanted nothing*, as Engels has so rightly put it, but simply *obeyed*, like sheep that graze without asking questions, because God has willed it so. That is the practical freedom of those who have been touched by God's "grace": the freedom to graze without complaining. Fortunately, God spares an increasing number of Québécois from his "grace." That is why Quebec has ceased to be a *quiet* colony of Washington and the Vatican. God and his Heaven are dying in the minds of the Québécois, who have at last awakened from the pious dreams of their childhood. Mindless obedience and sanctified servitude have ceased to be "virtues." They are becoming what they have always been: meaningless phrases, chains that must be broken. The political and economic decolonization of Quebec will be accompanied by the de-alienation of the Québécois. The Church will not make so much money, but the people will be free.

Many people in Quebec have understood at last that solidarity among the exploited, the humiliated, the oppressed, is nothing but slavery "sublimated" in common. Solidarity can exist only among free men. That is why, to the great despair of the bishops and the clerical aristocracy, there are fewer and fewer "religious vocations" and priests, and more and more rebels and revolutionaries.

In 1958, 1959, 1960, I spent months on end seeking reasons, the "why" of my existence. I went in for metaphysics. Through mysticism, I tried to seize God "by the collar" and make him *talk*. I wasted my time and a good deal of energy on the sport of "sanctification," the purification of the soul, prayer, etc.

For even if the great darkness of Duplessis had been transformed, thanks to God, into the "dark night" of the mystical theologies described by St. John of the Cross, Faith itself would have remained a "senseless," intangible thing outside reality. There are only two logical positions: to believe without understanding, or to leave God alone. I tried to believe and to understand. But the more I tried to believe, the less I understood, and the less I understood, the less I liked to believe; the more I began to think that, all things considered, the only thing to do was to forget God and try to understand human life in terms of the conditions of its development, by studying its history, its evolution. For if God had an answer to give to man, a meaning for human existence, was it not up to him to "explain himself," since we, on the one hand, could only reach him through a blind, mute faith that received no reply, while he, on the other hand—if he did exist and if he was really Love, as St. John said—knew our questions and our anguished doubts? Then why did he not take measures —he who was said to be all-powerful—to reach us? In order to further "purify" our faith, I was told. It was as if a man had said to the woman he loved: "You are suffering, darling? You ask me to reply to your long letters? You don't know what is happening? You are no longer sure of anything? But my dear girl, that's exactly the way I love you. When you are suffering. The more you suffer, the more I love you. Suffer, suffer, suffer! I love you like that."

"Fuck that kind of love," an American would say. "Fuck that" indeed! And long live poor little human freedom!

"Masturbate, Lord, and be crucified again, if you have such a *passion* for it! But for pity's sake, get the hell out as fast as you can!" That was the theme of my prayers less than two years after the Kierkegaardian "leap" into Faith, with a capital "F" to clearly indicate the "metaphysical" character of that absurd leap.

The rage that I had experienced at the *collège* took hold of me again. Since September 1959 I had been a philosophy student at the theological college of the Franciscans in Quebec, the heart and brain of traditional obscurantism ever since Bishop Laval had founded his state-within-the-Church there in the seventeenth century. (Even now, in 1967, the Québécois state has not yet entirely come out of the Church.)

I had come to know Christian spirituality and its masochistic practice a little better. Now I was going to become acquainted with the political and economic *institution* hiding behind that spirituality which is ostensibly founded on cha-ri-ty.

In the Church charity has the same function of fooling the people that illusory democracy has in the capitalist system. Every two or four years, capitalist democracy asks us to exercise "our" right to vote—the ridiculous right they leave us to choose which of two, three, or four thieves we "prefer" (!) to put in power; without, however, leaving us the freedom to call into question the foundations of this democracy which is supposed to grant equal "rights" to all men. The role of Christian charity is similar (and complementary) to that of the "right to vote." Christianity asks us to pray for the "wicked" and to give alms, from time to time, to help the "poor" and expiate our own sins, but it too is fiercely opposed to calling into question the capitalist system—which lets there be so many "poor" in the world —and is opposed above all to the practical consequence of a lucid and honest criticism of the system: its overthrow.

There can be progressive individuals within the Church, just as there are reformists in the capitalist state, but the Church as an institution is essentially reactionary (politically, economically, and ideologically) and doesn't have much to do with the Gospel of Jesus Christ, except, perhaps, for a rhetoric that has no practical meaning. The speeches of the Pope, like those of Lyndon B. Johnson, are filled with demagogy, and they have but one objective: to preserve the enormous privileges that the Church hierarchy derives from its cooperation with the businessmen and heads of state of the established Order. It is common knowledge today that the Church is one of the biggest financial institutions in the capitalist world and the surest "moral guarantee" of the system of exploitation of man by man. And to think that all that is in large part financed by the money of the deluded victims of exploitation, who buy indulgences, masses for the dead, masses for the souls in purgatory, medals, rosaries, statues, pardon for their sins, etc. With all this money, the "princes" of the Church make large and profitable investments in the great multinational corporations and draw fabulous dividends, which are either reinvested in those corporations or plowed back into the "business," the Church itself, which uses charity and "eternal salvation" to suck money from the people every day, with a patience and tenacity of which only these capitalist "churchmen" are capable.

At the Franciscans', who are supposed to be the poorest of the poor, I have been present at very mystical discussions concerning the sale of their house on Marie-Guyard Street to the University of Montreal. I do not know what agreement was reached between the Franciscans and the University administration. But I know—because I heard it from the lips of the very brother who was manager of the Order—that at that time the Franciscans were interested in making as much profit as possible (on the order of a million, if I am not mistaken) from the sale of this house, which they had once bought at a low price from a "charitable" rich person who became very sentimental and pious at the sight of the bare feet of the Franciscans. And yet according to their Constitution, the Franciscans are never supposed to make "financial speculations"! What then happens in the other communities whose constitutions, on the contrary, encourage investment?

In 1966 the curé-politician of Lake St. John, the Abbé Villeneuve, told a journalist from *Le Magazine Maclean* that the Québécois owed nothing to the Church. That is the exact truth. The Québécois owe nothing to the Church, unless it is three centuries of obscurantism. But the Church owes to us, to our ignorance and passivity, the fact that it has become the biggest French-Canadian financial institution, the only one the Americans "respect."

In Quebec I personally witnessed—and was sickened by—two incidents, among hundreds of others, whose meaning is easy to understand. First, on the eve of the 1960 elections, the campaign propaganda of the National Union Party was distributed to us. (I should make it clear that the only newspaper we could read was *L'Action catholique* of Quebec; we had to go steal *Le Devoir* and *La Presse* from the section reserved for the Fathers if we wanted to have a somewhat less "politicized" view of what was going on in Quebec!) Second, while the community gorged itself on abundant food and often enough drank Grand-Supérieur, the poor who knocked at the door of the monastery were given only one or two sandwiches of *"paris-pâté."* ° I was a door-keeper for one day, just one, and the "chief porter" took me to task for putting a little too much *"paris-pâté"* in the sandwiches. "After all," said he, "we're not rich!" I never went back to work at the door again, because I think I would have passed out revolvers to the poor instead of those lousy sandwiches.

I have read all the great theologians whom the Church has excommunicated over the last twenty years: Rahner, de Lubac, Congar, Daniélou. But I have never been able to understand why, after having so correctly criticized the *institution*, they did not make a clean break with the Church. It's all very well to appeal to the "mystical body" of the Church in order to justify one's faith in it. But in so doing does one not also justify, indirectly, the whole institution, its economy, its politics, its reactionary social thinking, and its fundamental conservatism? It is not ecclesiastical councils and liturgical reforms that the exploited and starving people of the world need, but a revolution. All the rest is only learned palaver between the "Left" and the "Right" of the same class of exploiters, conscious or unconscious. Faith in the "mystical body," like the "sincerity" and "honesty" of certain moralists, has never changed anything, and will never change anything, in the unbearable conditions of existence of the majority of men on the planet. The councils remind me of the parliamentary debates conducted by the so-called representatives of the people: they always end up ratifying little "deals" cunningly worked out for the purpose of *making people believe* that progress is being made, but they never propose radical changes. What will the people gain by praying in French rather than in Latin? Will that reduce the tithe? Will it increase the number of jobs and lower the cost of living? Will it make any change in the daily oppression?

Making over the face of the Church, like making over the face of the capitalist system, modifies its nature only very superficially! A witch who undergoes plastic surgery to get rid of her warts and her crooked nose still remains a witch.

The Church is the witch of God, and I hope the Québécois of the future will learn to get along without her, just as children today have

---

° *"Paris-pâté"* is a cheap brand of canned meat paste. (Trans.)

stopped believing in the boogie-man and take an interest in the real adventures of the astronauts instead.

2

As can be seen, my piety was pretty acid. And there were more times when I felt like smashing chairs, holy-water basins, alms-boxes, and statues than when I felt like imitating the canonized masochism of Thérèse de Lisieux. My philosophy professor, to whom I occasionally blew off steam, telling him what was on my mind, would break out into a great Rabelaisian laugh whenever I got angry. He had long since resigned himself to the human folly of the Church. In order to escape despair (and also, perhaps, to avoid the effort of an open revolt against those he called "the commissars"), he had taken refuge in philosophy and a kind of relativism or agnosticism which dared not speak its name, much less translate itself into action. In class he did more to initiate us into Einstein's theory of relativity and T. de Chardin's "forbidden" doctrine on the evolution of man than into the miserable Thomist philosophy as watered down by the nonsense of Dr. Grenier of Laval University. But his practical agnosticism remained an unhappy individualism, ashamed, tormented and, finally, hypocritical, since he "played the game" out of laziness, if not cowardice. And I found it all the more disgusting because in the pack of idiots who peopled that holy monastery, he was about the only intelligent being. But like many others, he had abdicated before he had even really done battle.

It took me a while to come to a firm decision to start wearing pants again and return to my former freedom. On the one hand, I was spending a lot of time over the works of Congar and de Lubac, seeking reasons for believing, for I was afraid to "return" to my atheism. On the other hand, I was studying certain works by Husserl and Merleau-Ponty, and this study was so absorbing that I easily forgot the foolishness that surrounded me. Finally, I ate well, I had no financial problems, and there were plenty of books available.

But all of that was beginning to smack a little too much of "sacrilege," that is, in common language: dishonesty with oneself. "The commissars" took up my case, for I was beginning to sow chaos in the theological college. I belched at table, farted during religious offices, slept at prayers, sang "dirty" songs in the shower, and even went so far as to dance rock 'n' roll in the reading room! Scandalizing these imbeciles made the barracks atmosphere of the place less oppressive to me, and I found it refreshing. After that, I could read a passage in Husserl more intelligently. But I was not very proud of myself, and I finally resolved to go study Husserl "in the open air." I had not finished my term in Philosophy and I would not take the examinations for the B.A. But what did I want with a B.A.?

I had decided to resume my philosophical search where I had left off before entering upon the novitiate, but this time using the method of phenomenological analysis. My plan was to apply this method to the analysis of human freedom—the behavior and motivations of men and their illusion that life had an ultimate purpose, conscious or unconscious—in order to discover the real, material, doubtless "relative" meaning of freedom . . . its "essence," as Husserl says, giving that word a very different content from the one it has in the Thomist "category" of the same name.

The commissars of God felt no regret at my departure. But as for me, I was knocking my fist against my head and repeating: "Idiot, what the devil were you doing in that galley? ° Decidedly, freedom —yours, at least—is not exempt from folly . . ."

3

I went back to Maurice, Gaston Miron, Ti-Guy, Yvon, and many other friends with indescribable joy. They found me "unchanged," as if I had returned from a long journey. Indeed I had not changed much, but the situation in Quebec, *that* was really beginning to change. "*Cité libre*" was in power, and the freedom of expression manifested in the press, on the radio, and on television, as well as in private conversations, was in sharp contrast to the timid thinking of the Duplessis era and the underground revolt that in those days had always led up a blind alley. Now revolt was coming up out of the catacombs, publishing reviews, building a "lay movement," and beginning to formulate the body of doctrine, still more or less confused, which was to give birth to separatism, the "quiet revolution," and

---

° This is a familiar quotation from Molière's *Les Fourberies de Scapin*, in which one of the characters (Géronte, Act II, Scene 7) repeats some half-dozen times, with increasing comic effect: "What the devil was he doing in that galley?" (Trans.)

the questioning of all the traditional institutions and values of the French-Canadian nation. But there was still only slim hope. Neither the RIN nor the PSQ had yet been founded.° The avant-garde remained "liberal," and thanks to the myth that had grown up around him, René Lévesque was the incarnation of rediscovered freedom. He had become the voice of a whole people who, for the first time since 1837–1838, were beginning to believe they had a future. They felt they were *alive* and making progress.

My plan was to introduce a progressive philosophy, a new vision of human existence, into this movement which was so unexpected but which people had been hoping for for decades. With the help of phenomenological reflection—rather than by revolutionary action—I wanted the Québécois to base their freedom as men on purely human values. But at the same time I remained obsessed by a certain need for an Absolute, a need to base these human values on some sort of transcendence and to define that transcendence. To try to persuade other Québécois to undertake this "fundamental" search, I wrote a few articles for *Cité libre* that had significant titles: "To Awake to the Depth of Our Existence," "The First Steps of Our Freedom," etc. I do not think the co-editors of *Cité libre*, Pelletier and Trudeau, really understood what I was writing. Besides, because I had a poor vocabulary and because the articles were brief, they could be variously interpreted, for they contained more than one commonplace thought dressed up in words to which one could give an almost unlimited number of meanings.

I realized later that Pelletier and Trudeau did not understand exactly what I was writing. Especially since my "existentialism" in search of freedom also called itself "personalist," and since in the beginning I avoided taking sides for or against belief in God.

A first divergence between us arose spontaneously when the co-editors of *Cité libre* decided to publish a special issue on separatism and strike a mortal blow against this new enemy of the Liberal, federalist bourgeoisie. I was asked to contribute, without being told that Pelletier and Trudeau's intention was not to *pose* the problem of separatism but essentially to demolish its arguments in favor of the independence of Quebec.

° The Parti socialiste du Québec (PSQ) was later founded by a group of Québécois nationalists who split off from the New Democratic Party. (Trans.)

According to my usual practice (at that time), my article was stuffed with philosophical considerations all turning on the central problem of human freedom. These considerations led me to affirm the legitimacy of separatism as a form of political thought and action. In my conclusion I even went so far as to admit that I was very happy that separatism was giving an increasing number of Québécois an opportunity to *assert themselves*, to take sides and to free themselves from the ancestral resignation to so-called historical inevitabilities. Instead of submitting to history, perhaps at last the hour had struck to begin making it *ourselves?*

The article was not published. It was not even read by the editorial board of *Cité libre*. For in my naïveté I had made the mistake of talking about it freely with Trudeau. Which was enough to keep my piece out of a special issue designed to nip separatism in the bud!

I must say that at that time, plunged up to my neck in philosophy, I knew absolutely nothing about the links between Trudeau and Pelletier and the Liberal Party. But the way they went about preparing and editing this famous issue (which read as if it had been directly ordered by Pearson and Lesage) disappointed me enormously.

I was not the only one who did not like their methods. I remember that at the editorial board meeting held before publication of this issue, the whole staff, with the exception of the co-editors, criticized the general tone of Trudeau's article (which made up practically the entire magazine) and certain aspects of his offensive against separatism. But Trudeau did not change his piece by so much as a comma; which shows how much consideration he gives to the ideas of others, even those of his friends, including Charles Taylor and Michael Oliver. The *"cité libre"* could allow many freedoms, but not the freedom to be a separatist. And to think that Pelletier dared to write about the "late unanimity"! Decidedly, the greatest madmen are those who do not know they are mad.

About the same time, the newly founded RIN held its first public meeting. The RIN was then only an educational movement, a little like the MLF.° This meeting was not a political assembly but a debate on separatism. Among the participants were, if I am not mis-

---

° The Mouvement laïque de langue française (MLF) promoted the secularization of public affairs. (Trans.)

taken, André D'Allemagne, Pierre Bourgault, Jacques-Yvan Morin, and Jean Marchand. I remember the statements made by D'Allemagne and Marchand very well. D'Allemagne's was a summary of the separatist arguments that are now familiar. It was not polemical but cold and lucid. Jean Marchand's, on the contrary, was flagrantly dishonest, for it assimilated separatism *a priori* into the old fascist nationalism that had put Duplessis in power immediately after the war. President of the CSN at the time,° Marchand presented himself as the "conscience" and the "voice" of the oppressed workers of Quebec. Now that he has become Pearson's right-hand man, we know in whose name and in whose interests (personal and class) he became one of the most virulent adversaries of Quebec separatism. Marchand's dishonest attitude is in large part responsible for the "split" that existed from the beginning between the Québécois workers' movement and the group that founded the RIN.

I attended this debate with some members of the executive of the Association générale des étudiants de l'Université de Montréal. We were all enthusiastic about the prospect of a "free Quebec," but we didn't dare believe in it too much. Even the founders of the RIN were far from suspecting the breadth of the movement—which, out of a concern for social peace, the Lesage crowd and their Anglo-Canadian friends were soon to call a "quiet revolution."

At this time I was a sales clerk in the now-defunct campus bookstore on Maplewood Avenue. I lived in a little room not far from the bookstore and took most of my meals at the University Student Center, where I found more than one former classmate from the *collège*. It was there that, for the first time in my life, I became acquainted with the university milieu, *Le Quartier Latin*, and the new-born student union movement. I envied those who were lucky enough to be studying biology, sociology, or economics and working in the movement. When they came to the bookstore, I would try to give them the biggest discount possible on the books they needed. The book trade made me sick. I was badly paid and every day I was asked to

---

° The Confédération des syndicats nationaux (CSN), or Confederation of National Trade Unions, is a Quebec organization. Like the larger Canadian Labour Congress (CLC), the CSN concerns itself with contract bargaining rather than social reform. However, unlike the CLC it has Catholic origins and takes pride in the fact that it is not affiliated with American unions or tied to U. S. imperialism. (Trans.)

bless the Dussault family for their "charity" in granting me a job! After a few months of this, I told the manager of the shop to go to hell and submitted my resignation.

I became unemployed . . . and free, for a month. It was the winter of 1961–1962. I took advantage of my leisure to improve my acquaintance with student society and to study Husserl.

But the preparation of the special issue of *Cité libre* on separatism put a distance between me and the "engaged" intellectuals. I saw Miron and Maurice only occasionally. I made new friends at the University among the pioneering members of the Chantiers de Montréal, who worked with the disadvantaged families of Saint-Henri. Several of them had spent some months in Latin America. They had "latched onto" the idea of practical charity preached by the Abbé Pierre and were trying to get the students to assume certain social responsibilities "as individuals," but without political commitment. They wanted to be a "presence" and a "support." They felt that to become involved in politics was . . . anti-democratic, for in their minds all politics were bad per se, unjust and immoral. Their goal was not so much to change the condition of the workers as to give themselves a clear conscience by showing that they "sympathized" with the misery of the exploited.

In the beginning I was attracted to this "applied" mysticism, for I had not yet rid myself of the morbid guilt that had driven me to make the "leap into Faith." Disappointed by the intransigent attitude of Pelletier and Trudeau with regard to separatism, disillusioned and unemployed, I decided to become a simple worker, a day laborer like my father, and to abandon my philosophical search.

Toward the end of March 1962, at the very time when Pelletier was offering me a job on *La Presse*, I became a laborer on a construction job. Through the Chantiers de Montréal I met the little worker-nuns who worked in the factories without proselytizing: Carmelites with dirty hands, without privileges, earning their own living, sharing exactly the same conditions of existence as the workers, living two or three together in miserable rented rooms, like everybody else. They showed me a new face of the Church. I met one sister in particular who was torn between the "contemplative" spirituality of her community and her need to take concrete, and necessarily political, action to change the living conditions of the workers.

One day she said to me: "Christ needs us to be his witnesses among the masses. But the masses don't need witnesses so much as revolutionaries and above all, right now, better union leaders. I think I would be more useful working in the union than suffering in silence . . . for nothing. What do you think?"

"To tell the truth, I don't know what to think. There are days when just about everything makes me sick. I haven't really got over the temptation to drop everything and . . . contemplate . . . my navel. You see, I work like you. I'm a day laborer. I'm friends with everybody. The work is very hard for me, because right now I'm on demolition. And I swallow a ton of black dust every week. The men gripe all the time. And so do I. But when you get right down to it, I want to *leave*. To get away as far as possible. To France, maybe. To try my luck over there. Never to set foot here again, in this country where there is no life . . . no passion . . ."

"There is much to be done here."

"I'm too sick of this country. I'm suffocating! In September if I've saved enough money, I'm going to drop everything and take the boat."

"I think you are wrong."

"I don't think so."

"What are you going to do over there?"

"I don't know. Maybe . . . I'll go to see your folks . . . ? Or maybe I'll go to Algeria. At least in Algeria the people *want* to get out of all the shit, to do something . . ."

"And what do you think the people of Saint-Henri want? To die in silence like rats? You don't really know the people around here . . ."

"That's very possible. I am still narcis—"

"And how!"

"Maybe that's why I have to leave . . ."

There was something masculine about her face and her tone of voice. She was still only a "postulant," and she had come from France about a year before. I had the impression that she no longer believed in the usefulness of the worker-priests, the worker-nuns, the "witnesses" . . . She would often begin her sentences like this: "As soon as you look at things from a worker's point of view, as soon as you *embark* on their existence . . . you cease to be a witness. You become a rebel, at least . . . The Church always looks at things from the point of view of God and *goes out* to extend a hand to the workers. The workers don't need 'our' charity, 'our' compassion. They respect us—out of superstition or habit. That doesn't mean anything. If tomorrow they shoot at us, they won't be wrong. Because I have the definite impression we're *deceiving* them . . ."

"Then what are you doing . . . in this uniform?"

"I'm a little like you, Pierre. I'm afraid of seeing clearly and above all of performing the acts that are called for. Two thousand years of Christianity, it's not so easy to get that out of your system! Then too, maybe when all is said and done misery blinds us instead of opening our eyes . . ."

"What do you mean?"

"That actually everything is *permitted,* as Dostoyevsky says, because in this life one can never be sure of anything. You see, I have to take sides and that frightens me. I would rather a God made the choice for me, so I would be *right,* so I would be *certain.* But everything is permitted; and that's why nothing is certain. And yet I believe in God. Do you?"

"I don't know any more. This morning I didn't believe. Now I don't know any more. Tomorrow I may say that I don't believe in Him, and the day after, that I believe in Him a little all the same. Everything is permitted, as you say . . . But what good does that do you?"

"It gives you the freedom to *choose,* I suppose."

I could tell that the little sister, a worker and a philosopher, had inwardly made a new choice.

"Everything is permitted . . ." For years I had been obsessed by Dostoyevsky's celebrated formula. What did he mean exactly? As in the days when I had been writing tormented novels, I was forever asking myself the same questions and going around in circles.

I discussed these problems with friends who were usually baffled by my torment. At work I contented myself with being like the others. Just the same, I tried to do a little "politicizing" during the federal elections of 1962, but without success. I was not prepared for it. Nor had I ever had any union experience. That year I was the only one who voted NDP. All my fellow workers voted Social Credit. The size of the *créditiste* vote in Quebec made the Montreal workers jump for joy. I was then living on Visitation Street, near Dorchester Boulevard. All my neighbors noisily demonstrated their delight. At last the old parties had got what was coming to them! The people had waked up. Gérard Filion wrote in *Le Devoir* that the *créditiste* vote meant only that Quebec was a "province more stupid than the others." But knowing those who had voted Social Credit, working with them all day long, I had an entirely different impression from Monsieur Filion . . . though I hardly dared believe that the Quebec winter was drawing to an end.

Not knowing if the little worker-nun had chosen to join the union movement; not knowing what, deep inside, my friends had chosen or would choose; not knowing if the *créditiste* vote meant a real and lasting collective choice or only an ephemeral one; not knowing if Quebec was getting ready to choose revolution or a greater integration with capitalist America; not knowing what I myself really *chose*, I decided in September 1962 to take the boat and go to seek the answer to my anxieties in France.

I embarked on the *Homeric*, one rainy day, intending never to return to Quebec again. From Montreal to Trois-Rivières I stayed on deck looking at the rain-washed landscape. Shortly afterward, night fell. I went to sit down at the bar of the liner. I had the feeling that the night was erasing my past and that a new, freer life was about to begin.

4

France, of which I had so often dreamed. The country of our ancestors. The home, it was said, of free men, of great thinkers. "Universalist" and Gaullist France. The France of the cathedrals and the Revolution . . . I spent the seven days of the crossing thinking about it, trying to form an idea of it from a group of Marseillais with whom I made friends at the bar. But I was not going to Marseilles.

The France I found was a dreary, disillusioned country which had been deeply rent by the Algerian war and was nourished on new illusions by Gaullism. True, I stayed in Paris most of the time, except for a few months when I lived in the "Red" region of Dijon. I made short visits to Lyons, Vézelay, and a few celebrated monuments of Romanesque art. I went to Chartres three times. My stay in France (I arrived in Paris with only $50 in my pocket) consisted mainly of work. During the last three months of 1962, I got to know the conditions of the agricultural workers of the Côte d'Or. First I worked for a week on the grape harvest; then picking beets; finally as a laborer among a group of "clandestine" Spanish émigrés. I obtained a one-year residence permit and a work permit from the mayor of a little village; he was also the largest entrepreneur in the region, which was entirely Communist. It was the first time I had met politicized workers who were ideologically trained and capable of understanding the system under which they lived, and who ardently desired its overthrow. Unfortunately, these workers were not organized. In France as in Quebec, less than 20 percent of the working class is unionized.

We worked at least fifty-five hours a week. The work-week was five-and-a-half days. No worker had an automobile. We went to and from work on bikes. We earned between $20 and $25 a week! But for all that, the working conditions were more human than in Montreal; we had an hour for dinner and two half-hour breaks (one in the morning, the other in the afternoon) to have a bite and a little wine. Of course, our wages did not permit us to free ourselves from daily enslavement to the *strictly necessary*. It was impossible for us to save any money, and all my fellow workers had just one thing in mind: to "go up to Paris."

It was at this time that there occurred "the big scare" about an American-Soviet confrontation over Cuba. To tell the truth, the people of the region were not greatly disturbed over this crisis. They made fun of both the Russians and the Americans, wishing they would each let the other have it. "That way," said someone, "we'll have peace at last and the General will be able to raise our wages instead of building atomic bombs that will be no use anyway."

I learned much from these men, some of whom had lived through the Spanish Civil War of 1936. Above all, I learned that no compromise with the present system of exploitation was possible. But even though this region was 100 percent Communist, I met neither union leaders, nor social agitators, nor full-time revolutionaries. Although laborers constitute a high percentage of the French working class, they were of no interest to the unionized "aristocracy of the working class" in Paris and the great industrial centers. The Côte d'Or (the former province of Burgundy) reminded me a little of our Gaspé.

The only ones who were really doing anything were some worker-priests, a few militants in Catholic Action, and a handful of disciples of Father de Foucauld who were content to "witness." The people liked them but did not believe in them. The workers did not want to redeem imaginary sins by offering their slave labor to God, but to fight to sweep away slavery itself. Nevertheless, these "witnesses" often helped them to stand up to the boss or the mayor who took advantage of their labor and their status as clandestine immigrants. In return, these workers, who were Communists and atheists, avoided making trouble for the preachers of redemption. Sometimes it all ended in a few "conversions": a group of "witnesses" would turn Communist! But instead of staying where they were to organize those who needed them, these new agitators could not resist the desire to go to Paris . . . to meet the heads of the union movement. Not one of them ever came back to the men who every day, from sunrise till sunset, did the same stupefying work over and over so as to earn the absurd freedom to *survive*—and be exploited by the boss until dead!

It was in this region that I came upon Marxism and revolution as "my" truth. I realized that revolution was not a gratuitous choice but a vital necessity for all workers. And that for *conscious* workers it was also a *responsibility*. But that still remained confused in my mind.

After a bicycle accident that paralyzed my right arm for a month and forced me to reflect a great deal, I too "went up to Paris."

The three months I spent in Paris were a veritable hell. I was revolted and disillusioned by the bureaucracy of the Communist Party. I looked around in various places for a revolutionary organization disposed to utilize my energy. I did not find one. I encountered dozens of men who talked revolution, but not a single revolutionary *organization*. I read piles of "incendiary" reviews, but I saw no place where a fire might start. The workers, powerless, contented themselves with cursing their fate—although they did not entirely cease to believe in revolution. They were prisoners not only of their factories but of their unions and the *Party* (the Communist Party). In 1958, when de Gaulle had taken power by a *coup d'état*, thousands of Parisian workers had been ready to fight de Gaulle's army, take power themselves, liberate Algeria, and put an end to chaos. But the *Party* had ordered the workers to disarm, suspend demonstrations, etc. And now the same *Party* was verbally condemning Gaullism after having helped it take power. Just as during the Resistance of the forties. What had the workers got out of all these compromises? Cracked heads, the maintenance of low wages and the five-day week, and the sacrifice of their welfare and liberation to the building of a mythical French *"force de frappe"!*

I thought the French Left had the stupidest leaders in the world. And all the brilliant intellectuals who were "the honor of France" were only impotent "critics" in the face of that crushing force of inertia which any fossilized, self-satisfied bureaucracy represents.

The young people, disillusioned, were going back to individualism and adapting themselves quite nicely to the social conformism bequeathed by the bourgeoisie. The student movement itself was going around in circles. And in the suburbs, the young workers were now dreaming of James Dean and Marlon Brando, while the Algerian refugees, the *pieds-noirs*, served as scapegoats for the French, who were disappointed by their defeat and, at the same time, ashamed of the ghastly war they had supported with a chauvinism comparable to that of the English ruling class at the beginning of the nineteenth century. As for the *harkis*, the Algerians who had collaborated with the French during the war, they dragged out a miserable existence moving from one shantytown to another on the outskirts of Paris. Many settled in Nanterre, a shantytown that can compete with those of Lima or Caracas.

It was a France full of sorrow and disillusionment that I found. Its cathedrals and its Revolution, Versailles and the châteaux of the Loire, the *grands boulevards* of Paris, the Louvre, the sidewalk cafés: all these were very interesting, but did nothing to change the slavery that was the daily lot of the majority of Frenchmen. Besides, only tourists and bourgeois had the leisure to contemplate the wonderful monuments to the daring and freedom of France's *past*. The workers were fed up with being crushed. What good did it do them to go take a turn on Sunday afternoon among the splendors of the very past against which their ancestors had risen up, arms in hand? The bourgeois might have secured for themselves the wealth of the kings, but as for the people, they were not deceived: the Revolution had in no way changed their condition, and Charles de Gaulle's nationalism was in no way changing it either. But the people's leaders didn't give a damn what the people wanted!

I often talked about all that with French or Québécois friends. Incidentally, since I had trouble finding work in Paris, I managed to subsist only thanks to the help and friendship of a few French Canadians whose uncalculating generosity I will never forget, a generosity that was in sharp contrast to the parsimonious "sympathy" of the Parisians, who "economized" even on their feelings. Without these Québécois friends—and two or three Frenchmen—I would have died of hunger on one of the quays of the Seine, where every day thousands of wretched beings lay stretched out like abandoned corpses, or moved slowly about, like big, weary insects with nothing to do, no longer living for anything but to savor among themselves the profound contempt they felt for the "universalist" France of the (American) tourists. I sometimes spent whole days among them, following a few of them as far as the shantytowns on the outskirts of the city, in particular to the one at Nanterre, where dozens of children died of cold that winter. I found vast Ville Jacques-Cartiers in this France that still called itself the heart of Europe. In this country where the workers were "politicized," why was a popular revolution not being organized? Decidedly, the bourgeois values (individualism, etc.) were being sustained and preserved by a truly coercive social structure for the purpose of preventing the workers from freeing themselves from exploitation . . . and even, in certain cases, from wanting to do so. Unfortunately, too many Frenchmen were content to gaze up at "their" great statesman like faithful dogs, the way Balzac's Nanon gazed up at her dictator, Grandet. They had had Saint Louis, Francis I, Louis XIV, and Napoleon. Now they had de Gaulle to nourish the illusion that their nation, their culture, their history still had meaning. They did not realize—not even those who belonged to the far Left—that they all partook of the same Hegelianism, which was oriented toward an uncertain future with a heavy baggage of values, categories, and habits inherited from a past that had long ceased to exist outside of schoolbooks.

The chauvinistic values poisoned and destroyed the values of the revolution, even in the anti-Gaullist Communists. That was not a very encouraging fact to record when you knew that in Nanterre there were thousands of illiterate, starving people, and that the Communists in Nanterre were wasting more time describing to you the mistake the Algerians had made in "separating" from Immortal France than they spent organizing the disinherited for the struggle which every day they preached in words. First-class imbeciles! Look, they would say, what a mess Algeria is in today *without us*. And so France was not "in a mess"?

Nowhere have I met imbeciles with such swelled heads as in the France of "pure reason" and learned palaver, the France that is stuck in its old bourgeois revolution and doesn't want to get out. The stupidity of the Left was demonstrated once again by the unanimous support it recently gave to the careerist Mitterand—which, by the way, it withdrew a while later. One would think the French Left was more anxious to find itself another de Gaulle than to change the society . . . which it only denounces now for form's sake.

One day Marcel, the only French Marxist I was able to make friends with, said to me: "Two centuries of working-class struggles to begin all over again. Everything has to be done over, Canadian, *everything*."

His voice was hard, implacable, but fraternal. He was thirty years old and came from Martinique. An unfrocked worker-priest, he had none of the complexes usually found in former curés. He had an adorable mistress, Françoise, who also became one of my best friends. He worked as a mechanic in a garage in Vanves, where he was organizing a clandestine union that he wanted to make the initial cell of a clandestine revolutionary movement, a new "Resistance," this one truly of the people. Françoise was busy educating the workers Marcel recruited and whom on two or three occasions I had a chance to meet.

Marcel and Françoise reminded me of the Curies. They worked with as much zeal as the two celebrated physicists, seeking ways to transform the working-class material, the exploited, into liberating action, into a revolutionary army.

"You know, Canadian" (that was what Marcel always called me), "France has aged a lot since Robespierre. Today she's in her dotage. The more bourgeois the old lady gets, the more she talks drivel. And the workers still listen to the drivel with respect. More than a hundred years of struggle to begin over again . . . It's unbelievable!"

Marcel dreamed of a new organization of the working class that would be totally independent of bourgeois institutions, including the present unions and the parties of the Left. But he was not sure how to structure it. He was thinking of the Resistance.

"We workers are still 'occupied,' but we don't know it. That's the problem. Everyone thinks he's free because there are no Germans around—as if exploitation could only come from a foreign 'race' . . . The trouble lies in our own system. But we French are under the impression that everything French is good and that consequently the trouble must come from Germany, Russia, or the United States. Sometimes I think we're too chauvinistic to make a true revolution. But I want to fight to the end to try and prove the contrary, together with the fellows in Vanves, and in other places later on. But it's no small job to 'de-chauvinize' the French!"

"There's a big difference," I said, "between the Spanish and the French. The Spanish are courageous and progressive anarchists. The French often seem to me to be self-satisfied individualists . . . who are cowards at heart and afraid. I'm talking about the rank-and-file of the Left—not the bourgeois."

"All we do is talk. We've learned to always think 'correctly.' But not to love. That's why it really doesn't matter much to our Communists if they win or not. It doesn't bother them in the least to betray their people, to betray themselves, so long as by a syllogism borrowed from some 'leading thinker' or other, they are able to justify their betrayal 'correctly' beforehand. Since the Frenchman always places himself in the domain of thought, he can never be wrong, for one can always think 'correctly' whatever one *wants*. So every Frenchman's right. The Spaniards have more guts. I quite agree with you. Sometimes I feel like going back to Martinique. But I still want to *hope* a little longer. One never knows . . . And you, what do you plan to do here?"

"I really don't know any more. I came in the hope of discovering true freedom—and I've discovered . . . an unbearable universe. How can one bear the fact that Versailles and Nanterre coexist? That's what I don't understand. Sometimes I think the French will be truly free when they are able to dynamite Versailles, the Invalides, the Arc de Triomphe, and the treasures of Louis XIV and Napoleon, instead of spending their Sundays gaping foolishly at the splendor of those who made their fathers the 'niggers' of their empire. As long as they take Versailles and Rambouillet seriously, the French will remain idiots. That's what I think."

"The French are too well educated . . ."

"Educated? You mean crammed with useless knowledge, historical dates, great names and so on, all having to do with France. The French are *too serious* to laugh at their society and analyze it correctly. That's why they are all so ready to rally around any Sun King who can once again give France (and their navels) the splendor it must have . . . if it's not going to 'degenerate' and become just another nation like the others . . ."

"But . . ."

"You yourself, Marcel, you believe you belong to a superior people, don't you?"

We would carry on discussions like that for hours. To no purpose.

I was becoming increasingly bitter. One evening when Marcel was out, I surprised Françoise in the act of washing herself in the kitchen. She was half naked. I could not resist the desire to go up to her, to pass my hands over her neck, her shoulders, her breasts, her belly. I leaned my head against hers and pressed her body tight against my own. I was crying.

She let her fingers wander through my hair, then over my back.

"Let me get dressed," she said gently.

I went and sat down at the little table where she prepared the meals. I folded my arms on the table, buried my face in them and broke into sobs.

"Found nothing today either?" she asked.

"Ah! It's not that . . . I want to kill myself!"

She broke out laughing . . . but without making fun of me. Her friendship for me was too real. She knew me well enough to know that at certain times I was capable of anything.

"Why tonight?"

"Why not tonight?" I answered, defying her.

"Come into the living room, we can talk more comfortably there."

I followed her into the living room.

"That's why . . . you jumped on me?"

"Yes."

"Then you don't really want to kill yourself. Because otherwise you wouldn't have come here."

"Actually, it was just before coming here that I almost threw myself into the water."

I told her about what had just happened.

For a week I had been roaming around Paris like a sleepwalker, though the sun was shining brightly. I was fed up. Fed up with French bureaucracy, fed up with filling out forms that went off to rot I knew not where, fed up with begging my friends for help without being in a position to really do anything for them in return, fed up with waiting for a reply from the Algerian government to my request to go and work in the literacy campaign, fed up with pointless discussions and with my solitude. I did not want to return to Quebec. I no longer wanted to remain in France. No reply came from Algeria. I was ready to jump out of my skin.

I had lost my appetite. Some days I ate almost nothing. I would walk around Paris until I was exhausted. My head was spinning. What had I ever come here for?

Never, even to my best friends, had I confided the despair that was spreading through me like a cancer. Like a dying man, I saw my whole existence reduced to an infinitesimal thing, a thinking and painful absurdity. I reread *The Trial*; Kafka's profound humor had often helped me take myself less seriously. This time, his modesty—for Kafka is a modest author, humble and disinterested—seemed to me to be a total indifference to the world, a reasoned suicide. His great love for men seemed to be an absolute contempt for human existence.

That night I had stopped on one of the bridges over the Seine. As in times past, in Longueuil, I gazed deep into the black water and wished I could disappear in it forever.

It must have been nine o'clock at night. I was alone. No witnesses. My whole body was being drawn by the mass of water. It was the second time in my life I had felt *that*. But this time my resistance was weak. I had not eaten since morning. My long walk had exhausted me. After looking long moments at the water, I let myself slip to the ground like a coward. For a while I remained motionless. A couple passed by, indifferent. I got up slowly and looked down at the black water again. "Why not?" I said to myself. "Why not?" There was nothing for me to do here. I could be of no use to anyone. As in Quebec. As in Algeria. No one needed me or my services. Men were satisfied with their shit. Why keep badgering them with ideas they didn't know what to do with? All countries, all peoples were the same. Why travel? There was nothing to be done anywhere . . .

Finally, I reached the Left Bank without having thrown myself into the water. And I went to the apartment of Marcel and Françoise.

After listening to me with great attention, Françoise said: "Pierre, you won't find the answer here. You must become reconciled with your country. Otherwise . . ."

"Otherwise?"

"You really will throw yourself into the water. And what good will that do you? You are wrong to despise your country so much. You must learn to *live* in it, even if it's in a mess, as you say. No country but your own can give you what you are looking for."

"What do you expect me to find in Quebec?"

"First of all—yourself."

" . . ."

"In the end you're going to have to accept yourself as you are, love yourself as you are. And in order to do that, you must go home, to your own milieu. Only there will you find yourself again. I don't think we—even Marcel and I, who love you very much—can really be of use to you. I advise you to go back to Quebec as soon as possible. You see, Pierre, we—Marcel and I—are not Québécois. When you talk about your country, it doesn't mean much to us because we've never set foot there. We don't know anything about your history, your way of life. You can be sure of our friendship, but it's of no use to you right now. It would be good for you to talk things over with a Québécois psychoanalyst, because even if I were madly in love with you, even if I left Marcel for you, I couldn't do anything to solve your present problems. Friendship, love, they don't help . . . when you can't accept yourself. What good does it do me to love you if you constantly despise yourself, eh? What do I want with an unhappy face to lay in my lap like a mother? I don't want to be a mother, because that's not what you need. It's too late for that. You have to learn to live with what you are, in your country as it is, nei-

ther better nor worse than the others. I am convinced that if you succeed in doing something for your own people, in fighting for them
and with them, your life will be completely transformed. I think it's
pretty much the same problem for Marcel. And that's why I want to
suggest to him that we move to Martinique . . ."

She went on talking to me for a long time. The things she said
were like what I had been hearing lately from the Québécois friends
I was staying with, both of whom were educators. It all seemed to
make sense. But to go back to Quebec . . . to the great darkness . . .
I was almost terrified to think of it.

When I left Françoise that night, I remembered that I had an appointment with Louis around midnight. Louis was a Québécois exile
in Paris who was unhappy but, like me, unable at that time to resign
himself to the inevitable: the return home.

We went to a little bistro on the Boulevard Saint-Michel to talk it
all over. Of course we knew that we were paralyzed by our alienation, but we found it difficult to admit that Europe could not free us
from it.

To act in Quebec . . . in the winter that Vigneault sings of and the
white dust that Langevin describes . . . ?

Did this country even have a future? Seen from Paris, Quebec
looked like a ridiculous provincial town whose inhabitants were
turned toward a past they had built into a myth and who had invented a heroic history for themselves out of the meager material
available. Dollard des Ormeaux, Madeleine de Verchères, Radis-
son . . .

I told Louis that I was going back just the same—so as not to commit suicide. He wanted to wait another year, to see if there was no
way to go into exile somewhere else, in a more hospitable country.

Next day I wrote my mother asking her to lend me the money to
come home. On the days following I bade farewell to my French and
Québécois friends. I spent the last days with two of them visiting
Burgundy, Vézelay, Lyons, Grenoble, and a few other tourist centers
in central France. This trip made it even harder for me to leave.

Then, one sunny morning, I went to the Gare Saint-Lazare. I
boarded the train the way one gets into a hearse.

As we approached Cherbourg, the train entered a landscape of fog
and fine rain.

I felt that all my dreams were forsaking me at once and that the future promised only mortal boredom in a boundless desert.

A few days after I came back, the Wolfe Monument was over-turned in Quebec City. I immediately said to myself that things had changed in the country of silence and winter.

I began to hope again.

Gérard Pelletier offered me a job at *La Presse* and I accepted with joy. I knew nothing about journalism, but it was not long before I felt as much at ease in it as a fish in water. It was at *La Presse* that I really became politicized, thanks to some older comrades for whom social revolution was still an objective.

The journalistic milieu gave me a better understanding of Quebec society. Political engagement, which was an integral part of my pro-fession, prevented me from letting myself be caught in the trap of comfortable ideologies, good jobs, careerism, and the soft life with an easy conscience.

In contrast to the institutionalized forms of dissent which journal-ists diligently report in the Establishment newspapers, my friends and I were soon involved in less peaceful forms of protest. Which quickly led me from *"cité libre"* to the picket lines, the protests against the war in Vietnam . . . and the Front de libération du Québec.

I have always felt myself to be, and I have always been, a proletar-ian. With the spotty cultural background of a self-taught man, I formed the ambition of acting directly on society, outside the estab-lished structures, and, together with my brothers in misery, of chang-ing it in accordance with the workers' desire for freedom. You must not expect me to join up like a bourgeois in the club of right-thinking socialists who have only read (so as to be able to quote it to the "hotheads") *Left-Wing Communism: An Infantile Disorder.*

Am I essentially a rebel? I have no idea.

I am certainly a man who has been flayed alive, like every clear-thinking Québécois. But contrary to what people might think, I have no predisposition for martyrdom or anarchy.

For me prison does not represent a setting-aside of political and so-cial engagement. Of course I don't want to rot here too long, al-though I am learning a great many things which some day will surely be very useful to me in *carrying on.*

A revolutionary must always be prepared to start over again and to live a life of continual danger. Revolutionary activity is never perfectly safe. When I am willing to make compromises, I will have murdered *our* ideal in my mind and heart. To my friends, I will then be ripe for the cemetery.

5
The Time of Action: Apprenticeship

The sociologist Fernand Dumont has said somewhere: "The complex societies we have inherited would inevitably appear to be governed by a weighty determinism if history did not enable us to understand their genesis and meaning and thus: *restore them to our freedom of choice.*" When he wrote that, Dumont was referring to the work of the French-Canadian historians, the great majority of whom are "nationalists." He was correctly affirming that there is a profound and necessary connection between the history still to be made and the history that has already been written by historians. I would add that there is also a connection between the history still to be made and the history that is being acted out at *present*, the history in which we are involved from day to day, the history that forces us to make a choice, to become engaged, to place our bets.

The destiny of the Québécois collectivity had often seemed to me to be that of a people doomed to slow death, or to prolonged mediocrity. Of course I did not really dare believe that, but unconsciously this vision of the destiny of Quebec was preying on my mind.

In March 1963 I had reluctantly returned to my native land, carrying away from France a certain amount of bitterness that I had doubtless picked up from the pessimism that followed the end of the Algerian war, and the disillusionment that my Parisian friends affected at all times. I too was blasé and ready to accept the vision of the world of a Claude Lévi-Strauss. No sooner was I back in Montreal than I was thinking about various ways to escape again, to flee the drabness I had rubbed elbows with ever since I was a child and above all, above all, that tense, snarling state of dependency to which we Québécois had become accustomed for lack of anything else. The Wolfe Monument was overturned in Quebec City, but so far the "quiet revolution" had nothing to say to me. I did not yet perceive any profound change in my country, but only a superficial unrest that was almost all talk.

I had thought I realized in Paris that *we did not exist* collectively, that we were of no interest to anyone. In books and newspapers we were associated with English Canada and the United States. People talked about the "U.S.-Canadian" economy, the "U.S.-Canadian" market, the "U.S.-Canadian" standard of living, or just about America—and America was essentially the "American way of life."

To remain in the country was to consent, once again, to suffocation, silence, effacement, a pointless death. Would this people one day awake? More and more of my Québécois friends were beginning to think so. Some of them even saw independence and revolution coming. As for me, I saw nothing at all. In 1962, in *Cité libre,* I had proposed a program: "To Awake to the Depth of Our Existence." At that time I believed strongly in philosophical action, in the power of ideas and reflection. Now I no longer believed in much of anything. There was a void.

That lasted for a few weeks. Gérard Pelletier offered me a job writing on world affairs for *La Presse* and suggested at the same time that I start working for *Cité libre* again. I accepted so as to keep from being consumed by despair, for I had a wild terror of sinking back into the state of a candidate for suicide that I had already experienced. I was not enthusiastic, but after all, I had to earn a living. And then, who could tell? Maybe it would give me new reasons for living . . . in Quebec.

1

For two or three months—perhaps longer—I went around in circles in my solitude, carrying on an inner dialogue with Kierkegaard, Kafka, and Lévi-Strauss. Then I moved on to more systematic philosophers, especially Husserl and Heidegger. With them, I hammered away at epistemological and ontological dilemmas. I kept asking myself Lucien Sebag's question: ". . . discourse or violence, affective chaos or reason, which should I choose?" [1] But there were also days when uncertainty gave me a pain in the ass. I would turn away from the "pessimists"—Kafka, Kierkegaard, Lévi-Strauss, and Heidegger —to concentrate on the study of Husserl's philosophy. There I found a demand for order, clarity, and meaning that also seemed to be a will to conquer despair, confusion, anarchy, and meaninglessness.

But after plowing through the abstruse works of the father of phenomenology, all I found was a camouflaged defense of essences that were dogmatically presupposed. I might have gone back then to Kierkegaard and despair. However, while I was still reading Husserl I had run across some short treatises by Marx, among them the famous *Theses on Feuerbach*. It had been a staggering experience. It was like a revelation. I suddenly understood that knowledge was inseparably bound up with practice, with experience, with life.

I had been seeking a reason for living in the abstract, whereas it had to be sought in life, in action. Not action for action's sake, as one says "art for art's sake," but action in the sense of engagement, of responsibility. It was not the first time, by the way, that I had made a "discovery" of this sort. But this time I was finding in the philosophical writings of Marx the connection between theory and practice I had been looking for. It seemed to me that I had just overcome the painful paradox that had paralyzed me until then. I felt as if I were at last beginning to live in the open air. I came back to social reality, no longer seeing it as a weight to drag me down or as an obstacle to freedom but as the locus of that freedom; no longer seeing it as a "spectacle" but as a responsibility to be assumed *together with other men*. Truth and freedom no longer stood outside our history, outside our past, present, and future. I was coming to understand that they are born, live, and die with us; that we affirm their reality and power through action, through practice, through continual transformation of the world.

I was coming to understand that to agree to live is to take responsibility for a collective history that is being made and at the same time always remains to be made, that is ceaselessly made, unmade, and remade, according to our knowledge and abilities, to our struggles, passions, hopes, interests, needs, and choices.

And for me, a Québécois, proletarian, white nigger of America, one of the "wretched of the earth," to take responsibility for our history was, inevitably, to begin by denouncing and exposing the inhuman conditions of our existence, to build up a body of concrete knowledge and orient it entirely in the direction of "the practical results of action," [2] of revolutionary action, of total liberation.

2

When I discovered Marxism, I felt as if I had found what I had always been seeking, what my father too had sought confusedly, what all proletarians seek: a truth, *their truth*, which can both reconcile them to life and enable them to work together for the only thing that is really worth living for—the revolution, the overthrow of capitalism, and the building of egalitarian social structures.

As I became reconciled with the world and with "other people," I became reconciled with the Québécois French nation, not the one that for centuries has been "blessed" with poverty, ignorance, and religion, but the one that is at last beginning to say "no" to exploitation, and is trying to emancipate itself completely.

What we have been *is* less important, in my eyes, than what we shall become if we want to.

For a long time our watchword was "The past is our master," and we idealized the bygone days when Catholicism, total resignation, and misery for all formed the basis of our unanimity and guaranteed both our survival and our isolation. Today we must take for a watchword "Our master is the future," and, going straight to the point, affirm our presence in the world through independence and socialism, through revolution and the building of a society run by the workers for the workers, a society without exploiters or parasites, without colonialists or puppet rulers.

A man is a man. It is only under certain conditions, Marx would say, that he becomes a sub-man. Up until now our conditions of existence have been imposed upon us from the outside, and the great majority of us have remained sub-men. It is in order to become men, free men, that we must change our conditions of existence. And we can do that only by overthrowing the established order.

Our future depends on this one step, which is objectively possible and which we either will or will not take. Our class consciousness is still on the level of an instinct. Together we must develop it by getting at the truth of our economic and political situation and then providing ourselves with the ideological and technical means of our liberation. It is not only *our* future (as the working class) that depends on our ability to see clearly and to organize ourselves accordingly, but the future of the whole Québécois nation as well, because the French-Canadian ruling class is absolutely incapable of opposing the imperialism and capitalism on which its privileges and institutions rest.

It is vital that we raise the necessity of our struggle as an oppressed class to the level of a conscious will, an active class consciousness. Of course the bourgeois and the pacifists are going to be indignant when they read that. But as Lukacs correctly says, "the pacifists and humanists in the class struggle who, intentionally or not, work to slow down this process which is already so long and painful and subject to so many crises, would themselves be horrified if they understood how much suffering they impose on the proletariat by prolonging this state of affairs. For the proletariat cannot escape its vocation. The only question is how much more it must suffer before it reaches ideological maturity, the correct knowledge of its class situation, class consciousness." [3]

The proletariat of Quebec can no more "escape its vocation," escape the necessity of making a revolution, than can the proletariat of the other countries. In the absolute, one can no doubt state that nothing is necessary in the metaphysical sense of the word; but in the reality we live in, *in the time we live in*, we are compelled to make a *choice*. For the working class, for all the victims of exploitation, that choice is revolution.

For the future of the vast majority of men, and hence the progress of all humanity, depends on revolution.

That is why I say with Lukacs that the working class of Quebec, like that of the whole world, "cannot escape its vocation."

I am well aware that this choice constitutes a sort of wager, and that it is founded not on a "natural" necessity but on the affirmation of trans-individual values, on a certain concept of human society and a need to realize an ideal of justice, equality, and freedom, an ideal whose truth will be proved only by its realization. But this wager is not a blind or contemplative faith. It is essentially an act, and a political act.°

° The concept of a wager, as it appears in this passage and below, is adopted from Pascal. Admitting that human reason was incapable of knowing for certain whether

There is a difference between the revolutionary wager and the religious wager, which is a bet made on a "supernatural," invisible, and silent God. There is also a difference between the revolutionary wager and that of the physicist who is certain that electrons exist (since they can be used technically), even though he knows that "the electron is not a thing susceptible of direct observation," that it is "the product of a *theory*," that it has no substance, is composed only of its qualities "and nothing else"; finally, that it can only be described by means of very abstract mathematical notions.[4]

The revolutionary wager is a combat, a struggle. It leads to victory or death. That is why those who make this wager do not enlist in the revolution "by the hour" or "by the week." Nor do they enlist just for a time—for as long as they are young or as long as the "combination of circumstances" is right. They commit themselves for life; they commit their lives.

It is therefore neither a "gratuitous choice" nor one of youth's "follies."

When, in the fall of 1963, I agreed after much hesitation to take on the editorship of *Cité libre*, I already knew that this act was only the first step of a commitment which would go much further and would allow no turning back. I was twenty-five years old—an age at which one can ill afford passing fancies.

3

I had at first conceived of engagement or responsibility as a primarily philosophical enterprise. In this I was following the example of men like Merleau-Ponty, Mounier, Camus, and Sartre. I had dreamed of intellectual action on the order of *Les Temps modernes* or *Esprit*. Since the founders of *Cité libre* considered themselves personalists (wrongly, by the way), I had thought of using the pages of the review for reflection in depth on the problems that men have to solve from day to day, and in so doing to base myself at the start on Mounier rather than directly on Marx, so as not to scare Trudeau and Pelletier.[5] But I soon came to feel that this ambitious dream went

God does or does not exist, Pascal argued (in *Pensées*) that it was to the advantage of the individual to make a wager on the affirmative proposition and to regulate his life accordingly, because by so doing "if you win, you win all; if you lose, you lose nothing." (Trans.)

beyond both my means and the immediate needs of the Québécois collectivity. Up until now, I said to myself, the Québécois have been satisfied to formulate disembodied "philosophies"; might not the time have come to try to *realize* a philosophy?

When I agreed, together with Jean Pellerin, to take over the editorship of *Cité libre,* I had it in mind to transform the review, which up to that time had served to promote the interests of the liberal bourgeoisie, into a weapon for the Québécois workers. It seemed to me that this was a legitimate ambition and the concrete extension of the defense of the Asbestos insurgents that Pelletier, Trudeau, and their friends were so proud of. But I was counting on a "socialism" that was more apparent than real, a "socialism" that was at most only a demogogic instrument designed to give a progressive image to conservatives who were eager to replace the men currently in power, at the federal as well as the provincial level. Certain *"citélibristes"* were already taking advantage of the fact that the Liberals had come to power in Quebec; others, including Trudeau and Pelletier, were biding their time, and while the Quebec government became increasingly "autonomist," were getting ready to "save" the Canadian Confederation from the "plague" of French-Canadian nationalism.

At that time I was far from realizing to what extent the traditional staff of *Cité libre* were linked with the Establishment, although some of my comrades on *La Presse* (of which Pelletier was editor-in-chief) had undertaken to enlighten me on the subject. Who could have sworn, in 1963, that in Ottawa, Trudeau would become the number one enemy of the French Canadians, that Pelletier would agree to occupy a stall in the federal stable he had so often indignantly denounced, that Marchand would forsake the union movement to ally himself with the official spokesmen of American imperialism: men like Pearson, Martin, Winters, Sharp, Hellyer . . . ?

One expected to see such men associated instead with the New Democratic Party. We were forgetting that at the time of the first convention of the NDP, Marchand was attending an important meeting of the federal Liberals. But even supposing that Trudeau, Pelletier, and Marchand had lined up with the NDP, would that have changed their attitude toward Quebec? There are only very slight differences between the federal Liberal Party and the NDP, and there is reason to believe that if the New Democrats come to power one day, they will be as reactionary as their predecessors.

So my plan was to turn *Cité libre* into a weapon and put it exclusively at the service of the Québécois workers. But Pelletier and Trudeau did not want the review to become separatist. I asked them if they had any objection to its becoming frankly socialist. They told me they had no objection to that. No doubt they thought the socialism I was talking about was the same as theirs: a label. Was I a separatist? I think so. But not in the manner of Marcel Chaput, for whom separatism must serve the interests of the French-Canadian petty bourgeoisie. Through socialism I wanted to justify a revolutionary separatism, a working-class separatism, a separatism that would be synonymous with social revolution and not merely with legal independence. Besides, could Trudeau and Pelletier—who in 1962 had refused to let me contribute to the issue on separatism because, they said, I was a "separatist"—not know in 1963 that I was a nationalist? The fact remains that they entrusted me, along with Jean Pellerin, with the editorship of the review.

Pellerin stood by passively while a new editorial staff was formed. From the very first issue, in which we took a position against the amendments to Bill 60 and for the secularization of education, we became suspect in the eyes of Trudeau and Pelletier. Then we denounced cooperative federalism, gave our support to the Parti socialiste du Québec, and began to define a policy which on all points was at variance with the *"politique fonctionnelle"* of Trudeau. What was more serious, we asked men who had formerly been "excommunicated" from *Cité libre,* like Pierre Vadeboncoeur, to come back to the review. Finally, we went so far as to attack directly the former co-editors of *Cité libre* in an article entitled "The Bumblers in Power" (March 1964), which was followed by a number of provocative pieces, such as "Charity, a Capitalist Hoax" by Jean-Claude Paquet and "Defense of the Iroquois" by Gérald Godin. This last was a defense of the "wicked, atheistic separatist" and a satire on the "good Huron," that is, the resigned, Christian, groveling federalist. That was enough to make Pelletier and Trudeau decide to put an end to the "experiment."

Even though *Cité libre* had become something other than a semi-official organ of the Jeunesse étudiante catholique, it was not yet a revolutionary review. But in the minds of Trudeau and Pelletier it had actually become the ally of *Parti pris*, a new pro-independence socialist review that had been founded just when Pellerin and I were beginning to assume responsibility for *Cité libre*.

Trudeau and Pelletier could not believe that the young people whom they had influenced from 1950 to 1960 had become separatist. It was as if they had given birth to a monster. And the young people, for their part, could not get over the fact that their former idols had aged so rapidly. One day some separatists burned Pelletier in effigy in front of the *La Presse* building. During the first wave of bombings, in 1963, Pelletier received threats against his life. Today in Ottawa, Pelletier and Trudeau cannot understand that they are traitors or that they are serving the imperialist aims of the United States and English Canada. But they are too intelligent to be considered irresponsible. That is why it is impossible not to regard them as traitors. Some day they will have to take all the consequences of this betrayal.

Because of Pelletier, who was afraid of the consequences of expelling us outright, the executive board of *Cité libre* finally gave me and the new editorial staff a choice between making substantial compromises and "resigning." I resigned in March 1964, together with most of the staff. But to prevent this affair from being kept "in the family," a long press release was sent to the newspapers. The so-called progressivism of Trudeau and Pelletier was further unmasked, and only a few moss-backs were left to keep the review from going under. *Cité libre* became frankly a review of the "center Left" and ideologically worthless.[6]

Around the group who had resigned, there gathered a few men who wanted to found a new review. This review was to be pro-independence, like *Parti pris*, but it would show a clearer will to dissociate revolutionary socialism from the reactionary nationalism of the French-Canadian petty bourgeoisie. It was to be called *Révolution québécoise*, to indicate both that its motives were revolutionary and that it was rooted in the reality of Quebec. It was to be separatist, although a minority envisaged the independence of Quebec in the form of an associated state, at least as a first stage.

The staff of *Révolution québécoise* was not absolutely homogeneous. It included both young and old—unlike the staff of *Parti pris*, which was made up exclusively of young people. The young staff members were separatists and revolutionaries; the old, some of whom were former members of the Canadian Communist Party and the Cooperative Commonwealth Federation, two federalist parties, were more moderate—there was still something of the traumas of the Duplessis era in them. Most of those at the review were engaged in direct action: unionism (CSN), student social action, the Union générale des étudiants du Québec, the protest movement against the war in Vietnam, committees of the unemployed, etc. Some even had relations with the FLQ, others with the CP, the Trotskyite Ligue ouvrière socialiste, or the PSQ.

Several of the founders of *Révolution québécoise,* the first issue of which appeared in September 1964, were members of the executive board of the Syndicat des journalistes at the time of the famous strike at *La Presse,* which lasted from June 1964 to January 1965.

In 1964 there were three important events that left their mark on me and taught me unforgettable lessons: first, the fight against Bill 54 (Labor Code, first version); then the long, hard strike at *La Presse*; and finally the convention of the Confédération des syndicats nationaux (CSN) in September 1964.

(1) The battle against Bill 54 exposed the blind alley into which the leaders of the Québécois workers, with Jean Marchand at their head, had led the French-Canadian union movement. As a delegate from the Syndicat des journalistes de Montréal (SJM),[7] I participated in the impressive assembly of the CSN that took place in Quebec City in the spring of 1964. The union members were ready to march on the Quebec Parliament and unequivocally denounce the anti-labor policy of the Lesage government. Addressing the assembly, which was vociferously demanding political action, Jean Marchand, then president of the CSN, declared that we must be satisfied with telling the government the union members would not accept Bill 54, and that above all we must not make a "political issue" of it. As if one could oppose a projected law without making it a political issue! From that moment on I understood the collusion between certain union leaders and the men who held political power. Moreover, shortly after the assembly, I learned from a "reliable source" that Marchand was not really hostile to Bill 54 and that he had gone along with the opposition solely because he was threatened with the immi-

nent resignation of the first vice-president of the CSN, a resignation that would have considerably diminished Marchand's prestige among the workers and would thus have been a serious blow to his political ambitions. Marchand was at that time a candidate for Favreau's old cabinet post in Ottawa and consequently a friend of Favreau's friends, including in particular Monsieur Jean Lesage. That was why Marchand preached apoliticalism for the unions. Marchand has now relieved the CSN of his despotism, and the Confederation is showing unprecedented vigor and dynamism. Nevertheless, one may still wonder if the present leaders of the CSN do not entertain ambitions similar to those of the Marchands, the Lefebvres, and the Jolicoeurs, who are now in the service of the Liberals in Ottawa or Quebec. Has the present president of the CSN, Marcel Pépin, broken with traditional corporatism? If so, why does he not advocate the formulation of a working-class policy and urge the establishment of an independent political organization for the workers of Quebec? Why does the CSN still leave a monopoly on political activity to the parties of the bourgeoisie? And then, is it a minor matter that the present secretary-general of the CSN, Monsieur Robert Sauvé, is the brother of the federal minister Maurice Sauvé? Is it an accident that there are almost no workers, no rank-and-file union members, in the *bureau confédéral?*

The Fédération des travailleurs du Québec (FTQ) side of the picture is much darker. Not only is the Federation more conservative and much less democratic than the CSN, but it is not even independent. It is at most a poor and timorous branch of the Canadian Labour Congress (CLC) and the AFL-CIO. The Québécois workers can expect nothing from the present FTQ, which must either break its connections with English Canada and the United States or disappear. Besides, the FTQ has begun to disintegrate. In the present circumstances, there is every likelihood that the disintegration will increase. I do not understand why the "Leftists," of whom there are quite a number in the FTQ, still refuse to pose squarely the problem of their Federation's independence from American and English-Canadian union imperialism. Their affiliation with the NDP shows that their so-called socialism is pretty much a thing of words. There too they have become adept in the art of deceiving people.

(2) The strike at *La Presse* (June 1964–January 1965) was a rough

experience not only for the journalists but for the other employees of the newspaper, who outnumbered the "stars" of the conflict four to one. There again, collusion between Marchand and the Liberal government and the financial circles of the Rue Saint-Jacques was one of the main reasons for the resounding failure of this famous strike. Marchand had no more cause to love the journalists than Monsieur Lesage did—and for the same reasons. The corrupt exercise of power does not thrive on a free and critical press. So everyone—the financiers, the government, and the CSN (certain of its leaders, I mean)—was agreed that it was necessary to break the backs of the journalists of the most powerful daily in Quebec. From the first weeks of the conflict, the employees of *La Presse* felt isolated and defeated. By the time *La Presse . . . libre* appeared, at the initiative of Marcel Pépin, it was already too late. Since most of the journalists and other employees of *La Presse* were up to their necks in debt, it was easy for the bosses to impose their conditions on the strikers after seven months of lonely struggle which had come to seem a "dubious battle" they could not win.

I learned from this experience: (1) that a union must never count on the support of the congress or confederation to which it belongs, even though *under normal circumstances* such support would be provided; (2) that the organization of a strike is of greater practical importance than the negotiations themselves—the mistake made by the journalists at *La Presse* was to be content to negotiate without bringing pressure to bear on the adversary by demonstrations and reprisals against, for example, the property of the company's administrators.

By negotiating "with kid gloves" and with respect for bourgeois legality, the strikers at *La Presse* lost a great deal. Unfortunately, their experience was not unique in Quebec.

Nevertheless, I think the failure of the strike at *La Presse* woke up many people in the CSN and may have precipitated Marchand's departure . . . for Ottawa. Furthermore, I am convinced that when the day comes for the employees of *La Presse* to go on strike again, they will not repeat the unfortunate experience of 1964.[8]

(3) In the middle of the strike at *La Presse*, the convention of the CSN took place in Quebec City. A convention whose outstanding features were: the personality cult of Marchand, timid support for the employees of *La Presse*, a scathing denunciation of the sectarian-

ism of the FTQ, and a decision to raise the wages of the chaplain and the officers of the CSN. A ton of papers was distributed to the delegates, who hardly had time to figure out what was in them before they were called upon to "approve," or slightly amend, the resolutions prepared by the *bureau confédéral*. The convention was a monumental farce, more like a plebiscite than democracy in action. I came away disgusted.

It was a non-political and even non-union convention. The participants had received no kind of education in political or union affairs. The few delegates who were political to start with were afraid to oppose Marchand and his clique.

A minor but significant incident illustrates pretty well the atmosphere of the convention. The review *Révolution québécoise* was launched at the time of the opening of the convention. In the first issue I had devoted a paragraph to Marchand, whom I accused of spending more time looking after his own political ambitions than after the needs of the union members of the CSN. Since I was a delegate from the SJM, I took advantage of the fact to sell *Révolution québécoise* to the delegates. The paragraph concerning Marchand very quickly made the rounds of the whole room, and a group of pious souls immediately got the idea of presenting a motion demanding my expulsion from the CSN and proposing, furthermore, that no resolution of support for the *La Presse* strikers be adopted by the convention! The other delegates from the SJM were seized with panic. Marcel Pépin told me that if I didn't like Jean Marchand, I had only to quit the CSN! Gérald Picard, counsel for the SJM, informed Pépin that the convention did not have the power to expel a union member, that power being reserved to the unions, according to the Constitution of the CSN. After a day of suspense, Pépin agreed to nip in the bud any motion for expulsion. But I was forbidden to sell *Révolution québécoise* to the delegates.[9]

Certain "progressives" in the CSN, who *today* denounce Marchand's attitude in Ottawa, never forgave me for having called his integrity into question when he was still president of the CSN. Yet they are "democrats" and humanists; one may wonder what is the good of their democracy and humanism.

As can be seen, dissent was not highly esteemed in the CSN three years ago. The situation has greatly improved since the departure of

Marchand, but there is still a long way to go before democracy is anything more than an "aspiration" for the union members of Quebec.

It was in this climate of reaction that *Révolution québécoise* was born. The strike at *La Presse* ruined several of the staff members financially; others, students for the most part, begged for state aid, as they did every year, in order to pursue their studies in the social sciences, literature, or history. We had less than a thousand dollars in the till when the review was launched.

4

After the strike at *La Presse*, I set about organizing a series of anti-American, pro-Vietcong demonstrations in front of the United States Consulate on McGregor Street. Each time I had to be absent from *La Presse* because the demonstrations generally coincided with my working hours. A little later there were demonstrations to protest unemployment, then "strike backings" organized jointly by *Révolution québécoise* and *Parti pris*. In the spring of 1965, the death of the patriot Gilles Legault in Montreal Jail was the occasion of an impressive demonstration in the center of town. Then came the famous demonstrations of May 24 (Victoria Day) and July 1 (Dominion Day), which were very violent and almost turned into riots.

All these demonstrations provided an opportunity for the most dynamic elements of *Révolution québécoise* and *Parti pris* to meet in the field. *Parti pris* had the idea of forming a mass movement, and the majority of the staff of *Révolution québécoise* decided to cooperate with *Parti pris* in getting the movement under way. Later, other groups also decided to join together for more effective action. This union gave birth during the summer of 1965 to the Mouvement de libération populaire (MLP).[10]

Meantime, along with other comrades, I had secretly joined the Front de libération du Québec. We met frequently to lay the foundations of a revolutionary movement that would exclusively serve the exploited of Quebec. This did not mean that we neglected legal action. Far from it. But we always tried to orient such action in the direction of the progressive radicalization of worker and student demands. We thought it useless to work within any of the traditional parties, including the parties of the Left and the RIN. We were (and still are) convinced that on the ground of electoralism, the battle is always lost for the wage-earners, that is, for the vast majority of the nation. As Duverger would say, every election, organized at the cost of millions of dollars, expresses not so much the real participation of the masses as the means by which they are "legally" excluded from power. The people, who are the "theoretical and fictitious sovereign," are manipulated every time by the political machines of the parties most favorable to the interests of the local and foreign capitalists. Within these parties, which function like corporations of share-holders, the "little" people have no place. How could these parties, which exclude the workers from their ranks, admit them to power? Capitalist democracy is only a farce which, at election time, makes the citizens choose a government that, by its very essence, is beyond their control and represents only the ruling minority. We are told there are "third parties" which oppose the "old parties." To be sure, the third parties oppose the old parties, the way the Liberals oppose the Conservatives, that is, respecting the rules of the game that have been established by the bourgeoisie. The third parties in Quebec do not oppose the system; they oppose a political clique— not structures, institutions, the economic and social regime, and the illusory bourgeois democracy. That is why the workers can hope for nothing from them. When the third parties, like the NDP, seem to be coming closer to power, it is because they are beginning to serve the interests of the financiers. Besides, the closer they come to power, the more conservative and "respectable" they become. The evolution of the NDP is eloquent on this point; and so is that of the RIN, even though the party has only been in existence for five years. Because in order to take power through elections, one must have a great deal of money; and in order to obtain money, one must give guarantees to the capitalists. But supposing the miracle occurs and a socialist, radical party is carried to power by elections. If that happens, the "revolutionary government," which has taken power without having overthrown the existing structures by a mass revolution, will soon be liquidated by a *coup d'état*. Or else it will be forced to lean for support on the existing bureaucracy and the infrastructure of capitalism, and in order to endure it will have to repudiate the interests of the workers in favor of those of the capitalists—unless it takes to the *maquis* and calls upon the masses to rise up, weapons in hand, against capitalism and imperialism. But is there an example in history of a party that came to power through elections and then staked everything on armed insurrection?

So my friends and I were convinced of the futility of electoral struggle. We also knew the limits of legal or para-legal social agitation, and we thought it urgent to set about immediately laying the foundations of a clandestine revolutionary organization, an organization that could give the masses of Quebec both the means (ideological and technical) and the opportunity for economic, political, and cultural liberation.

For a while we were able to combine our clandestine activity with the organization of fairly widespread para-legal social agitation, particularly among the groups of workers on strike in Montreal. But at the end of 1965 we had to make a definite choice in favor of clandestine action. This decision was also encouraged in part by the *rapprochement* and then fusion of the Mouvement de libération populaire and the reformist, "senile" Parti socialiste du Québec. We thought this fusion would be accomplished at the expense of the MLP; and the MLP was in fact swallowed up by the inertia of the PSQ. We are far from rejoicing at this turn of events, and we think the MLP should be put back on its feet. We had not left the MLP because we considered its policy of social agitation useless, but because it had become physically impossible for us to work at the same time for both the FLQ and the MLP. But it is true that our choice was precipitated by the decision of the majority of the members of the MLP to fuse their party with the PSQ. The unity of the Left is indeed a fine thing, but it must not be achieved in such a way as to benefit the Left's most reactionary elements. To my mind, the PSQ is a reactionary party and will remain so as long as it is run by the graybeards who use it to make a little political capital for themselves and keep themselves from dying. It is possible that some day the PSQ will pass into the hands of the workers and young people and get rid of the relics from the CP and the NDP with whom it is now encumbered. When that day comes, the PSQ will be able to play a positive role in the Quebec revolution. Up until now, like the (pro-Moscow) Communist Party of Quebec, it has done nothing to serve the interests of the Quebec working class. At most, it has served as a vehicle for illusions and has encouraged the development of organizations harmful to the workers of Quebec, such as the FTQ, which is only a screen for American big-business-style unions. But just as it is not impossible that the FTQ should some day sever its connections with the "international unions," so it is not impossible that the PSQ, animated by new forces, should some day become radicalized; it is even to be desired that this will happen as soon as possible.

It may be hoped that the new generations of workers and students, seeing every day the impotence of the unions and political parties which are integrated with the system—and which, consciously or unconsciously, are forced to serve the interests of the exploiters—will soon come to understand at last the necessity of organizing revolutionary unions and political movements.

One of the objectives of the FLQ was and still is to accelerate this process of becoming conscious, to make men aware of the necessity of fighting *to the death* against the despotism of the capitalist system, the despotism experienced daily in the factories, the offices, the mines, forests, farms, schools, and universities of Quebec. The sooner the Québécois unite to sweep away the rottenness that poisons their existence, the sooner they will be able, in solidarity with the exploited, the niggers of all the other countries, to build a new society for a new man, a society that is human for all men, just for all men, in the service of all men. A fraternal society.

It is not by adding up little reforms that we will succeed in realizing this ideal.

Did I lose interest in philosophy in the fall of 1963? I did not stop reflecting, but let us say that I began to think differently.

From that time on, having understood the necessity of putting my ideas into practice, I studied in particular the writings and deeds of the revolutionaries of our time: Lenin, Rosa Luxemburg, Mao Tse-tung, Castro, and "Che" Guevara. I was more impressed by the thought of Mao Tse-tung and the ideas of Guevara than by the work of Lenin. It must be said that the unfortunate evolution of the Soviet Union, of the International, and of Western Communism obliges us to question several of Lenin's theses, for I do not think we should consider Stalin alone responsible for it.

I also read a number of works on history, sociology, and economics. And finally, for the first time in my life, I began to study the society of Quebec, its history, geography, and economy, its ideologies and opposing social classes.

As for philosophy, I do not consider it useless. Quite the contrary. I think that philosophy, or rather "critique," has a fundamental role to play in history. What I am most preoccupied with at present is the formulation of a critique that will challenge the "scientific" pseudo-objectivity which, in the social sciences, rests on the dogmatic and ideological *a priori* assumption that man's creations, such as capitalist economy, have become "natural forces" which now lie outside man's control.

I believe (along with Charles Gagnon, who is doing research in this direction) that today one of the essential roles of critical (dialectical) thought is to unmask the scientific spirit, including the spirit of "scientific socialism," the reified spirit of objectivity, and in so doing to restore the social sciences—economics, politics, etc.—to our freedom of choice. Of course the social sciences, from phenomenology to structuralism, from psychoanalysis to sociology, teach us many things essential to know, but most researchers cannot resist the temptation of turning their research into an explanatory system that is supposed to be definitive. Most of them, like Husserl, fix essences or *nature* in the hope of escaping from relativism and ending up with something permanent, eternal, transcendent. The same method is found in linguistics as well as economics and, in fact, characterizes all the present sciences. We delude ourselves by thinking that knowledge escapes the force of history. We refuse to see that everything must be constantly called into question. To be sure, one never completely escapes from the temptation of the absolute. It might even be said that constituting an absolute is a process that is linked to the essential relativity of our historical existence. But while we may need to reach a certain balance, a certain coherence, in our knowledge as in our activity, should that prevent us from seeing that that balance and coherence must crumble and give way in turn to more perfect knowledge and activity? It seems to me that alienation consists of an accommodation that one makes, willingly or unwillingly, to a particular balance, to a particular order, to what we call the *established Order*. There are sciences of accommodation, such as American psychology, whose basic aim is to promote the "adaptation" of the individual to the system. One of the best examples of reified science is without doubt American psychology.

We do not fully recognize the fact that the social sciences are controlled by the bourgeoisie and put at the service of capitalism, even if the researchers themselves are not always aware of it. That is why the researchers seek to install objectivity everywhere, an objectivity that consists of justifying the nature of the established Order, that is, capitalism.

It is therefore urgent to restore scientific research to our freedom of choice, and those who try to unmask the "scientific spirit" of our time are working for the collective de-alienation and liberation.

I do not think that I personally will be able to accomplish much of this work that I consider so important. It is true that periods of imprisonment, of enforced rest, can be the most productive periods for revolutionary philosophy. But revolutionary action has taught me that I am not first of all either a philosopher or a thinker. Which, however, does not incline me to underestimate (quite the contrary) the importance of what Amilcar Cabral, the leader of the guerrillas in Portuguese Guinea and Cape Verde, calls the "ideological weapon."

My greatest desire is to again become, as soon as possible, an active militant, an organizer and propagandist of the Quebec revolution.

Notes

1. *Marxisme et structuralisme*, Petite bibliothèque Payot. Sebag, a French Communist, committed suicide in January 1965, at the age of thirty-one.
2. Paul Nizan, *Les Chiens de garde*, François Maspero, Paris, 1960. To be published in English by Monthly Review Press.
3. Gyorgy Lukacs, *Histoire et conscience de classe*, trans. K. Axelos and J. Bois, Editions de Minuit, Paris, 1960, p. 102.
4. Arthur March, *La Physique moderne et ses théories*, Gallimard (coll. "Idées"), Paris, 1965, pp. 211–214.
5. I had not forgotten the sectarianism shown by the founders of *Cité libre* when the famous issue on separatism was being prepared in 1962.

6. Jean Pellerin remained at the head of *Cité libre*. Anyway, he had only been named co-editor by the "old crowd" in order to prevent the "new wave" from working freely.

7. To my great surprise, I had been elected secretary-general of the SJM a few weeks earlier.

8. It would be extremely interesting to write a detailed history of the strike at *La Presse*. If I did so now, however, I would be afraid of being too unjust toward certain persons. I have not yet sufficiently "digested" this lost strike.

9. I must say too that, having spent two days denouncing the lack of democracy within the FTQ, the delegates to the CSN would have lost face somewhat if they had expelled from their ranks a union member who had dared to criticize their "great leader."

10. Cf. my article "The Unity of the Left" in *Parti pris*, July-August 1965; also the "Manifesto of the Mouvement de libération populaire and of the Review *Parti pris*" in *Parti pris*, September 1965.

6
The Time of Action: Our Ideal

The conditions under which we live were created by men who lived before us. These conditions (from the relations of production and property to the organization of leisure, education, and culture) can be transformed or destroyed, and other conditions of life that are better, more human, can be created by the power of united men and collectivities (the men and collectivities of *today*) in order to serve other ends than those served by the existing conditions of life.

In the present state of things, these conditions of life constitute an essentially economic organization in the service of a minority. Upon this organization, whose principal end is the search for and accumulation of maximum profits—of money—by means of the exploitation of the labor of the immense majority of human beings, depend political life, intellectual life, education, religious life, and even artistic life, to the extent that these various spheres of human activity are controlled, monopolized, and directed by the ruling minority, in accordance with its economic class interests.

In this world, every individual is supposed to have complete freedom to do as he likes. But in fact, this freedom belongs only to those who have the money to take advantage of it and to *realize* it in their personal activities. Freedom exists only for the dominant minority. The vast majority of individuals are enslaved to work and to conditions of existence over which they have no control, which give them no real power of decision or right to enjoy the wealth produced, and which deprive them of the ownership of their means of production and, consequently, of the concrete freedom to satisfy their true needs—their own needs, and not those of the capitalist market. For the vast majority who live under these conditions—the conditions of present capitalist society—freedom is nothing more than a word, a hoax. The members of the minority can afford to have a *personal* life. The others, the mass of men, have no chance, no right, no concrete possibility of achieving this personal life within the conditions of existence of society today. In order to "assert themselves as individuals," [1] they must abolish their present conditions of life, which are also those of the whole society. They will achieve this only through the practical, collective action of a total revolution,[2] which will not only overthrow the capitalist state but at the same time abolish everything that for centuries has perverted and poisoned social relations, life in society: private ownership of the means of production and exchange, the accumulation and concentration of capital in the hands of a few, the commodity categories, the market economy, exchange based on the "law of value," [3] and even money itself. It is a question, in short, of "de-capitalizing" social relations and replacing the present forced cooperation (which profits only a few) by a social solidarity that gives every individual the means of developing his faculties, of concretely realizing his personal freedom. Isolated individuals are contingent, dependent upon the demands of competition, labor, etc., upon the conditions of life created by the bourgeoisie to serve its class interests. The bourgeoisie extols individualism because that individualism subjugates each of us to its economic, political, and ideological power, because that individualism alienates each of us and makes the bourgeoisie invulnerable. It is to the extent that we join together in solidarity that we will free ourselves from all our alienations and that each of us will become more of a *person.*

In the so-called free world we know at present, concrete personal freedom exists only for individuals who succeed in developing themselves within the (small) ruling class and under the conditions created, desired, and maintained by that class. In the so-called independent nations the same conditions of existence often remain, because the economic bases of the division of society into classes and of the exploitation of man by man have not been abolished by the "accession to independence" of this or that colony.

Only a revolution carried out by the majority of the men in a given collectivity can lay the basis for a true, radical transformation of the conditions of existence of the majority in that collectivity (which can just as easily be the entire world as a country or group of countries).

1

Our ideal, the ideal of the Front de libération du Québec, is based neither on the opportunistic pragmatism of the capitalist parties, nor on the obsession with "revolutionary inevitabilities" (*sic!*) of the parties that call themselves Communist.

Our ideal is based solely on what is human, on men, on their activities, their capacity to produce and create, to destroy and recreate, to transform, to unmake and remake, etc. . . .

If there is a certain determinism in history,[4] even within the framework of the universal relativity discovered by Einstein, and notwithstanding (perhaps) Werner Heisenberg's "principle of the indetermination of matter," [5] this "determinism," in my opinion, cannot consist of an "*autonomous*, necessary, and natural (determined) development of the productive forces," a *natural* development that would deliver whole centuries of humanity up to Chance or Necessity.

I believe, rather, that the development of the "productive forces" is an essentially human activity and that man himself is without doubt the most important "productive force" of all. Of course, the men of each generation, each collectivity, each class, and each social category "act on material bases and within material conditions and limits that are *determined*," as Marx and Engels declare; but I understand this word "determined" in the sense of "particular," of *particular* material conditions and limits which are partly independent of the will of men but are also, in part, produced, created, or at least accepted by them . . . and which they can therefore change themselves.° [6] These material conditions of existence of individuals and

---

° The question of the interpretation of the word "determined," as used here by Marx and Engels, arises only in the French translation from the German. Vallières quotes the French version as "agissent sur des bases et dans des conditions et limites matérielles *déterminées*." The English translation of the same passage uses the word "definite," thus confirming Vallières' understanding of "*déterminées*" in the sense of "particular": ". . . individuals . . . as they are . . . active under definite material limits, presuppositions and conditions independent of their will." (*The German Ideology*, New York, International Publishers, 1939, p. 13.) (Trans.)

collectivities—both the conditions which they find ready-made (those that were created by preceding generations) and the conditions which arise out of their own activity (those that are imposed on them by the oppressing class or created on their own initiative, through union activities or revolutionary activities, for example)—are not, and have never been, the necessary product (in the sense of absolute necessity) of an "autonomous" development of non-human forces of production. They are essentially the product of the activity and struggles of men. And that is why revolutions are possible.

If today we say that the "proletarian" revolution is possible and that it has even become necessary, it is because we believe there are limits to the exploitation which the workers have been enduring for centuries, exploitation to which they are subjected by other men who are organized economically, politically, and socially to make as much profit as possible from the labor of the majority.

We believe that these limits, this multiform, multiracial, and multinational oppression, must today be left behind, that it must be dynamited all the more violently because scientific and technical progress provides the contemporary masses—at least *can* immediately provide them—with the means of becoming conscious, through a daily experience of exploitation that is opposed to (and contrasted with) the wealth of the "free world" as displayed by the mass media; the means, I say, of becoming conscious of the many disparities and injustices of the present system. But neither the mass media nor electronic machines nor even big-business-style unions are going to rise up in place of the exploited, or even give the exploited the opportunity, the intellectual means, the finances, and the arms necessary for the victory of a popular uprising. No. It is men who are going to accomplish this work . . . no matter what the level of development of nuclear energy in their country or in the world!

The consciousness of injustice exalted to a system calls for revolutionary action, for radical changes in the relations of production and property and in social relations in general. But this action cannot spring automatically out of mere awareness of injustice. It must be organized—intellectually, morally, politically, and militarily—into a really revolutionary force, that is, a force which is at the same time militarily effective; psychologically, intellectually and economically de-alienating; democratic; and, morally, founded on solidarity, equality, justice, and honesty.

Such a revolution cannot be accomplished without war, without violence. For the established Order will try to the end to wipe it out in blood. Such a revolution, therefore, means the organization of an anti-capitalist, anti-imperialist, and anti-colonialist war that can end only with the victory or defeat of the working class. Now if we make war, it is in order to win it, and not in order to be martyred in vain in the name of freedom. That is why if there can be no revolution without war, there can be no victorious war without technique.[7]

Every combat technique requires a discipline, an ensemble of means capable of giving maximum effectiveness to fighting units of collectivities. In the age of imperialism, in which we are living (whether we like it or not), there can be no social transformation without a popular revolution, nor any popular revolution without a technique and a discipline conceived for the people and adapted to their means and capacities (present or potential).

Left to the spontaneity of their revolts, which must always be begun over again, the people possess no military strength because they do not see clearly and their class consciousness remains on the level of an *instinct*. That is what the anarchists (who have hearts of gold) always forget. Popular violence does not automatically lead to the overthrow of the established Order, and it can even be an additional factor of political alienation—for whole generations of individuals. The overthrow of the established Order, and the collective de-alienation of the working class that must accompany it, is a problem of conscious and collective organization of the people.

2

The foregoing already shows clearly that our ideal of a society has nothing to do with the electoral programs of the traditional parties. Our program is nothing more nor less than a complete transformation of society and of the men who compose it. It is total revolution.

The political programs of the capitalist parties (Conservative or Liberal, Republican or Democrat) claim to be "pragmatic." This pragmatism is nothing but political opportunism which dares not speak its true name. It is determined by "circumstances," that is, fundamentally, solely by the economic interests of the ruling class or classes.

As for the political programs of the so-called Left parties (traditional Communist, Labor, Socialist, Social Democratic, etc.), most of the time they are based on the same pragmatism but with slight differences, the most important of which is the belief that the revolution will someday come about of its own accord, through electoralism, unionism, and state capitalism. The parties of the Left are forced by their revolutionary past to periodically revive the "future revolution" and the obsession with economic inevitabilities (as Malraux would say)—failing which, these Leftists would find nothing original to put into their programs.

History demonstrates that revolutionaries (including those of the FLQ) are not wrong in thinking that the emancipation of the workers will be achieved by the workers themselves.

The important thing, for the revolutionaries of the whole world as for those of Quebec, is not to expect the revolution to come from the *natural* and so-called *autonomous* development of the productive forces, but to organize immediately the spontaneous violence which in various ways (from workers' strikes to student demonstrations to juvenile delinquency) springs from the profound and cruel frustrations generated by the present organization of society.

The spontaneous and increasingly fierce violence of the people, in particular of the farmers, workers, and youth, is the response called for (and obtained) by the violence that has been systematically practiced for centuries by the minority ruling classes.

This violence can only increase with the consciousness which entire masses have today that they are being unjustly deprived of the ownership of *their* means of production, as well as of the wealth produced, culture, etc., and that they are being maintained in slavery in the name of democracy, the democracy of free enterprise and the exploitation of man by man.

The essential thing is to prevent this justified violence from periodically getting bogged down in despair or from strangling itself in the collective self-destruction that the fascists know so well how to organize, at the opportune moment, for the greater benefit of the Democrats: high finance, the great multinational corporations, the bourgeoisie, and the Church. And the only way to avoid such a misfortune (which is always possible) is for the revolutionaries to organize the people's violence into a progressive force *before* the fascists (who never sleep) take control of it in order first to poison it and then to crush it. And this must be done on an international scale as well as in each country.

Besides, these days there are no more national problems. Santo Domingo, Vietnam, German neo-Nazism, etc., following upon hundreds of similar events, are proof of that.

Revolutionary violence is not, strictly speaking, *ideological*. I mean by "ideological" or "ideologized" violence, a violence based on absolute principles, on the unconscious or the irrational, on the negation of reality, etc., such as fascist, racist, and anti-Semitic violence. Revolutionary violence is nothing but the organized and conscious violence of a people, a class, a national or multinational collectivity that has chosen to confront, combat, and overcome the violence—it too, organized and conscious—of the established Order that is crushing it.

This popular, organized, and conscious violence is based on the needs, aspirations, and *rights* of the majority of men. It is demanded every day by the age-old negation of those needs, aspirations, and rights by a minority of thieves, exploiters, and murderers whose economic, political, military, and legal strength (Capital, the State, the Army, Justice) has been built, over the centuries, on the pitiless oppression of billions of men.

This violence does not force individuals and masses into irrational actions, by means of immoral propaganda, as does Nazi violence, which has no scruples about exploiting the instinct for murder that dwells in all the oppressed. In the foregoing account I have repeatedly emphasized the savage hatred that inhabits humiliated men, a hatred without any definite object. Fascism bases its irrational violence on this strong frustration and on the ignorance in which the mass of humanity is deliberately maintained by the classes in power. Fascism liberates hatred the better to destroy the working class.

Revolutionaries, on the contrary, organize the people's violence into a conscious and *independent* force. Fascism, it must be remembered, is also corporatist: in the end it always encourages the collaboration of classes to the advantage of capital and the bourgeoisie. In working to develop a conscious and independent popular force, revolutionaries organize—out of the natural violence of farmers, workers, petty white-collar workers, students, and young people which constitutes the raw material of every revolution—the de-alienation of the masses. In short, a victorious popular revolution is a successful collective psychoanalysis. And by victory I mean here much more than the mere taking of power. The taking of power is only the first in a long series of collective activities that must transform every sector of human life from top to bottom. I shall return to this later.

Any psychoanalysis (individual or collective) is frightening. And that is a normal reflex. For an "honest" psychoanalysis soon proposes acts for us to perform, acts that radically contradict our old habits of behaving and thinking. As Freud has demonstrated, the more resistance and anxiety is provoked in the "patient" (the individual or collectivity) by an act to be performed, the more that act is *necessary*. To de-alienate oneself is not a romantic enterprise . . . Only dishonest demagogues can promise the masses happiness the way Santa Claus, at Eaton's, promises the children toys.

Revolution is frightening to the masses, who nevertheless spontaneously desire it. For revolution makes its demands. But at the same time, violence attracts the masses, fascinates them as ritual dances fascinate certain so-called primitive collectivities. The oppressed masses ask nothing better than to have *someone* give them the opportunity and means of "unloading" all the frustration, hate, and poison that present society has built up in them. That *someone*, unfortunately, is often fascism. And compared with the Nazi machine, the "authority of the people," my dear Vadeboncoeur, is a little thing indeed!

The big problem is that the fascists have the capital in the beginning while we, *in the beginning*, have only right, justice . . . and poverty. But the fascists rarely give their lives for the people. They do nothing out of solidarity, without a material objective. They break strikes and shoot the workers who want to take possession of the factories. They are on the side of the police and the judges. But unfortunately, the people often realize this too late . . . And then, once again, resignation, submission, and shame win out over violence and the desire for liberation.

All this is not simple, nor can it always be physically "controlled." In time of crisis, theory is a very small weapon. It is *before* the crisis that it is necessary to see clearly and to organize the foundations of a popular revolution. One must always bear in mind that the economic, political, and social crises that encourage the development of an authentically popular revolution are the very ones that at the same time encourage the emergence of fascism. And the ruling classes always have recourse to fascism when they are seized with panic. Because in time of crisis, fascism is their best instrument of combat and repression. When the crisis is over, the fascists become "democrats," "liberals," "Christian socialists" . . . Illusory democracy can begin to exploit the people again in a climate of "social peace"!

3

In the twentieth century fascism has been the permanent temptation of the French-Canadian petty bourgeoisie of Quebec. In the climate of social ferment that is shaking Quebec today, that fact cannot but arouse certain anxieties, even if an important faction of the new petty bourgeoisie calls itself "socialist" and even if the young intellectuals of Quebec, unlike those of Greenwich Village in New York, do not draw swastikas on the walls and write "Bomb Hanoi Now!" all over the place. In 1965 we saw with what enthusiasm a thousand students of the University of Montreal burned an issue of the "socialist" *Quartier Latin,* and with what alacrity Judge Laganière congratulated them on this courageous and Christian gesture!

The presence of fascist elements within the separatist movement is also very disturbing, for we all know that fascism is the art of transforming, sublimating, and then crushing popular discontent in the name of a false "national renaissance" which is only the renaissance of the most frustrated elements of the petty bourgeoisie, that is, of a tiny minority. Quebec separatism in itself is an excellent thing, and I support it 100 percent. But that does not mean that I close my eyes. And I am not unaware of the fact that the Québécois separatists do not all pursue the same objective, that they do not all defend the same interests. Unfortunately for those who advocate a States-General of French Canada, a "dialogue among all parties and all classes in the nation" such as Maître Jacques-Yvan Morin desires[8] can only be a fraud. There might be unanimity on the "unsuitability of the present structures," but certainly not on the new structures to be set up. I notice that the advocates of a States-General mainly attack the present political structures and do not really call into question the most fundamental structures, the economic ones. To be sure, their objective seems to be the "economic independence of Quebec," since Monsieur Marchand himself, chairman of the Council for Economic Expansion, affirms that it is "impossible for Quebec to become economically independent without conquering political independence as a *preliminary*." I underline the word *preliminary*, because that is precisely where the fascist temptation lies: first achieve unanimity on this preliminary, and after that we'll see. See what, *after that?* The factories turned over to the workers, or the unions turned into corporations?

I believe there is only one way to escape the fascist temptation: to organize the majority—that is, the workers, farmers, white-collar workers, progressive intellectuals, students, young people, and clear-thinking petty bourgeois—into a revolutionary force that is openly and radically anti-capitalist, anti-imperialist, and anti-colonialist. It is a question of siding with 90 percent of the population against the 10 percent who want to seize the opportunity offered them today to increase their domination over the "ignorant" and by so doing augment the profits and privileges associated with that domination.

I admit that the Sarto Marchands of Quebec do not appear, at first glance, to be fascists. But it will not take long for them to become fascists if Ottawa persists in its present attitude. And since Quebec is a rich country, Washington might manufacture itself a little Tshombe, a little Ky, or a little Balaguer to prevent our country from "toppling" into the enemy camp. The fascists have a very good press in Washington, notwithstanding the monumental hypocrisy of the kings of the White House.

Only a long experience of revolutionary struggle, requiring an ever higher level of consciousness and responsibility, can enable the oppressed and humiliated masses to escape fascism, to escape the magic of a fanatical nationalism manufactured to serve the needs of a minority of individuals who are seeking a greater measure of economic and political power.[9]

Those who now speak to the masses, taking care not to tell them the whole truth and, above all, preaching nonviolence, electoralism, etc., are imposters who are preparing the way not for revolution but for counter-revolution.[10] "Is it possible that fascism will one day sweep Quebec?" you ask. Yes, it is possible, even after the "quiet revolution." For the "quiet revolution" has also awakened *that* . . . If the conscious workers,[11] the clear-thinking petty bourgeois, the students, and the young people do not do more to translate their progressive ideas and political convictions into practical action, it is entirely possible—alas!—that Quebec may become not another Vietnam but another Portugal.

Certain facts already raise very disturbing questions: the lightning popularity of Caouette, Grégoire, and Marcoux in 1962; the renaissance of Adrien Arcand's party; the "vogue" of the magazine *Aujourd'hui-Québec* in clerical circles and institutions controlled by the clergy (schools, *collèges*, convents); the fusion of the separatists of the Regroupement national with the nationalist *créditistes* of the extreme Right; the presence of notorious fascists in the very ranks of the RIN; the recent transformation of the Order of Jacques-Cartier into two other secret societies with clearly fascist tendencies;° the victory of the National Union and the "Duplessist renaissance"; finally, the plea for a one-party system made by the mayor of Montreal, Jean Drapeau, shortly before the last municipal elections. Jean Drapeau and Daniel Johnson (together with Pierre Laporte) are, in my opinion, the most cunning of the leaders of the Right. Jean Drapeau is perhaps the one who enjoys the broadest financial support at present. Will he someday become our Führer?

The present situation is somewhat reminiscent of the one that enabled Houde and Duplessis to become the puppet rulers of Quebec immediately after the Second World War.

But this time the workers and Leftists are better organized and stronger than in 1945. They represent a definite threat to the system. That is why it is very possible that, in Quebec as in the United States, the extreme Right is arming. There is talk of Arcand's organizing a para-military training camp in the Louiseville region, and of an intense propaganda campaign in Berthier County and in the working-class quarters of the East End of Montreal. One of my friends was "approached" by a senior officer of the well-known private detective agency Phillips, which was recruiting for a para-military fascist organization. My friend refused the invitation but has not forgotten it; that happened two or three years ago.

One could also mention the speeches by the Abbé Gravel of Que-

---

° The Order of Jacques-Cartier was a secret society composed of the traditional élite of lawyers and businessmen and reputed to have played an important role in politics. (Trans.)

bec; the little Brother of Christian Schools who dispensed Hitler-style education in Montreal; the remarks of Judge Laganière on the occasion of the auto-da-fé of *Le Quartier Latin* by students; the anti-union statements of Lucien Tremblay,° the Association profession-nelle des industriels, the Chambers of Commerce, etc.

One thing is certain: agitation on the Right has increased in intensity over the last two years. And this agitation clearly shows that the established Order is now *afraid.* It is not yet in panic, but that is not far off.

4

The renaissance of the Right in Quebec is not a national phenomenon but part of the vast counter-revolutionary movement that is spreading across the world with surprising rapidity (and almost with the complicity of the Russians). The escalation of the war in Vietnam; the crushing of the Dominican revolution and of the black insurrection in Watts; the *coups d'état* in Brazil, Algeria, and Indonesia; the massacre of millions of Indonesian "Communists"; the Johnson-Eisenhower alliance in the White House; the assassination of Ben Barka; the rise of Nazism in Germany, Austria, and Flanders; the recent events in Ghana and Guinea; the repression of the students in India, Brazil, Argentina, and Chile; and even the condemnation of the Jesuits by Paul VI: these, among thousands of others, are so many events that clearly show the determination of the old Order, of imperialism, to halt the world revolution that threatens it on all sides.

Fortunately, the need for freedom is stronger than the fear generated by the nuclear blackmail of the United States. In all parts of the world, groups of peasants, workers, and young people are rising up against the ruling classes. And every time a revolt occurs—in Harlem, in Atlanta, in Chile, the Congo, India, Holland, Spain, or Japan —the workers and the youth of the entire world are immediately informed of it. More and more, despite all the efforts of reaction, the workers and young people feel *involved* in all the struggles carried on by their brothers the world over; and they also know that their own struggle involves the others. Thus little by little there is developing a

---

° Lucien Tremblay is an organizer of company unions. (Trans.)

multinational class consciousness which sooner or later will call for, will demand, the organization of a world revolutionary movement. Not a movement directed from Moscow, Peking, or Havana, but a movement run collectively by the peasants, workers, intellectuals, and young people of all countries, without distinction as to language, culture, color, or privileges (privileges of the sort: *I'm* a Russian, *I'm* Chinese, *I'm* a Cuban, *my* country did this, did that, etc., etc.). Moreover, it is only through the revolutionary action of a multinational people's organization that imperialism (whatever its name, form, or color) can be liquidated once and for all.

Is all that utopian? I think there is no dream of mankind that cannot be realized, providing it is pursued on earth (not on an imaginary planet or in a heaven inhabited by angels). I believe that man possesses the capacity to make an ever more human world and that there are no limits to the progress of humanity. I believe neither in the Apocalypse nor in the eternal domination of the Barbarians. I believe that revolution is possible . . . and at the present stage of humanity, logically necessary. Indeed, the historical development (material and human) of the "productive forces" has now reached such a level that it should enable all men to enjoy a very high standard of living. The scientific foundation of this ideal lies in the present technological revolution, in man's utilization of space, air, nuclear energy, etc., and in the development of communication techniques, the world market and so forth on a planetary scale. But there are two principal obstacles to the realization of this ideal. The first is the concentration of capital, knowledge, technique, and power[12] in the hands of the international bourgeoisie (chiefly American, Soviet, and European). The second is the absence of a multinational revolutionary organization capable of conducting a struggle for liberation under the conditions of existence in the society of the last third of the twentieth century—not the first half of the nineteenth century!

I often feel uneasy watching the evolution of the international revolutionary movement. Evolution toward what, exactly?

We desire, we say, the total liberation of man, and we risk our lives for it every day . . . in Guatemala, in Vietnam, in the Congo, in Angola, in the United States itself, and in Quebec. But despite what some people call our "heroism," do we really know in detail what society we want to build? Do we know what kind of men we want to create? And the men whom we consider it our duty to "awaken" and organize—do we even know what they are? Do we know what the reality around us is made of? What if, after all, too often we were merely agitators . . . ?

It is not unusual to meet revolutionaries who think only about overthrowing the bourgeois state, as if that act had some magic power and could spontaneously create overnight the practical conditions for the liberation of individuals and collectivities from all their present alienations, and for a new movement toward a greater measure of freedom for each and all.

If our ideal is really to see to it that, by a practical action called a revolution, every exploited man, every humiliated man, every frustrated man is placed as soon as possible in a position to "assert himself as an individual," we must, as revolutionaries and conscious beings, think *now* about a great deal more than merely overthrowing a bourgeois state. And we must concern ourselves with more than just problems of military strategy and tactics. We must propose to the workers, farmers, white-collar workers, students, and young people of today a new model of human society, and we must begin to lay its foundations right now, with them, within the revolutionary movement itself, which must not only put them in power, but at the same time fit them to build this new society for the advent of which they will have (or have already) risked their lives a thousand times.

It is sometimes said that nothing is more difficult than to make people think about what they must do in order to be consistent with their principles and, first of all, with themselves. The truth of that statement can be seen in even the most passionate, generous, and disinterested revolutionaries. That is why it sometimes happens that they have no very clear idea of the kind of society they want in place of the one they are working with all their energy to destroy. Their "negligence" in this respect entails enormous risks. Among other things, we might mention that for certain persons, without their even realizing it completely, action becomes an absolute, a mystique that is sufficient unto itself. "Possessed" by this mystique, they gradually agree to perform the most gratuitous acts—providing they have the consolation or justification of paying for them with their lives . . .

I think I demonstrate in this essay that the FLQ is not a terrorist movement whose action is in the service of blind passions. We know rather precisely what we want. In the following pages I shall describe in detail the content of what we call "our ideal." You will easily see that we have no predilection for adventurism, nihilism, or martyrdom (even if we happen to have made mistakes and even if we should happen to make more).

If some day, like so many revolutionaries before us, we die for this human ideal that has become our reason for living, it will not be as martyrs or heroes but as simple soldiers in the daily and universal struggle of the peasants, workers, students, and young people. We shall die the way one dies in war—the victims of enemy weapons or of a stupid accident. We shall be neither the first nor the last, neither the best nor the worst. Men like you.

5

It has become a cliché to say that Quebec is a colony, a sub-colony, a sub-sub-colony, a triple colony, etc. The dependence of Quebec in relation to foreign countries is a constant in its history. Its economic, social, and political development, continually subordinated to foreign financial interests, has never had an independent evolution. For ever since Champlain established a trading post in Quebec in 1608, Quebec has always been subject to the interests of the dominant classes of the imperialist countries: first France, then England, and today the United States.

Because Quebec has been a political colony for more than 350 years, its economy has always been directed, controlled, and organized by factors other than the needs of its population. First, commercially, Quebec has always "lived" and still "lives" on the export, to a limited number of countries (actually, to a single country and a few of its big satellites), of a limited quantity of raw or semi-finished products: furs, under the domination of the French; furs, lumber, wheat, and copper, under the domination of the English; lumber, newsprint, electricity, aluminum ingots, asbestos, iron, under the domination of the United States. This sector of the economy belongs to foreign capital—today American—which transforms the raw or semi-raw products, imported from Quebec at an extremely low price, in the factories of the United States (or sometimes one of its European "colonies," like Norway or England).

As for the "transformation" sector, covering the needs of the domestic market or of a part of the foreign market (textiles, furniture, shoes, clothing), it is poorly equipped and rests on the exploitation of cheap labor (which is all the more abundant in Quebec because agriculture is scarcely easy or flourishing there). This sector too is in great part controlled by American capital, with the forced cooperation of English-Canadian capital, Italian-Canadian capital, etc., which cannot match American power. Quebec, and especially the region of Montreal, is in a situation of *absolute financial dependence* with regard to the United States which, like France and England in the past, cannot but oppose the autonomous development of the Quebec economy. The bankruptcy of the Sidbec project, the purchase of Quebec-Telephone by American interests, the financial dependence of the State of Quebec on American credit are current illustrations of this. This is the essential fact today: Quebec, manipulated by the United States, is compelled to sell its natural resources and its cheap labor at prices much below their real value and to buy products manufactured in the United States, Japan, or England at prices much above their real value—thanks to the limitless exploitation of its resources and of the labor of its population (which is now approaching six million)!

The conclusion is clear: the United States derives enormous profits from its economic domination of Quebec (as it does from the domination of a number of other countries) and, unless it is forced to do so by the violence of the Québécois, it will never consent to end its domination. On the contrary, everything indicates that it is in the interest of the United States to increase this domination still more, even though it may be given a "French face" so as to calm the "patriotic" sentiments of a petty bourgeoisie with no imagination, which dreams about the New France of Canon Groulx, like the beggars of the Carré Viger in Montreal who give themselves the illusion of transforming reality by telling each other "stories"! It passes the time, as the saying goes, but it makes absolutely no change in reality. And the fact that the oil imported from Venezuela is refined in Montreal to be sold afterward on the Canadian market is not a sign of prosperity but of underdevelopment. For this oil stolen from the Venezuelan people by the American corporations is transported to and refined in Montreal East (the suffix "East" has a real economic content; see note 13) because taxes are not so high there, wages are lower, and profits are consequently greater than if the oil were refined in the United States and subjected to customs tariffs before being sold to Canadian consumers. One can say essentially the same thing of the airplanes that the Americans manufacture at Canadair (Montreal) for the Canadian Ministry of Defense, and of the explosives that are manufactured here at lower cost and sold to the United States Defense Department at a higher profit than if they were made in Detroit or Chicago. There is no lack of examples of this kind, and they only illustrate the fundamental fact that, in the present state of affairs, there simply is no "Quebec economy."

"Then how do you expect to build a strong Quebec, an independent Quebec, on a void?" one may ask all the Jean Lesages, Eric Kieranses, and Daniel Johnsons of Quebec who are asking for *still more* American investments! If we are going to be underdeveloped, what difference does it make whether or not it is within the framework of a pseudo-republic?

Political independence is only a myth (a luxury we can do without, bled white as we are!), except on condition that it is preceded by: the expropriation of foreign capital (American and other) and the nationalization of natural resources, banks, and other enterprises that presently belong to foreign capital; the modification in depth of the monetary, financial, commercial, and customs relations that enslave us to the United States; and a social transformation that can lead to the disappearance of the parasitic classes (the English-speaking and French-speaking petty bourgeoisies of Quebec) which are tied to imperialism and profit from the sale of Quebec to foreigners. This condition is therefore tantamount to the necessity for a total revolution.

Those are the prerequisites of true independence. They want to make us believe—the Québécois petty bourgeoisie of trade, industry, the professions, and the Church want to make us believe—that on the contrary, it is legal, formal independence that is a prerequisite of economic independence. This is crude demagogy, pure and simple, designed (like the "return to the land" in the old days) to—excuse the expression—"screw the people"!

One does not decolonize a country by proclaiming it a republic and designing a beautiful new flag for it. Especially if that "republic" separates from the colony—that is, English Canada—but makes no change in the fundamental economic relations which Quebec, like Canada, maintains with its Yankee "partner." If the separatism of the petty bourgeois is only the separatism of a colony, if it represents only the desire of a colony to live out its destiny as a colony of the United States without the intermediary of English Canada, well then, let them stop talking about economic independence—and even about political independence!

I have no objection to our all getting together and telling Ottawa to go to hell. Because we have no use for its cumbersome paternalism which, by the way, costs us pretty dear in taxes and helps to confuse matters. OK. Let's tell Ottawa to go to hell. And then? What's going to change? We'll have one tax return instead of two? A direct telephone line between Quebec and Washington? A comic-opera army integrated with NORAD? A delegate to the UN, another to the OAS, a third to NATO, and our very own ambassador to the Vatican? And then what? The iron of the North Shore, the asbestos of Asbestos, the mines of Abitibi, our forests and hydraulic resources, our commerce, finance, and industry—and the political machines: will not all that still be the exclusive *property* of the Americans? Then what does the majority of the population of Quebec stand to gain from this paper independence, apart from one more political alienation and, probably, a still greater measure of economic servitude?

Understand me: I am not against the independence of Quebec but against the *illusory* independence of Quebec which, dressed up in various guises (from an Associated State to a Republic), is now being proposed to us by the parasitic petty bourgeoisie of French Canada. And that is why I am for revolution, because only a revolution in depth can make us independent. That is not a question of ideology but of fact . . . And one must voluntarily close one's eyes and one's mind to pretend not to recognize it.

But, gentlemen—you who are for "political" separatism—intellectual dishonesty is likely to cost you dear one day; for a revolution, especially a revolution conducted by the majority, is not too tolerant of the hypocritical and cowardly exploiters who play into the hands of its adversaries. And the adversary of the Quebec revolution is not Ottawa (which does not have the means to oppose it!) but Washington. Yes or no, gentlemen, are you for separation from Washington? Are you for or against imperialism? I know how embarrassing this question is for you. But it can't be helped, dear compatriots!—it's the only question today that makes any sense.

It's not 1837 any more, and we're fed up with the Louis-Joseph Papineaus! We find the Papineaus of 1967 as disgusting as the one of 1837. Just as we find the Cartiers of 1967 as disgusting as the one of 1867.

We are disgusted with 350 years of being bargained over by "indigenous" and foreign capitalists. This time we are demanding *everything*, independence and economic power included. And if, in order to get that, we have to confront L.B.J.'s Marines, weapons in hand, well, we will take up arms against the Marines, we will follow the example of the Vietnamese people. Then you will have no choice but to go out into the street with us and *follow us* . . . or else seek refuge, comfort, and B-52's in Washington, as General Ky and his clique of traitors are doing. As a number of cliques of traitors did before them. As you yourselves may do tomorrow, you who today demand: equality or independence.[14]

6

This revolution that Quebec needs—as do all the countries that are enslaved by capitalism and colonial imperialism—implies nothing more nor less than the disappearance of capitalism itself. That means transformations that are even more profound than those required by the nationalization of foreign capital. It is a question, in fact, of abolishing capital itself, the basis of present society.

Present society, you know as well as I do, rests on what the specialists call a "market economy," that is, an economy in which the real decisions affecting the whole collectivity, workers as well as nonworkers, are made by a handful of financiers (in scholarly language: "individual economic agents") in accordance with their personal economic interests: the accumulation of constantly increasing profits. This capitalist economy exploits the majority of men by means of a labor market in which the workers (the real producers of wealth), deprived by force of the ownership of their means of production, are compelled to sell their labor (when there happens to be a demand for slaves!) in order to obtain from the system that exploits them the minimum which they and their families must have to subsist, that is, to consume (and so "reimburse" the system) the products which the capitalists, through advertising, force them to buy at the highest possible price.

In short, a minority of financiers has monopolized the means of production and has organized human labor and society in general (relations of production, relations of exchange, and social relations) in such a way as to appropriate for itself, in the name of allegedly free competition and an illusory equality of individuals, the greatest possible share of the wealth produced by the daily labor of the majority of mankind. These financiers and their army of ideologists call this "democracy." The workers call it organized slavery.

We want to replace this economy based on the exploitation of the majority of mankind not only by a new economy but by a new society, in which the category "economy" will not have the same content it does now. We want to replace it with a society in which the producers (the workers) collectively own and administer their means of production and create, organize, and plan their relations of production and the distribution of their products in accordance with ultimate goals that they choose themselves, for the satisfaction of their true needs, in the framework of an absolute equality of rights, opportunities, and benefits.

In this "economy," this new society, there will be no more "free competition," that is, no more capital market and labor market, no more accumulation and concentration of the collective wealth in the hands of a few individuals who are the strongest and richest, no more exploitation of the workers, the immense majority of mankind, by a handful of men who accumulate profits. Rather, there will be an egalitarian (and not totalitarian) social structure without non-workers, without exploiters, and without parasites. A society without classes, therefore, and as soon as possible without a state. For in the last analysis, capitalism is determined, developed, maintained, and periodically renewed, rejuvenated, programmed, etc., by the strongest social class (today the bourgeoisie of big business, of the American or Soviet type), to whom the state belongs and who profit to the maximum from the class nature of present-day society (a nature which, throughout history, successive ruling classes have arbitrarily defined as inalienable). It is this class nature of society and of its legal form, the state (whether it be of the American, British, French, or

Soviet type), which the workers and young people—all the progressives of the twentieth century—must destroy. For otherwise how can we make sure that a "new ruling class" will not be built into a state in which equality would be as much a myth as the "democratic freedom of individuals" is in the present system? °

Only an egalitarian social structure can make it concretely possible for the workers to actively participate and enjoy to the full the products of their activity, which is free and yet disciplined. It is not merely a question of "permitting" from above (from the heights of some supreme "presidium") the free circulation of suggestions, proposals, and criticisms "at the base," but of a great deal more. It is a question of setting up, through this egalitarian social structure and by a collective effort, the machinery of a concrete and effective democracy, a democracy for all that will enable the workers and the entire society to make the fullest possible use of the potentialities not only of the economy but of the whole range of human activity and the energies at work in the known universe, energies which men have unlimited power to control and use for human ends, for progress, happiness, and the satisfaction of needs known and as yet unknown.

It is understood that the concrete, local, particular forms of such a structure (which in my opinion can exist securely only on a continental or even world scale—for economic and political reasons that I shall explain below) may have many accidental "variations," good in themselves (or rather, immaterial to the foundations of the structure), according to the specific historical development of the different countries, nationalities, minorities, or "races." But these "variations" only give local color to the essential thing: the establishment of an egalitarian social structure, of a classless society.

In order for this society to exist and endure, three sorts of conditions must be realized, conditions which we shall now sum up as clearly as it is possible to do within the narrow framework of this essay.

They are: first, economic; second, administrative and political; third, subjective and intellectual.

(1) *Economic conditions*. These conditions, which are fundamen-

---

° The phrase "new ruling class" refers to the French title of the book by Milovan Djilas that appeared in English as *The New Class* (1957). (Trans.)

tal, can be summed up in the disappearance of the following: the commodity categories; calculation in terms of "value" (which expresses itself through the price system and whose purpose or utility is not, as certain persons affirm, to express the labor time required for the production of the various products or goods, but to accumulate as much profit as possible); money; the system of national accounting connected with the capitalist commodity categories; and the financial and credit system.

The functioning of the commodity categories and the utilization, by a bureaucracy of technocrats, of the law of value make no sense in an economy that calls itself "socialized." For that is wanting to socialize the economy without de-capitalizing it. That is putting a new coat of paint on an old automobile. It is being satisfied with an economic revolution in name only. At most, it is making private-enterprise capitalism evolve toward state capitalism. It is leaving in place, as if they were vital to humanity, the roots of the accumulation and concentration of capital and of ever increasing profits in the hands of new social categories, new ruling classes which, by means of their state and of their exclusive control of economic decisions, plans, etc., will not be slow to monopolize in their own interests, as the new class in power, the so-called revolutionized use of the law of value and the commodity categories. The great (American) multinational corporations have socialized "their" economy too, have planned wages, prices, investments, etc. The USSR of 1967 has become the biggest trust in the world,[15] the corporation with the most widespread activities. General Motors is beginning to court it for an amicable Soviet-American agreement over the heads of the workers, whose conditions of existence have not been fundamentally changed by the revolution of 1917 and who are now faced with having to prepare the overthrow of a new bourgeoisie, less feudal than that of 1917 but more clever and hypocritical. A bourgeoisie which I would call a "state bourgeoisie." A bourgeoisie which plays a prudent game in Asia and asks the American and European capitalists to come help it "reform" its system of planning and reintroduce into the Soviet economy the notions of profit and free competition, so that the USSR may become the number one imperialist power of the year 1980, and the Brezhnev-Kosygin clique the Rockefellers of the year 2000! Is that really what Lenin was prophesying when he naively said that "With socialism (appearing) at every window of contemporary capitalism," it was an "infantile disorder of communism" to refuse any compromise with that system? Today one can say that capitalism is reappearing at every window of Russian and East European socialism. That is what the pragmatism of revolutionary phraseology leads to, once it is in power.

Our ideal is not to turn out a new edition of the "realism" of the Lenins, Stalins, and Kosygins. Because today that "realism" has shown itself for what it is. And decidedly, after fifty years of Soviet history, it appears that out of the popular insurrections of 1917 the Russians have made a bourgeois revolution, a revolution that has had recourse to planning (like postwar France) in order to concentrate— massively, and as quickly as possible—the capital and talent inherited from the old regime on the building of a basic industry and a state capable of "competing" with the United States. And after fifty years of unparalleled privations imposed on the workers, General Motors and Ford are finding in the USSR and Eastern Europe a market all ready to receive American cars assembled in Moscow. It is Saint-Bruno (SOMA) on a gigantic scale, and Kosygin is the Gérard Filion of the Soviet Union's "quiet revolution," of peaceful coexistence and cooperation with American fascism! °

All that because after October 1917 they accepted as a "necessary" and "temporary survival" the use of commodity categories in the economy. From Bolshevism they quickly passed to planned reformism, and from that to state capitalism. That is what the *autonomous* development of capitalist forces of production leads to!

The Soviets have not understood that the "law of value" is not a law of nature but a man-made thing, and that the commodity categories and everything connected with them (money, the financial system, credit, the price system, etc.) are man-made things and not natural forces like light, nuclear energy, and so forth. If man is capable today of converting matter into energy and one element into another, how can one deny that he has the capacity not only to "revise" the law of value but to challenge it?

° The Société de montage automobile (SOMA) is a Quebec state enterprise that assembles Renaults and Peugeots from parts bought from the French firms. Its plant was set up in Saint-Bruno, near Montreal, when Gérard Filion was both vice-president of the company and mayor of the town. (Trans.)

The "Marxist" economists, in their libraries crammed with statistical tables, try to "determine the objective conditions for the withering away of the commodity categories." [16] But when they pose this fundamental problem, they forget to put it back in the context of the modes of activity that have been generated by the development of capitalism and the bourgeoisie. They abstractly isolate the commodity categories from the capitalist social structure and its class nature. That is why they forget to pose the problem in the concrete domain where it is located.

First of all, there can be no "withering away" of the commodity categories unless there also is a "withering away" of the system of which they are an integral part and in which they serve as an instrument for achieving economic goals set by men—by the classes that have created and constantly perfected that system. To pose the problem of the withering away of the commodity categories is to pose the problem of the withering away of capitalist society itself. Now, can capitalist society "wither away"? To be sure, it is frustrating for the majority of men. To be sure, it is incapable of adequately meeting the vital needs of hundreds of millions of men. But can this society "wither away" like a man growing old who, *in spite of himself,* withers away and dies? For my part, I believe that capitalist society can only be *overthrown.* It cannot wither away by itself, any more than the bourgeois class can commit suicide. Only practical action, a revolutionary movement, can sweep away the old society and at the same time the commodity categories, the law of value, etc. There remains to be determined the total content of this revolution, which I shall attempt to do further on in this chapter.

But the essential thing for the moment is to remember that the commodity categories and the law of value, which have been created by men through their activities, can be abolished by men through new activities that are called "revolutionary," in the sense that they radically change the social relations (of production, exchange, etc.) established by preceding generations or, more precisely, by the ruling classes of those generations. It is impossible to imagine that an egalitarian social structure can emerge from the planning of *capitalist* relations of production and exchange, which have been created precisely for the accumulation of capital—of wealth—in the hands of a ruling minority which alone is favored by the system. The planning of capital investments, prices and wages, various types of production, etc., can exist only under state capitalism. In an egalitarian social structure, all that remains is the planning of *distribution* (and not "exchange" in the capitalist sense of the term) of the goods produced by men to satisfy their needs. That planning is done on a basis of equality for all, an equality which can only be achieved through a long experience of solidarity in the struggle men are compelled to wage to rid themselves of the system that oppresses them economically, politically, militarily, legally, religiously, and ideologically.

The truth of this statement rests on the assumption that two other economic conditions have been realized in the revolutionary movement which has abolished, in this or that part of the world, the traditional commodity relations that are based on monetary exchange and are therefore "capitalizable." (Which no revolution, to my knowledge, has yet accomplished.)

These two conditions are:

(a) An identity, as nearly perfect as possible, between the "juridical subjects" (those who possess the effective *right* to order the means of production and work out new relations of ownership, production, and distribution of products) and the "economic subjects" (those who are *capable*, practically, of managing these activities). This identity cannot be achieved so long as the different centers for the appropriation of the means of production and the centers for the appropriation of the political and technical powers of distribution remain independent, separate, or opposed, dealing with antagonistic interests (real or artificial).[17]

(b) Absolute economic independence from foreign capitalist markets, should any still exist at the time when an "economy without capital" can appear.[18] For any extension of the distribution of goods to capitalist markets or any penetration of a de-capitalized economy by foreign capital would soon reduce to nothingness the fundamental objectives of the revolution.

These two conditions, complementary to and inseparable from the preceding ones, bring me to the "administrative and political" conditions for the establishment, by the majority itself, of an egalitarian society (2), and to the "subjective and intellectual" conditions for the realization of this human ideal which at first glance appears utopian (3).

The conditions described in (2) and (3) are as important as those enumerated in (1) and are part of what might be called the ensemble of objective conditions for a total revolution. Such a revolution cannot result from a *natural* development (natural in the sense of being independent of the will of individuals and groups) of blind and autonomous forces of production, but solely from a long process of human—that is, conscious and responsible—activities, collective activities of sufficient duration and depth to replace traditional individualism by an effective solidarity. For solidarity is the only foundation on which it is possible to build a truly egalitarian social structure, a social structure which is free for all, fraternal and cooperative and within which each individual can become more of a person, as I said above.

(2) *Administrative and political conditions.* It is an illusion to think one can build an egalitarian social structure while retaining the political categories and the administrative modes of functioning inherited from the development of capitalism by the bourgeoisie. For such a structure must be, can only be, built *collectively.*

The abolition of free competition, of the commodity categories, and of the accumulation of capital through the exploitation of man by man must coincide with the abolition of the traditional state, in which personal freedom is reduced to the "right" to *enjoy*, within the limits of one's individual fortune and the conditions of existence of one's class, certain very limited powers that are subordinated to the interests of the "objective power" of the system set up by this or that ruling class.

Even in a state in which opinion and criticism were freely expressed, an egalitarian social structure could only be a myth unless the "national" and then the "multinational" collectivities possessed the instruments enabling them to command the state, with full knowledge of all the facts—that is, to *govern themselves*, directly, without going through the intermediary of a state "detached" from the conditions of everyday life.

These instruments are: management of the processes of production and distribution of goods, control of planning (the coordination, in the interest of all, of central and local managements) and control of the division of functions among individuals and groups, and power to set human goals independent of the requirements of the old market economy. This last implies the power to orient policy in the direction of the common interest, the collective and individual interest, which is for every man to assert himself as a person (in present society, a privilege reserved for those who hold economic and military power, the "state-as-arbitrator" being only a screen to disguise that power).

In order for there to be an egalitarian social structure, the division between the "base" and the "presidium," if you will, must disappear. The difference between the "mass" and the "élite," and even the distinction between the "people" and the "party-as-guide," must disappear. Furthermore, so-called democratic centralism must give way, on the economic level as on the political level, to democracy itself.

It is therefore necessary that it be materially impossible in this structure for individuals or groups of individuals to enjoy political power, economic power, etc., at the expense of other men. The abolition of capital and the replacement of capitalist relations of exchange—which function through a "price system" that is arbitrarily based on a supposed calculation of man-hours necessary but that deliberately departs as much as it pleases from the levels allegedly fixed by that socially necessary labor, so as to ensure maximum profits for the ruling class!—the replacement of these relations by true relations of distribution based on the needs of each and all (of which I spoke in (1) above) render the exploitation of man by man if not impossible, at least unprofitable. But these new relations of production and distribution must be disciplined (for otherwise you have anarchy) by an administrative and political structure that makes the traditional state obsolete. This structure should make it possible both to decentralize the real decisions and to centralize the information enabling each social group to coordinate freely with the others (which are cooperative and no longer competitive) the allocation or utilization of available resources with a view to obtaining the maximum yield from those resources (material and intellectual) for the greatest benefit of all.

How can that be achieved? By the socialization of modern technology, which is the perfect instrument for the *unification* of the process of appropriation by men of nature (energy, mineral wealth, etc.) and the process of reproduction and transformation of those resources by the *same* men—a unification, at both the local and the international levels, necessitated by the creation of an egalitarian society.

Modern technology makes it possible both to calculate the maxi-

mum yield of resources, wherever they are located, and to dissemi-
nate the information to the decison-making units scattered over one
or several territories. It gives everyone—it *ought* to give everyone—
increasingly exact scientific knowledge of the potentialities of exter-
nal nature and of man himself (who is also a part of "nature," of the
universe). Bringing men face to face, so to speak, with the true
knowledge of their capacities, it also gives them the technical means
of fulfilling those capacities and of planning them in accordance with
one or more of the collective, social objectives that have been freely
chosen by men united in a single effort at progress. Which presupposes that *beforehand* these men have learned to unite and to utilize,
with maximum efficiency and for their real benefit, all the possibilities of modern technology, which are now monopolized by the same
individuals who control capital, the state, the law, etc. And that in
turn presupposes that these men have taken possession of technology, which is not accessible to them now but which they are in an
objective position to make the basis of their emancipation from enslavement (in all its forms: economic, political, moral, religious, cultural).

This leads me to the "subjective and intellectual conditions" for
building this egalitarian social structure which constitutes "our
ideal" and which—allow me to emphasize it again—presupposes a
violent and total revolution.

(3) *Subjective and intellectual conditions.* These conditions are required by our ideal of a society itself, which must be achieved by de-
alienated men who have learned to rid themselves of everything that
now blocks their individual and collective development: ignorance of
modern science and technique; enslavement to routine; the habit of
abdicating; individualism; the psychological frustrations that harden
man, blind him, or gradually destroy him; the absence of a highly developed, lucid, organized class consciousness; a weak sense of responsibility; ignorance of the possibilities opened up by active solidarity; lack of confidence in the success of a popular revolution and
even in the prospect that it will soon be launched; the many disappointments accumulated over decades of betrayals by the unions and
compromises by the socialists; fear of overt action; lack of self-confidence; etc., etc.

Man is the principal "productive force" and the only "natural" power capable of giving to the ensemble of known and used productive forces a particular goal and a particular organization (which may be changed from one generation to another). He must therefore make the effort to transform himself in order to be really in a position, as Marx and Engels say, to sweep away, by revolution, "all the rottenness of the old system and to become *fit* to build society on new foundations," fit to organize an egalitarian social structure, without non-workers, without exploiters, and without parasites—a society without classes, whose primary social objective is to make it concretely possible for *all* men to assert themselves as individuals without exploiting one another, as they are now forced to do by the conditions of existence created by capitalism.

That is why the "subjective and intellectual conditions" are the ones it is most important to bring about, for without them nothing can be done. In order to realize these conditions, the revolutionaries of the twentieth century must make use of social techniques: group psychology, "social animation," ° the development of creativity by the "gratuitous" exercise of the arts and of writing, the development of manual skill by the practice of domestic mechanics (repair of household objects whose workings, although very simple, are too often not understood), reading, and reflection based on everyday life and current events, both local and international.[19]

The most profound alienation is no doubt the one expressed in the common remark we have all made at one time or another: "I wonder what the world is coming to . . . I honestly don't know where we're heading."

This spontaneous expression of "disorientation" reveals to what an extent *we are not free*, in this world that is supposed to be ours.

In the age of interplanetary travel and nuclear energy, we are like primitive people lost in a universe of mysteries.

We do not understand a thousandth part of the contemporary scientific discoveries whose practical applications serve as instruments of domination and exploitation for the capitalist bourgeoisie, which alone possesses the knowledge, the men, and the technology

---

° In French-Canadian radical movements, "social animation" is a group sensitization process led by trained group leaders whose purpose is to help people relate to each other and understand social and political issues. Ideally, the group reaches a consensus on analysis and strategy and formulates actions accordingly. (Trans.)

necessary to apply those discoveries to its own ends or interests. Because it alone monopolizes the money that is the cement of present-day society, it can "buy" the scientists, their discoveries, and the technical instruments for using them practically. It thus possesses increasingly perfected means not only of reinforcing its domination and its system of exploitation, but of *justifying* them "scientifically," through magazines, reviews, newspapers, radio and television broadcasts, and courses in the *collèges* and universities, whose real function is not to socialize scientific knowledge but to pervert that knowledge and make it work for the ruling classes by transforming it into an ideology justifying the status quo. For pure science—that is, science that is consistent—can only demonstrate that the universe (and therefore human history) is subject to a "natural" process (which also governs human activity) of continual revolutions. To be sure, it is virtually impossible for the contemporary ruling classes to *freeze* the "relativist" and "dialectical" science of the twentieth century into a rigid, monolithic system of knowledge like that of the Middle Ages. Therefore the policy of the bourgeoisie today is to pretend that capitalist society is in perpetual revolution and is capable of resolving all the contradictions and problems raised by contemporary scientists and thinkers. "Progressive conservatism," in other words! °

Nevertheless, the social failures of the system (unemployment, war, poverty, economic insecurity, etc.) give the lie to this official optimism and to the opportunistic relativism of the "science" pages—or broadcasts—of the capitalist press. And in order to crush the practical reactions produced by social injustice, unemployment, racism, war, etc., capitalism must have recourse—on the "politics and ideology" pages of that same press—to *necessity*, just as the ruling classes did in the Middle Ages. And it is not long before necessity, which is also supposed to be "scientific" (even though it is nonsense from the point of view of authentic science), is transformed into a police state, as soon as the economic interests of the big bourgeoisie begin to be challenged by the "ignorant" masses. Then the police and the army quickly supplant science as the justification for the social status quo.

° The name of the conservative party in Canada is the Progressive Conservative Party. (Trans.)

A reactionary ideology comes to the assistance of the police state, and the law takes responsibility for imposing on the malcontents a forced respect for necessity! Einstein is sacrificed to Hitler. Engels to Stalin. Curie to Laval.

But between the oppressed people and the "liberal-totalitarian" big bourgeoisie, there is a petty bourgeoisie which is caught in a dilemma. It cannot really understand Einstein, and it cannot "swallow" the philosophy of Hitler. Applied fascism (although consistent with the conventional ideas that fill the petty bourgeoisie's "acquired" or "consumed" knowledge of the universe) constipates it. It feels sick. It has *nausea*. And—fortunately for capitalism—it takes refuge in irrationalism, either passive or willful (according to circumstances and tastes). The neutralism of individual cowardice becomes "lucid" existentialism, "being and nothingness," a room with no exit, that is comfortable in spite of the smell given off by the corpses of the millions of men who are crushed and incinerated—"scientifically" —by the fascist panic. The smell finally makes them sick, these gentlemen who want to remain "free" in a universe of barbarism. They begin to shout and ask the fascists to go home. They become engaged! But their "ethics of ambiguity" forbids them to take sides openly and clearly with the workers against the bourgeois, just as their "lucidity" forbids them to take sides openly with Hitler and his irrationalism, stained as it is with the blood of millions of men.[°] Bloody irrationalism has given them gooseflesh and a guilty conscience. That disturbs their "clear ideas" about the ambiguity of (petty-bourgeois) human behavior! They give their support to a new liberal and pseudo-democratic government, and their "engagement" finally boils down to demanding that the state provide "social peace" without the stench of incinerated corpses, and restore to them the individual freedom momentarily compromised by the necessity of "resisting" fascism, which has decidedly gone too far: Nietzsche did not expect all *that* of the Führer! "Beyond good and evil," the absurd once again becomes the quiet philosophy of the melancholy petty bourgeoisie, still caught in the same dilemma, while the big bourgeoisie, re-established on the solid base of capital after a good paying

---

[°] The reference to the "ethics of ambiguity" is an allusion to Simone de Beauvoir's book *Pour une morale de l'ambiguité* (1947), which has appeared in English (translated by Bernard Frechtman) under the title *The Ethics of Ambiguity*. (Trans.)

war, entrusts to the "scientism" of the charlatans of *Planète* and similar publications the "historic" task of repeating the same old pack of nonsense in a new and currently fashionable vocabulary. A whole collection of digests comes along to supplement this "scientific information" that is served up to men who are starved for knowledge but have slim pocketbooks, few tools of learning, and scanty leisure!

Thus we daily consume a pseudo-science the way we consume the bread made by Weston, not in order to nourish ourselves but in order to make profits for those who exploit even the most elementary needs of man.

The existentialist "superstructure" (Christian, nihilistic, neutralist, sadistic, Marxist, etc.—something for every taste, so to speak!) has its "popular" counterpart in the mass of sentimental romances, detective stories, pornography, scandalous gossip, tales of sadism, gangsterism, and violence, war adventures and murder stories that fill a considerable number of publications and radio and television broadcasts. Plunged into this irrational merchandise with which we are daily inundated by the mass media—the property of the businessmen—we are taught, under pressure, to accept the absurd, to despise existence, we are trained in delinquency and the amoral individualism of the "struggle for life," and by this means are deflected from our political and revolutionary tasks.

Contemporary science, from psychoanalysis to sociology, while unmasking these processes of an alienation directed and scientifically programmed by the bourgeoisie, lets itself be used like a commodity, and the scientists offer only scant and feeble resistance to the utilization of their discoveries about man for anti-human purposes. When it is "honest," science is too expensive and remains inaccessible to the majority of men, who cannot afford psychoanalysis or prolonged studies at the universities and great technical institutes. Since science is not truly socialized, in spite of the fact that present-day technology makes such socialization objectively feasible, the businessmen, who are the kings of our democracy, go unchallenged as they plan and socialize stupidity.

And how can one defend himself against this cunning debasement of the mind when one does not possess the intellectual means to combat it? Intellectual means which, in our society, depend on our economic and political power. Power which is nil for the majority of men. Power which is daily negated in the name of free competition, the most widespread and effective myth of the nineteenth and twentieth centuries.

It is one of the most important tasks of contemporary revolutionaries to give the farmers, workers, students, and young people the means of freeing themselves from intellectual debasement; and this must be done by perfecting a process of conscious integration of the masses in the collective revolutionary struggle, whose duration may be long and whose end may be very difficult to foresee, but which must begin today. Which, in fact, has already been going on for over a century, starting with the first revolts of the English and French workers of Europe in the early nineteenth century and continuing up to the present Vietnamese revolution, which the Americans are desperately trying to destroy with weapons that in quantity and sophistication go beyond everything we have yet seen in the history of wars and class struggles.

This arduous collective task has *already* been undertaken wherever a serious, clear-sighted effort is being made to teach the masses to think about the world and history, starting not with the abstract creations that the ruling classes have invented to alienate them but with the very conditions of their existence, with life as they have experienced it.

Beginning with the techniques of "social animation," films, and simple conversations about everyday realities, revolutionaries must teach the masses to produce by themselves, so to speak, the science that has hitherto been reserved for specialists. Otherwise, science will never be socialized and man will never be de-alienated. Because the socialization of scientific knowledge, understood in its continual evolution (its dialectical movement of affirmation and negation of contradictions) and assimilated in its reality, is a fundamental condition for the de-alienation of the majority of humankind and for the achievement of what one might metaphorically call the transition of humanity from prehistory to history.

In order for this transition to take place, science must not be dissolved into a new kind of witchcraft sold in the form of "products of the mind" that have been emptied of content and offer the deceived consumers only a collection of hollow phrases without practical implications. Science must cease to be enslaved to the capitalist bourgeoisie's accumulation of profits and carry out at last its true function of liberating all men from the so-called objective powers which presently oppress them, but which can cease to exist as blind and oppressive necessities if they are "possessed" through knowledge and utilized through technology for determined goals and interests. This role, which has hitherto been reserved for the richest (from all points of view) faction of the bourgeoisie, must become the daily activity of humanity, for that is the real and constantly renewed content of what we call human freedom. This freedom must become the practical exercise of all men, and in order for that to happen, it must cease to be the privilege of a minority exploiting the majority.

In short, the number one objective of the total revolution is to give all men the opportunity and the means to acquire knowledge, to understand the discoveries of the scientists, and to use them intelligently and effectively and, in addition, to participate in their turn in scientific research, the perfecting of technology and the exploration and enjoyment of the universe, which belongs to all men . . . and not just to the bourgeois.

It is only by means of this concrete, *conscious* freedom that humanity will be able to fulfill itself, leaving behind the frustrations that make it the slave of international capitalism, and turning to account the many "forces of nature" which influence its behavior and which it does not yet use for its liberation because it is just beginning to learn about them, through contemporary biology and physics in particular. And the beginning, or apprenticeship, of this freedom coincides with the beginning, or apprenticeship, of revolutionary action.

For man can acquire the power to determine his activities advisedly—that is, he can acquire true freedom—only by means of a practical, collective, radical revolution, which no Messiah can bring about for him.

7

This ideal—which is also a product of our social activity, of our evolution—seems very far off, vague, even theoretical. But like any ideal, like any objective, it is a working tool, a hypothesis, a hope born of the felt need to *realize* it. And far from being an obstacle to our immediate daily activities, it is indispensable to them, as light is indispensable to a man descending into the depths of a mine. This ideal was not born spontaneously in the mind of a single unparalleled genius. It is a weapon, a tool, an implement forged by conscious men with a view to finding the road to the creation of a better world, in which every man and every human collectivity can flower. It is not for nothing that throughout history men have taken up arms and accomplished revolutions. It is not for nothing, or spontaneously (in the pejorative sense of the word), that the workers, peasants, and young people of today are taking up arms here and there the world over. And if they are taking up arms *today*, it is because *today* they have a glimpse—even if it is often confused—of this ideal, this "utopia," for which millions of proletarians have fought and died.

I believe that the more precisely one can define this utopia—with the help of the accumulated experience of the many political and scientific revolutions that constitute our collective history and our common "production"—the more effectively every revolutionary, every group of revolutionaries, every multinational organization of revolutionaries, can carry out his or its historic task, all the way from such humble activities as the printing of "subversive" tracts to the organization of a true revolutionary army capable of defeating imperialism.

I cannot conceive of conscious and effective revolutionary activity which does not have a clearly perceived end in view (an end that is, in fact, only the beginning of something else), and which does not at the same time—starting *now*, from day to day, even within actions that are seemingly insignificant—attempt to integrate individuals and their problems, etc., into an ever broader community of common interests.

In short, a "utopia" is necessary for the emergence of class consciousness and collective revolutionary action. But this "utopia" is not a divine revelation but the material and theoretical product of human needs felt by men, one of whose most fundamental characteristics is the *hope*, the *will* for "more," for progress, for an ever greater measure of freedom, happiness, creativity, and joy. These are ideas to which the men of today are as responsive as were the men of yesterday. And personally, I find it difficult to conceive that men—that is, the vast majority of them—will one day renounce their need to create, to love, to live in happiness and complete freedom. I do not know *why* men exist, love, suffer, and do not want to die. But I know that they exist and that, everywhere and in everything, they seek to fulfill themselves as *persons*, through fraternity, love, solidarity, and so on. The system under which we live has invented a multitude of obstacles (economic, psychic, etc.) to the fulfillment of this need, or these needs, which everyday observation leads us to believe are fundamental for men.

Perhaps I am wrong to believe in these things? But have you yourselves ever felt you were to blame for loving and wanting to be free?

To my way of thinking, the danger for humanity—and this danger seems to me to be "complementary" to the level of consciousness that men have now reached—is that it may cease to believe in itself. But that is not a new phenomenon. Every great historic change has been accomplished in fear, risk, and anxiety, which I think are inseparable from hope, the will to power, and revolutionary action itself. And every revolution is made of thousands and millions (soon billions) of human lives composed of emotions, feelings of joy or sorrow, of hopes, disappointments and fresh starts, of fear, courage, consciousness and unconsciousness. And in my opinion, any revolutionary action which does not have as its objective the realization of the material conditions (including the "intellectual" conditions) that can enable each and every man to assert himself as an individual—and to do so from the outset of the revolutionary action—is not worth undertaking.

Oh, I can hear you muttering: "More dreams that are impossible to realize. We were born to suffer and die," etc. But how can you be sure that we were born for what you say? God has told you so and the curés tell you so. But what does that prove?

I do not want to *be right* but to *live*. Like you, when all is said and done. And that is why the purpose of my ideal and my action is not to prove to you what is true and what is false, but together with you to make a world that is more habitable for me, for you, for us all. The important thing is not to be right metaphysically but to overcome everything that oppresses us, to overcome first the forces that we consciously know are crushing us, hemming us in, suffocating us, so as to be able afterward to overcome and tame the forces of nature that are acting on us without our yet really knowing how. Individually we can do nothing, but *together* we can realize our dreams, which will in turn give birth to other dreams in the generations that follow us.

Nothing has begun with us and nothing will end with us, unless it be our individual existence. And even if some day individuals succeed in overcoming death, that will only be the beginning of a new era, a new history, also made of "revolutions." Will there come a day when life can evolve without death?

Now I've launched into some pretty profound reflections, into questions which neither you nor I can answer, but which remain. I should like to get rid of all these questions. But it seems to me that if I did, I would quickly change into an apathetic clod, moved at most, from time to time, by transitory adventures, superficial and soon forgotten.

My dreams are "measureless," and yet I am an ordinary man, I think. I cannot "live my life" without working to make the revolution, and it seems to me that it is pretty much the same for you. It is not a question of playing at being heroes—besides, who can do that, in the era of the atomic bomb and the agonizing war in Vietnam?— but of getting *together* to build a new world in which ordinary men, like you and me, will no longer be the niggers of the millionaires, the warmongers, and the preachers of passivity, but will be free at last to subject the world to their "whims": love, scientific curiosity, creation . . . in solidarity and equality, in modesty and pride.

Notes

1. This is not the expression of a personalist but of Marx and Engels. Cf. *The German Ideology*, New York, International Publishers, 1939, p. 78.
2. We shall see below everything that is implied by the expression "total revolution."
3. A little further on we shall take up briefly these difficult questions, whose solution is of *vital* importance to the success or failure of the total, completely human revolution carried out by and for man, which constitutes "our ideal."
4. My comrade Charles Gagnon has undertaken a critique of Marxist historical determinism. This critique, which is still in the embryonic stage, al-

ready contains many positive aspects that are capable of completely renewing Marxism, or rather, I believe, of making it disappear as an independent, self-sufficient system of thought. In the hands of the commissars of the Soviet and Western Communist parties (in the East no less than in the West), Marxism—alas!—has become an ideology enslaved to the economic and political interests of a new bourgeoisie whose instrument of economic domination is state capitalism. Marx, Engels, and Lenin are in part responsible for this state of affairs, which is called "revisionism." But only in part. The positive aspect of their critique of philosophical idealism and of illusory capitalist democracy deserves to be better known and studied in greater depth. But their vision of the world, it must be remembered, dates from more than a century ago. And Marx and Engels never read—could not read—Freud, Lévi-Strauss, Einstein, Heisenberg, and the great contemporary physicists, biologists, psychoanalysts, structuralists, sociologists, anthropologists, and psychologists. But the "Marxists" of today do not have the excuse of being unaware of the giant strides made by contemporary science.

I am personally very grateful to my friend Charles Gagnon for having introduced a certain dose of "relativism" into my Marxism (which to me was at first an instrument of struggle rather than an object of research). I hope that notwithstanding the very hard conditions of prison life, Charles will be able to pursue his research and someday give us the benefit of the results of his arduous labor.

I think that in these days, taking into account the present results obtained by science, one should speak of "historical relativism," that is, of a determined relativism (cf. Einstein), perceived, conceived, and reconceived, and applied concretely, through individual or collective acts, by the men of each particular historical period.

This "historical relativism," which to me is an intuition rather than a system of thought and a clear vision of reality, seems to me to leave man his full measure of freedom, the freedom given him by his nature as a conscious, acting, social being, capable today of converting matter into energy and so on.

5. This principle can be crudely summed up as follows: the more precisely the speed of an electron is measured, the less certainly can its position as a particle within an atom be determined.
6. Because that which is determined is not necessarily determining.
7. What I mean here by "technique" and "discipline" goes far beyond the meaning usually given those words by professional military men. Thus, the study of the pure sciences can be as much a part of revolutionary technique, as I understand that term, as the study of the handling of weapons, of purely military strategy and the tactics of guerrilla warfare.
8. See *Dimanche-Matin*, Montreal, September 18, 1966, p. 4.

9. I condemn here only the nationalism of the exploiters and not that of the exploited, the poor, the humiliated. Cf. footnote 13 in Chapter 1 on American black nationalism.

10. Whether they are aware of it or not makes no difference.

11. Especially the union leaders (those at the base and the others), who have an immense social responsibility and who have no right to wash their hands of it.

12. By "power" I mean here not only the power to oppress the masses politically and exploit their labor, but also the power to *force* them into buying, through advertising; into racism, through films, comics, radio, and television; into guilt, through the invention of various moral systems based on sin; into indebtedness and insecurity, through the deification of credit; into the illusion of living in a democracy, when, carried away by huge party machines, they mindlessly exercise "their" right to vote; into an unhealthy delight in the contempt for sexuality and love, through obscene "slick" publications; lastly, into self-destruction, through the refined "culture" of sadism, masochism, etc., presented as the behavior of liberation (individual liberation, of course).

13. Taxes are lower and "privileges" more numerous in Montreal East than in Montreal itself. Nearly all big industry is located in the suburbs. And that is not the result of chance.

14. A very important struggle is going on at present within the RIN between the Left and the Right of this separatist party. The RIN's support of the Lachute strikers in 1966 suggests that the Left is in power right now, but only by a slim majority. If the influx of young people into the RIN continues to increase, the Left will probably be strengthened. But a movement to the right remains possible, and a "grand coalition" of the RIN, the RN, and the National Union would be enough to place Quebec under the yoke of an out-and-out fascist government.

   One thing troubles me: that the RIN hesitates to take a position radically opposing the war in Vietnam and American imperialism, which nonetheless controls 80 percent of the country this party wants to "liberate."

   It is up to the rank and file of the RIN to orient their party in the right direction while there is yet time. Pierre Bourgault seems to me to be a little too wavering. That may be because he has no solid base of support either on the Left or on the Right. And is he himself sure on whose support he wants to base his policy?

15. Primarily in so far as basic industry is concerned. In the other sectors of the economy socialized production coexists with cooperative and individual production; especially in the consumer-goods sector, where the USSR is calling more and more on foreign capitalist corporations.

16. Cf. Charles Bettelheim, *Planification et croissance accélérée*, Paris, François Maspero, 1964, p. 25.
17. This somewhat difficult, but precise, vocabulary is borrowed from Bettelheim.
18. For my part, I believe that in order to achieve what Marx calls "a community of free individuals, carrying on their work with the means of production in common, in which the labour-power of all the different individuals is consciously applied as the combined labour power of the community" (quoted by Engels in *Herr Eugen Dühring's Revolution in Science* [*Anti-Dühring*], trans. Emile Burns, New York, International Publishers, p. 149), there must be a multinational revolutionary movement capable of definitively crushing imperialism. And unlike Marx, I do not believe that such an overthrow has anything in common with an imaginary "withering away" that is tied to the very development of capitalist production, as death is tied to human life, with, as Marx puts it, "the inexorability of a law of Nature" (*Anti-Dühring*, p. 152). I do not believe in inexorability. I believe in revolution.
19. All that, of course, in addition to agitation, propaganda, political action both legal and illegal, etc., etc.

7

After the Trial*

In a political commentary on the Palestinian armed resistance to the Israeli occupation, Monsieur Jean-Marc Léger, one of the most prominent journalists in Quebec and the leading representative of the nationalist petty bourgeoisie, wrote in Le Devoir of January 16, 1969: "All the resisters of history have been terrorists."

The petty bourgeoisie, liberal or social-democratic, accords to the Arab "terrorists," as to the Vietnamese fighters, the political status of "resisters." But when it comes to the Québécois "terrorists," the nature of their actions, so to speak, is regarded as radically different by the indigenous petty bourgeoisie, which feels its own privileges threatened by the "terrorism" of the Front de libération du Québec (FLQ). That is why the petty bourgeoisie of Quebec, notwithstanding the political struggle it is waging against Canadian colonialism, insists on considering the partisans of the FLQ as "criminals" or, at best, as irresponsible and dangerous "anarchists."

Of course, it would be very different if the FLQ were the armed avant-garde of the nationalist petty bourgeoisie and were content to demand legal, formal, purely political sovereignty for Quebec. But the FLQ is, on the contrary, the armed avant-garde of the exploited classes of Quebec: the workers, the farmers, the petty white-collar workers, the students, the unemployed, and those on welfare—that is, at least 90 percent of the population. The FLQ is struggling not only for the political independence of Quebec, but also and insepara-

---

* This chapter, written from Montreal Jail, is dated February 6, 1969, or two years after the rest of the book was completed. In the interim, the first edition of Nègres blancs d'Amérique had been published in Quebec, by Editions Parti pris. (Trans.)

bly for the revolution, a total revolution which will give all power to the workers and students in a free, self-administering, and fraternal society. Only a total revolution will make it possible for the Québécois, in collaboration with the other peoples of the earth, to build a Quebec that is truly free, truly sovereign.

The nationalist petty bourgeoisie is incapable of leading this revolution, or even desiring it, because it is completely dependent on American imperialism, in whose hands—in the framework of the Canadian Confederation, or in the future framework of a "sovereign" republic—it is only an obedient puppet. A parasitic class *par excellence*, the French-speaking petty bourgeoisie of Quebec can demand and obtain only the appearance of power. The true masters are on Wall Street and in Washington, for only total revolution will be able to destroy the economic, political, and cultural bases of the domination of Quebec by the U.S.A. The nationalist petty bourgeoisie, caught between American imperialism, which tomorrow may use it as a screen—in place of the English Canadians—and the exploited classes whose interests are radically and definitively opposed to its own, can survive as a semi-ruling class only on the condition that it becomes the *sole* manager of imperialist interests in Quebec. For the Québécois, petty bourgeoisie separatism is the only means that will enable it to play the same role in Quebec that the Anglo-Saxon petty bourgeoisie plays in Canada as a whole, the parasitic role of prison guard and policeman of American interests. That is why the petty bourgeoisie of Quebec is separatist.

The exploited classes of Quebec are also separatist, but for quite different reasons. For them, separatism, along with the destruction of the capitalist structures, is the means of wresting Quebec from the clutches of American imperialism. It is a struggle for both the national liberation of Quebec and the total social liberation of the Québécois.

The petty bourgeoisie may achieve its ends by means of elections, an invention of the capitalists designed to give the masses the illusion of a certain degree of democracy. But as in many other so-called decolonized countries, it may also have to resort to violence to overcome the stubborn resistance of the "Rhodesians" of Quebec, the Anglo-Saxon minority which has hitherto been all-powerful.

The exploited classes, on the other hand, have no choice. The only way in which they can oppose the organized violence of imperialism and its local representatives (English-speaking or French-speaking) is by the revolutionary violence initiated by the FLQ in 1963.

Ever since revolutionary violence broke out in Quebec, it has haunted the sleepless nights of the ruling classes (American, English-Canadian, and Québécois), and they are trying every means to crush it, or at least discredit it. But since this violence is the product of the very contradictions of the colonial, capitalist system, it can disappear only with the system itself. That, of course, is something the ruling classes want neither to believe nor to see. And one cannot blame them for systematically refusing to envisage their own more or less imminent disappearance!

Hence the ferocity with which the Establishment hounds political prisoners, whenever it can use them as scapegoats. For to the Establishment the economic and political crisis rocking Quebec (and the world) is obviously provoked by the FLQ, the unions, and foreign "agitators" who have come to "corrupt" the youth of Quebec.

Whenever partisans of the FLQ are brought before the courts, the bourgeois treat them as if they were common criminals or mentally ill. Of course there is no question of officially according them the status of political prisoners because, for the ruling classes, that would be to admit that one can radically and practically challenge the present system without necessarily being a gangster or a lunatic. But the established Order has every interest in making revolutionaries out to be gangsters and lunatics.

In Quebec, at least in the upper spheres, the FLQ itself is not considered a political movement. At most, people sometimes speak of a political "gang," as if it were a ramification of the local underworld. But if officially the partisans of the FLQ are considered criminals, in practice they are treated so much more harshly than real criminals by the courts, the government, the police, and the bourgeois press that the political and revolutionary character of their struggle readily appears to the masses who read the newspapers, look at television, and attend the caricatures of trials that partisans of the FLQ have been undergoing periodically since 1963. The masses recognize the partisans of the FLQ for what they really are, and that is all that matters. As for the ruling classes, their behavior toward political prisoners is so arbitrary that it continues, by its very ferocity, to draw the attention of the exploited to these new "heroes," and to confirm by concrete examples the injustice inherent in the system. Thus, the more relentlessly the established Order pursues the FLQ, the more the FLQ's prestige increases and the more its influence spreads, especially among the most disadvantaged, whom everything daily incites to armed rebellion. In vain do the authorities multiply rewards; the population does not collaborate with the police in the hunt for "terrorists." On the contrary, the population is always giving the police additional headaches by daily turning in dozens of false bomb alarms in the city of Montreal alone, and by sending the investigators off on false trails. While the police waste time and the government grows impatient, the FLQ (which with each arrest the authorities consider to be definitively broken) constantly expands its action.

In the meantime, of course, as in all countries where armed struggle has begun, there are revolutionaries mouldering in prison where, notwithstanding their isolation and the foul conditions of detention, they are pursuing their education as militants and ceaselessly preparing themselves for the combats that await them. For prison will end some day, but the struggle will go on; and then they must be ready, no matter how much time they have spent behind bars.

I am one of those political prisoners, members of the Front de libération du Québec, on whom the Establishment angrily spews its contempt and fear.

Arrested in New York on September 28, 1966, together with Charles Gagnon, while we were demonstrating in front of the United Nations in order to draw the attention of world opinion to the liberation struggle developing in Quebec and to the fate reserved for Québécois political prisoners who are members of the FLQ, then deported illegally to Montreal on January 13, 1967, I waited more than a year for my first trial. At the end of this first trial, which lasted six weeks, I was condemned on April 5, 1968, by Judge Yves Leduc of Montreal, to life imprisonment, having been fraudulently found guilty of manslaughter. Half a dozen other accusations were drawn up against me, and if the Attorney General does not withdraw them in the meantime, I shall have to go through at least six more trials (when?) and doubtless see myself sentenced six more times to life imprisonment! For no matter what charges are brought against me, I am judged *solely* for my activities in the FLQ, and therefore I must automatically incur the maximum penalty provided by law—that is, life imprisonment, capital punishment having recently been abolished except for the murder of a policeman or prison guard in the performance of his duty.

I consider my trial to have been a great political victory for the Front de libération du Québec, because the Prosecution found it impossible to conduct a case in accordance with the regulations of the British Criminal Code (which is still in force in Quebec) and was obliged to fabricate illegally, with the complicity of the judge, "proof" of a political nature, based particularly on my writings (including *White Niggers of America* and the pamphlet "Qu'est-ce que le FLQ?") Now, as I had not been accused of inciting to violence or of an attempt against the security of the state, but of murder, no proof of a political nature could legally be brought before the Court, but only *facts* that might connect me directly or indirectly with the murder. Of course, the Prosecution could not produce any facts relevant to the case. The few "accomplices" called by the Prosecution unequivocally cleared me of the accusation of murder, a fact which under ordinary procedures should have automatically led to my acquittal without my even having to present a defense, for in fact *there was no case!*

So during the six weeks my trial lasted, from February 26 to April 5, 1968, very little was said about the murder charge that had been brought against me. It was not a trial of an alleged murderer but of the Front de libération du Québec and the Quebec revolution in general. The exhibits placed on record by the Prosecution were almost exclusively political writings: copies of the clandestine newspaper *La Cognée*, mimeographed lectures by professors at the University of Montreal, political analyses published by the Parti socialiste du Québec and the Mouvement de libération populaire, pamphlets, books, etc.

To make things easier, the original indictment was changed twice: the first time during the first few hours of the trial, and the second time *after* the Prosecution had rested its case and the Defense (in this instance, the accused) had moved that the case be dismissed for lack of evidence. The second change in the indictment was made in order to include the following clarification: I was henceforth accused of having participated in the murder of Mademoiselle Thérèse Morin, who died in the course of a bomb attack in May 1966, "by my speech, *writings,* attitudes, etc." This modification, which transformed the very nature of the accusation, was made by the judge, Yves Leduc, even though the writings produced by the Prosecution in the course of the trial were purely theoretical and could in no way connect me with the bombing which took place on May 5, 1966.

But neither the Prosecution nor the judge, both of whom represented the established Order, could act otherwise unless they agreed to my being acquitted and set free. Now to the established Order, Charles Gagnon and I are the leaders of the Front de libération du Québec and obviously constitute a "security risk." Neither of us denies our membership in the FLQ and our complete solidarity with the FLQ's actions. On the contrary! Even in prison, we never stop being active propagandists for the FLQ and the Quebec revolution. But in the face of the obstinate refusal of the authorities to grant us the official status of political prisoners, we for our part refuse to plead guilty to committing common crimes, and in court it is we who defend legality, that is, the rules of the Criminal Code, and it is the Prosecution and the judge who are forced to resort to illegal maneuvers!

I should make it clear at this point that, like Charles Gagnon, I decided to undertake my own defense, as I am authorized to do by the Criminal Code, and this enables me to *attack* the established Order on both the legal plane and the political plane, which is something no Québécois lawyer could allow himself to do without being automatically disbarred, for the Bar is directly and solidly controlled by the all-powerful caste of English-speaking lawyers, who are intimately linked with high finance.

It is the duty of every revolutionary who is arrested and tried by the bourgeoisie to make every effort to use the Court for his ends by vigorously attacking the established Order. A trial, if it is well conducted, can be a very important political act and can even have a determining influence on the course of the revolution. No situation is ever hopeless and everything can be used for revolutionary ends.

There had not been a political trial in Quebec for a very long time until the authorities decided, under pressure of public opinion, to bring my case to trial on February 26, 1968. (Charles Gagnon, who was to have been judged with me, is still awaiting trial after two and a half years of incarceration! ° Since my trial, the authorities have realized that they cannot have the partisans of the FLQ condemned without at the same time providing them wonderful opportunities for spreading their ideology among the masses, discrediting the lackeys of colonialism and imperialism, and carrying the class struggle into the courtroom itself. Some judges are now wondering if the state will not have to institute special tribunals, courts martial, to judge the partisans of the FLQ. But the authorities fear the consequences of such an initiative which, from my point of view, would at least have the advantage of clarifying things.)

Before my trial opened, no one seriously believed that I would succeed in turning the legal debates into a political battle. All but two of the lawyers whom Charles Gagnon and I had consulted believed it was impossible to politicize a trial in Quebec. Above all, they did not want to be implicated in such a trial, and they put pressure on us to plead guilty from the opening of the case, even trying to persuade us that by fighting to the end we would be breaking with those of our comrades who, yielding to this sort of pressure in a moment of panic or discouragement, had consented to plead guilty to the many and multi-sectioned charges brought against them. In so doing, our comrades had only followed the example of many a political prisoner brought before the courts of Quebec. Since 1963 it had become almost a tradition for political prisoners to plead guilty. Because any legal battle seemed lost in advance. The attorneys for the defense (even those who were highly paid by the relatives of certain partisans) periodically tried to convince them that there was nothing to be gained from a trial and openly collaborated with the prosecuting attorneys, the judges, and the police to prevent the opening of trials which could not fail to be political. Like the government authorities, the attorneys for the defense feared political trials more than anything else. They presented their "clients" as romantics and delinquents. They supplied "psychological explanations" for their acts and asked the courts for a false indulgence, paternalistic and hypo-

---

° Charles Gagnon has since been tried, after twenty-seven and one-half months in prison. The trial lasted ten weeks, and as the jury was unable to reach a unanimous verdict, the judge ordered a new trial. (Publisher.)

critical. There is nothing surprising in that: practically all the Québécois lawyers form a caste of privileged men who are not in the least
interested in serving the revolution and revolutionaries, because that
would automatically eliminate their chances of someday becoming
judges or members of Parliament.

In Quebec, therefore, a political trial cannot be brought about by
the lawyers for the defense but only by the accused, providing he un-
dertakes his own defense. In the jungle of legal procedures, the political prisoner is thus terribly alone. His only allies are the audience (silent on pain of being expelled), a handful of journalists, and one or
two legal advisers who are sympathetic to his case but gagged by the
Court.

To assume my own defense during six long weeks was a task at
once exalting and very heavy. Of course I had had no experience on
the floor of a court and I had only a theoretical knowledge of the
rules of procedure. At each session I had to present the legal arguments, make the motions, examine or cross-examine the witnesses as
the case might be, alone. Between sessions I had to analyze the testi-
mony of previous witnesses, interview my own witnesses, prepare my
address to the Court (which lasted a day and a half) and search the
Code and the abundant British jurisprudence for arguments that
might be used to counter the illegal maneuvers of the Prosecution
and the Court, maneuvers which came up anew every day throughout the trial and which were profoundly instructive to me as to the
perfidy, hypocrisy, and dishonesty of those who, under the present
regime, incarnate what they call Justice.

I was assisted by two legal advisers, Maître Robert Lemieux and
Maître Bernard S. Mergler, who gave me total support but whom the
bench had forbidden to open their mouths in court. All that they
were authorized to do was give me hasty advice between arguments
or examinations of witnesses.

I was therefore alone opposite a hostile judge, two fierce prosecuting attorneys, and several tenacious police officers who effectively assisted the Court in this trial. The jury had difficulty following the debates because every time a point of law was argued they were sent
out of the room, the judge being sole master of the law under the
English system. As for the press, it did not have the right to report,
much less comment on, what was said or done in the absence of the

jury. As half the trial—the most political half—took place in the absence of the jury, persons who did not attend the whole trial could not completely understand the battle that went on there. Nevertheless, in the course of the many examinations and cross-examinations —which absolutely *had* to take place in the presence of the jury and which were extensively reported by the press—it was relatively easy for me, thanks to the great number of political exhibits offered in evidence by the Prosecution, to engage and win the political battle I had deliberately sought.

Very often during the course of the trial I made a particular effort to unmask the arbitrary nature of the system. For example, on several occasions I reminded the judge and the Prosecution that they had publicly committed themselves to judge me as a common-law criminal, in this instance as a common murderer, and that consequently it was illegal and dishonest to try to have me condemned for murder on the basis of my political writings or the fact that I openly acknowledged myself to be a partisan of the FLQ. I asked the Prosecution either to be consistent and limit itself solely to those facts which were relevant to a murder case, or else to try me for inciting to revolution and attacking the security of the state. I repeated many times over, during the course of the trial, that I was ready to be tried for my ideas, my membership in the FLQ, and my political activity as a whole over the last five or six years, but that I could not agree to their trying to have me condemned for murder on the basis of proof of a political nature. Of course, as I expected, my arguments were systematically rejected by the Court, although from a legal point of view they were irrefutably sound. The essential thing was not to obtain the assent of the Court or its good will, but to use these arguments as a springboard for carrying the debates to the highest level, the political level.

In fact, by placing my writings, ideas, and political activities at the center of the debates, the Prosecution and the judge gave me powerful assistance in attaining the objectives I had set for myself when I decided to undertake my own defense to the end. Throughout the trial I never stopped denouncing their hypocrisy, but at the same time I made no secret of the satisfaction they afforded me by thus trying my ideas and political activities while claiming to judge me as a common criminal. The innumerable irregularities they were forced to commit day after day constituted an irrefutable demonstration of everything the FLQ has been denouncing and combating since 1963. What the established Order feared would happen in an officially political trial occurred anyway in the framework of a trial that they wanted at all costs to be "ordinary." For the sole fact of summoning a revolutionary before the courts, no matter what charge is brought against him (was not Mulele accused of rapes and murders?), in itself constitutes a political act. How could it be otherwise, since where a revolutionary is concerned, all things—his ideas, actions, motivations—are of a political nature? A revolutionary cannot be made to undergo a common-law trial unless he renounces all consciousness and honor. Whenever a revolutionary is put on trial, the very nature of the court is transformed by contact with him. The Court, whether it says so or not, automatically becomes an exceptional tribunal because it finds itself faced with an exceptional case. A thief or a killer does not oppose the system even if he violates its laws from time to time, while every revolutionary wants and seeks to destroy the system, to replace it by a new society and, consequently, to overthrow the ruling classes that the Court represents.

As I stressed in my address to the Court, my trial can be called historic because for the first time since the Louis Riel affair at the end of the nineteenth century, revolutionary violence was put on trial in Quebec. Judge Yves Leduc himself notes in his report to the Court of Appeals: "We are dealing in this instance with a case that is of a public interest unique in our legal annals. This trial will have serious consequences, and the Court has a heavy responsibility; it is important that both Justice and Peace reign in our tormented society." And further on, commenting on my sentence, the judge declares: "As for the sentence, it is with unspeakable sorrow [oh Tartuffe!] that the judge thought it his duty to impose on the accused the maximum penalty provided by law. Indeed, it is manifest that the accused, behind walls, has continued to publish and is still publishing incitements to violence and revolution in this Province [of Quebec]." Etc. . . .

Shortly after my condemnation I wrote my friends and comrades a long letter which sums up well my feelings at the time, feelings I have always had, from the beginning of my incarceration to this day.

I take the liberty of reproducing this letter below in its entirety.

Montreal, April 29, 1968

Dear friends and comrades,

First of all, know that I am in the best of health and that my condemnation to life imprisonment has in no way affected my determination to fight to the end everywhere, even in prison, for the liberation of the white niggers of Quebec.

All I want at this time is that my trial and condemnation should make you even more aware of the arbitrary nature of the accursed system that oppresses us and fortify you in your convictions and your action.

It was a very important victory for the FLQ and for the Quebec revolution to have driven the Crown and the Court to politicize my trial themselves, beyond anything we could have hoped. In imposing this murder trial on me, the established Order unmasked itself and was forced to reveal its true face to the people—the face of dictatorship and despotism.

Now, it is important to exploit this historic event to the maximum so as to demonstrate to the exploited masses the fundamentally arbitrary character of bourgeois laws, laws which it is the function of the judicial apparatus, together with the police and the army, to use in the defense, maintenance, and promotion of the privileges and political and economic interests of the ruling class alone, the capitalist class which is bound by allegiance to colonialism and Anglo-American imperialism.

You must not be left stupefied or crushed by the very heavy sentence that Judge Leduc has had the eminently Christian and bourgeois kindness to grant me at the end of this long political trial. (The established Order must not feel very secure in 1968 if it treats my insignificant person with so much severity and honor!)

Nor must you be content to cry out your revolt, indignation, or nausea. You must act. And act quickly.

The time for recriminations within the family, around a table littered with bottles of beer, is over. It is in the streets and in action that battles are lost or won. And we must win! Our freedom, our dignity, our very existence are at stake. Are we going to resign ourselves in practice, all our lives, to slavery (hard or easy) and humiliation, sounding off about the evils of the system in our spare time?

If we are to free ourselves completely from the slavery in which we are trapped by the present system, we must first cease to be slaves to our fears, our cowardices, our hesitations, and all the little habits of men who are resigned or benumbed. It is time to take the leap and plunge deep into struggle.

It serves no purpose to shout about the treatment of Québécois political prisoners by the colonialists and their local watchdogs unless you yourself are ready to fight as they have done—and as they will do again, once they are freed from the jails of oppression and contempt.

Perhaps you will say that I am going too far, that I am soaring in the realm of the absolute without taking into account the everyday realities in which each individual is necessarily more or less entangled. As a matter of fact, I know all that very well . . . and all the rest too. But just the same, one must face up to the fundamental questions and answers, and also to the tasks imposed by those questions and answers—which you know as well as I do.

Our liberation is essentially a practical problem. And it is by practice, through action, that it will be resolved. Theories and speeches are of value only to the extent that they illuminate and stimulate action. Without action, without practice, they ring hollow and produce nothing.

It is up to you to define and carry out the action which, in the milieu where you are working, is most likely to accelerate the process of our decolonization and our emancipation as a people and an oppressed class. I am counting on you—my comrades in prison are counting on you—to see to it that this action is never exchanged or abandoned for some borrowed comfort, for an illusory promise of victory without combat, or for a nonviolence that is ineffective and too often the accomplice of oppression and the exploitation of man by man. Even if violence is a phenomenon detestable in itself, it is nonetheless true that for exploited and colonized people like ourselves, freedom grows out of the barrel of a gun. The so-called social peace that the bourgeoisie wants to impose on us with nightsticks is itself continuous violence exercised against our freedom and our right to call the capitalist, colonial order into question, to destroy it and replace it by another order more in conformity with our aspirations, more worthy of man. Those who become the accomplices of this false peace help to maintain the dictatorship, to reinforce illusions of democracy, and to delay the development of a revolutionary class consciousness among the exploited masses.

We shall really be able to "build peace" only on the day when revolutionary violence, armed and conscious, counters the violence that the capitalists, colonialists, and imperialists, the exploiters of the people, exercise daily against the workers, students, young people, and progressive intellectuals, against 90 percent of the population of Quebec. When the present system is destroyed we shall build peace together, and at the same time fraternity and justice. But in order to attain this objective, we must first build a revolutionary movement and a people's army together. We must first organize together a violence—a force—capable of liberating us all from the multiple forms of slavery, domination, and alienation that subjugate us collectively and individually from the time we are in the cradle. We shall become free to the extent that, together, we have the courage to take up the weapons of our liberation and to fight to conquer. We shall be able to build peace, equality, fraternity, and justice to the extent that, together, we find the way to win the war imposed on us by our condition as white niggers. We must win the war, and not just a battle here and there every fifty years.

We are not the only ones who are struggling to win our freedom! Far from it! Our struggle is linked to the many peoples' wars that are developing in the four corners of the world against the common enemy: American imperialism. Our battles—the battles of the Québécois, the French-speaking people of America, the white niggers—interest the other oppressed peoples as their battles interest us and concern us directly. We are all interdependent and responsible for each other. None of us, without betraying his brothers, can exempt himself from the tasks which the construction of a more human world imposes, on a planetary scale. Not to be engaged is always to collaborate with the enemy. Neutrality does not exist anywhere.

Dear friends and comrades, these words are not new, and other revolutionaries, much better qualified than I, have shouted them the world over. Some of us, indeed the best, have paid with their lives for having put these elementary truths into practice.

I wanted to greet you today by reminding you, once again, of the profound meaning of our struggle and our sacrifices. That seems essential to me if my trial and its temporary dénouement are to be placed in their true perspective. My trial was also yours. My trial was the trial of the anger of the exploited of Quebec. My trial was the trial of the workers, students, young people, and revolutionary intellectuals just as much as it was the trial of the FLQ and one of its members. My condemnation to life imprisonment is precisely the sentence that the established Order thinks it has imposed on the Quebec revolution, which is guilty of wanting to overthrow capitalism and destroy imperialism. But by condemning an individual, a member of the FLQ, the established Order has not abolished the overall situation that created the necessity for a revolution in Quebec. On the contrary, by this trial and condemnation, the established Order has even contributed to the acceleration of the revolutionary process.

My friends, my comrades, my brothers, I am certain of it,
WE WILL WIN!
Let us not look back but plunge ahead. Forward!

Long live free Quebec!
Long live the revolution!
Long live the FLQ!

Although my trial has been the climax so far, it is not the whole story of the political and revolutionary battle my comrade Charles Gagnon and I have been fighting ever since we were arrested in New York on September 28, 1966.

This long battle, which began at the United Nations building more than two years ago, is still going on. It demands constant effort, high morale, and an enormous amount of patience and faith.

Charles Gagnon and I were practically alone when, in September 1966, we went to the United Nations to cry out our appeal on behalf of those who are fighting in Quebec for the liberation of their country. At that time Quebec had not yet received the visit from General de Gaulle and, consequently, was almost unknown. Quebec, as the saying goes, had not yet been put on the map. In the United States, a few hundred persons at most knew of the existence of a liberation movement in Quebec.

Of course, knowing that the Canadian police were actively looking for us, we could have gone into hiding in the United States, Mexico, or Cuba, instead of appearing at the United Nations. We thought of that. But reading the Quebec newspapers, which at the time were dragging the partisans of the FLQ through the mud and deliberately distorting the meaning of their struggle, we soon became convinced that a practical reply had to be made to this campaign of vilification. The Montreal police had just arrested fifteen or sixteen of our comrades. The newspapers were telling all sorts of more or less fantastic stories about them. They were also saying that Gagnon and I, "the leaders," as they put it, were hiding out in the woods north of Montreal and starving there. The whole dismantled network was being described more or less as a gang of anarchists.

I, personally, had been in the United States for two months and Charles Gagnon for a month. We were actively preparing to return to Quebec, having made contact with the principal revolutionary and progressive organizations in the United States, when we learned from the newspapers that our comrades had been arrested. One of them had been held for a week, secretly and under a false name, and had finally talked. The others had been arrested very quickly.

A few days later, Charles Gagnon and I drafted a statement of solidarity with our comrades in prison in Montreal and went to the United Nations to distribute it to the various delegations. At the same time, we began a hunger strike. At the United Nations some American friends and Canadian and Québécois journalists helped us a great deal. On September 25, 1966, from the United Nations television studios, we launched a five-minute appeal which was broadcast live by the Canadian Broadcasting Corporation from the Atlantic to the Pacific. Our statement of solidarity was widely disseminated by the wire services, and we recorded interviews for radio.

No one knew we were at the UN, and our sudden appearance on Canadian television had the effect of a bomb. And immediately the attitude of the newspapers toward the FLQ partisans who had just been arrested began to change.

The next day, September 26, after a night in a New York hotel, we returned to the United Nations, this time to picket, demand political asylum, and continue our hunger strike. Dozens of journalists and policemen were there. The Canadian police urged their Yankee allies to arrest us on the spot, but they dared not do so because they had no warrant. Our picketing was perfectly legal. After about two hours the New York police made up their minds to "take us in" without a warrant. Once we were at the police station, they made the fantastic accusation that we had entered the United States illegally. Then they offered us voluntary deportation. We refused for political reasons, even though we knew the United States would never grant us political asylum.

We decided to use all legal and political means to fight deportation and, if it came to that, extradition.

We were taken to the Immigration Office to be photographed and card-indexed, and then conducted to the Manhattan House of Detention for Men, known as the "Tombs," where we were to remain for more than three months.

In the Tombs we continued our hunger strike for twenty-nine days, drinking only water and even refusing all medication. Montreal friends contacted two New York lawyers who pretended to defend us but in reality collaborated with the American authorities to "organize" our deportation to Montreal.

Life in the Tombs was not exactly restful, but we were immediately accepted and supported by the prisoners, who often did us precious services. Our hunger strike brought us many letters and unhoped-for expressions of support. While preparing for our return to Montreal, we took maximum advantage of our stay in the Tombs to write letters, newspaper articles, etc. We were afraid that once we were back in Montreal we would be deprived of all means of self-expression and struggle. After the hunger strike, I wrote my book *White Niggers of America* straight through from beginning to end, finishing around January 10 or 12, 1967.

On January 13, 1967, we were kidnapped by the Immigration police and taken to Montreal by plane. Before that, we had appeared in court many times on two charges: illegal entry into the United States and "disturbing the peace" opposite the United Nations building. Two equally ridiculous charges. The Court never proceeded against us on the second charge, and there was one postponement after another, for form's sake. On the charge of illegal entry into the United States, they put us through a parody of a trial in *closed session*. Of course we were found guilty, even though we were able to prove that we had crossed the border openly, passports in hand. We immediately appealed the verdict to the Supreme Court. On Friday, January 13, 1967, at 4:00 P.M., our lawyers were notified that our appeal had been rejected. *At the same time*, a New York judge was annulling the charge of disturbing the peace. We were informed of this "deal" around 7:00 P.M., and they were very careful to advise us that we could undertake no new procedures concerning the deportation case until the following Monday, January 16. We were immediately "liberated" from the Tombs and turned over, handcuffed, to the Immigration police who, refusing to give us any explanation, took us to Kennedy Airport. About 9:00 P.M. the American police turned us over to the Montreal police at Dorval Airport.

We were questioned by officers of the anti-subversive squad of Montreal until around two in the morning. To no purpose. We had nothing to say to them.

Our arraignment was set for Monday, January 16, 1967. There were nearly a dozen charges against us, ranging from stealing dynamite to committing murder. The preliminary investigation of our case, which had been set for the following Monday, was postponed several times and did not take place until March 21, 1967—for the murder charge only—and in June 1967 for the other charges (some of which were withdrawn).

Our trial, which we were to undergo together in May or June, was postponed to September, then to November, to December, to January, and finally to February 1968.

In November 1967 one of our comrades, Richard Bouchoux, was acquitted of the charge of murder. The witnesses in his case were the same as in ours. The Prosecution then began to fear that we might be acquitted and did everything it could to postpone our trial indefinitely. Finally, under the pressure of public opinion, our trial was set for February 26, 1968, nineteen months, to the day, after our arrest.

Charles Gagnon and I were to stand trial together and we had prepared ourselves accordingly. On February 26, to the general surprise, the Prosecution decided to proceed only in my case, postponing Charles' trial to an undetermined date.

I have described my trial above. I will not go back over it here, except to say that it drew the attention of the International Federation for the Rights of Man, which has its headquarters in Brussels. In September 1968 the Federation sent to Quebec Maître Roger Lallemand and Alain Badiou, who had already headed a delegation to Bolivia at the time of the trial of Régis Debray. At the same time a Committee to Support the Political Prisoners of Quebec, headed by Maître Nicole Dreyfus, was created in Paris. A number of French in-

tellectuals, including Jacques Berque, J.-M. Damenach, Alain Res-
nais, Jean-Luc Godard, the staff of the review *Partisans* (Maspero),
Roger Garaudy, Michèle Ray, *et al.*, signed a petition in our behalf.
In Montreal, as far back as November 1966, a Committee to Assist
the Vallières-Gagnon Group had been formed. Over the last two-
and-a-half years this Committee has done an enormous amount of
political work among students, unionized workers, and intellectuals,
constantly explaining our fight to them. The Committee has often
gone out into the streets to demonstrate and has not been content
simply to draft press releases. Today it no longer limits itself to defending political prisoners: in collaboration with the most radical
Left movements, such as the Front de libération populaire and the
citizens' committees, the Committee is working to achieve in action
the unity of the revolutionary forces of Quebec and to formulate a
revolutionary ideology adapted to the situation in Quebec. (It must
be said that the ideological baggage of the Québécois militants is
generally too scanty for the tasks imposed on them by the present situation. There is an enormous lag to be made up in this area.)

In the United States also we have received support, especially
from *Monthly Review*, Stokely Carmichael, many partisans of the
Black Power movement, the Black Panthers, Youth Against War and
Fascism, certain "draft dodgers," etc. . . .

I have appealed the verdict and the sentence in my case, but I
have not yet been able to obtain a hearing before the Court of Appeals of Quebec. As for Charles, his trial for murder has not yet taken
place *after two and a half years of detention.* The Prévost Commis-
sion, which was set up by the Quebec government to investigate the
administration of justice, has recently denounced the treatment of
Gagnon, and the "Gagnon affair," as it is now called, has taken on
the proportions of a veritable political and judicial scandal.

In September 1968 Gagnon and I went on a seventeen-day hunger
strike to protest this state of affairs. The strike, which was supported
by 400 other inmates of Montreal Jail, forced the Ministry of Justice
to make written promises—promises which, however, it later failed
to keep.

Will Gagnon be judged at last or will he remain illegally imprisoned on charges that the established Order is unable to prove?

Since my trial and condemnation, the Québécois judges seem afraid to compromise themselves in a new political affair. Perhaps, sensing the change in the wind, they are thinking of their future . . .

On the other hand, since the summer of 1968 there has been a great expansion of revolutionary action in Quebec. In Montreal alone there have been more than sixty bombings. In October 1968 tens of thousands of students occupied the educational institutions for several days, and the workers of the Domtar company occupied their factories, weapons in hand. Violent demonstrations have multiplied and agitation has become considerably more radical. The sudden death of Premier Daniel Johnson has weakened the government party—the National Union—which is now divided into two factions, the nationalists and the federalists. On the economic plane, there is total stagnation. Unemployment is increasing, investments are decreasing, the state coffers are empty. At all levels of government one finds only instability and panic.

Meanwhile, the independence current is growing stronger from day to day, and in the next few months the quarrels over language in Montreal might well lead to street fighting.

The newspapers, radio, and television talk about nothing but violence, rebellion, protest, and revolution. The ruling classes are desperately trying to find themselves a dictator. The police are preparing the ground for a Québécois Hitler who could restore "law and order." Fortunately, Quebec has no army and no colonels! But the police are increasingly conscious of the political role they may soon feel it their "duty" to play if the unrest continues and if the economic and political crisis is not solved.

It is against this background that one must place the "Gagnon affair." If the Establishment "grants" Gagnon a trial, will that trial not be the opportunity the revolutionaries have been waiting for to throw the high priests out and rouse the people to revolt against the established authorities? Never since 1837 have the ruling classes had such a feeling of panic. But how much longer will they be able to keep Charles Gagnon in prison awaiting judgment, without provoking the wrath they fear?

And what will become of all the charges that were brought against

Gagnon and me in September 1966 and are still pending? Are they determined to put us through six or seven trials apiece? At the rate at which cases come to trial in Quebec, we have another fifteen years of court battles ahead of us!!

Charles Gagnon and I have no illusions. We expect absolutely nothing good, nothing just, nothing clean from the established disorder. But we are convinced that in a few years the coming to power of the advocates of independence will free us from prison. Of course the coming to power of the *indépendantistes,* now led by the liberal reformist René Lévesque, will not coincide with the revolution we want to make. We will still have to fight. For we shall not be truly liberated until the day capitalism and imperialism are vanquished.

Meantime, while waiting for the day of our liberation, we are not wasting our time in prison. We are studying and writing a great deal. We are completing our education as men and as militants.

We enjoy no special status or privilege in prison, unless it is that we are subjected to closer surveillance than the other prisoners.

We can receive almost all the books we want, including political and revolutionary works. We get the newspapers every day. We do not feel too isolated from those who are fighting "on the outside." But we are impatient to take up the struggle again beside our comrades.

My experience as a political prisoner has enriched me considerably so far. It has taught me a great deal about men, about individuals, about society in general and Quebec society in particular. I do not regret the time I am spending here, even if I could be more useful elsewhere. I mean to take the maximum advantage of prison life to better understand Man, whom it is our ideal to transform, to de-alienate, to liberate completely.

Some day I shall write a book recounting in detail everything I have experienced in prison, everything I have seen and understood there, loved and hated. My story, like the experience I have been living through for more than two years, will no doubt be very hard, but also very human. For here in prison man has no more secrets from man. He takes off all his masks. He is naked as a worm. He is *true*.

And this man—my double, my brother, as Baudelaire would say—

never have I loved him so much as now. And never have I hated so much the system that oppresses him.

I am completely reconciled with my country, Quebec, which in former days I thought only of fleeing and forgetting. But like Guevara, I would not hesitate to go and fight imperialism in another country if some day the "great darkness" once more descended upon Quebec and made all action impossible. But the situation in Quebec would have to be truly hopeless.

I am 100 percent Québécois, and it is in Quebec first that I want to pursue the struggle against imperialism. It is in Quebec that I hope with all my heart to overcome tyranny with my comrades, or else to die with them, weapons in hand.

If I were a citizen of the United States, it is in the United States that I would fight first. Revolution is not impossible anywhere. It is necessary in all countries, including today most of the so-called socialist countries.

It does not matter what country is our "native land." It does not matter what difficulties we are daily confronted with: *our duty as revolutionaries*, wherever we may be, *is to make the revolution*, as Guevara so well reminded us before he was vilely assassinated by the CIA in Bolivia.

And even in prison, this duty must take precedence over everything else.

By Way of Epilogue*

Often, in writing this book, I have asked myself: Am I right? Am I wrong? But really, what do I care about being right?

It is not a question of being right, my friends, but of overcoming the exploitation of man by man, of overcoming without betraying oneself or one's people. And if we are to overcome tomorrow, we must begin to fight today. To be sure, we must make every effort to see clearly. That is essential. But we must avoid the trap of imaginary certainties, of postwar dreams. We are at war, and have been for centuries, against those who exploit us. Let us not think that we shall win someday by a divine miracle. Neither let us wait until we know precisely what our world will be like after our revolution. But starting now, let us organize ourselves in such a way as to make this world as human as possible. Because we are forced to *make* history every day; we are not going to wake up one morning and find ourselves in a radically transformed society without having brought the transformation about ourselves. And which of us can describe what does not yet exist? We make plans, but we know that those plans will be modified, improved, and perfected by our action, as we become more clear-sighted and more experienced in struggle. And it is by giving the maximum of ourselves today, by practicing today the principles which have become ours, by translating into action the consciousness we have today, that we shall develop both our strength and our consciousness, that we shall become truly responsible and free.

Let us not wait for a Messiah to bring us a magical solution to our problems. Let us reflect, let us sharpen our tools, roll up our sleeves and *all together* set to work! The revolution is *our* affair, the affair of

* This final chapter was written at the same time as the bulk of the book, while Vallières was still in the Tombs, and was included in the first edition. (Trans.)

the niggers. Let us not wait to get started on it until the Pope or the President of the United States gives us the word. The word can come only from us, the niggers: white, black, yellow . . . the men with dirty hands!

We are the strongest, my friends, but we do not know it because we are still dominated by fear.

I can understand that we are afraid of freedom when we see the price the Vietnamese are having to pay for theirs!

But we have no choice. Slavery is not a life. Others are doing all they can to free themselves from capitalism and imperialism. Why not us? Can it be that we are cowards, my friends, men of delicate constitution who shiver when winter comes? No. We are not cowards, but we are still a little too much like sheep.

Everything, in this world, belongs to us. We must abolish the inequality of privileges usurped and accumulated by force. By force, I repeat.

And it is by force that we too—the men with dirty hands, the hewers of wood, the drawers of water, the bootblacks, the laborers, the anonymous and underpaid pencil-pushers, the waitresses, the miners, and all the "cheap workers" in the textile mills, shoe factories, clothing factories, and canneries, in the industries, department stores, and railroad companies, in the ports of the St. Lawrence, on the rocky land of Quebec, and in the cooperatives strangled by the trusts—it is by force, and not through resignation, passivity, and fear, that we shall become free.

The struggle will be long and hard, but *it will be*. I am convinced of that.

We are not done with suffering, with being clubbed down, with going to prison . . . but we will win, for we are the strongest.

We shall pay dearly for our struggle, but it will win us a better society, one which will at last be *ours*.

Workers, students, young people, intellectuals of "the land Quebec," as Paul Chamberland calls it, in the Tombs, in my cage of steel and cement, I have nothing—to help me communicate with you and to unite me with your efforts—except this faith in the capacity of men to create a world more human than the present one. My faith is not a religion but the choice of a nigger who is fed up with slavery.

The sooner we who are niggers arm ourselves with courage and rifles, the sooner our liberation from slavery will make us equal and fraternal men. Utopia?

It is because I cannot bear to be a nigger that I joined the FLQ; that I will stay in the FLQ until the victory of the white niggers of Quebec over capitalism and imperialism; that I will stay there *on my feet*, in or out of the prisons of the established Order; that in every possible way I will bear witness to our will, the will of all of us, to free ourselves from our condition as niggers.

I have enough confidence in you—in us—not to be afraid of the future.

The Quebec revolution will not stop.

We are not the only ones who are fighting. Our struggle is part of man's long march toward liberation from the exploitation of some by others.

The long march of the niggers of the entire world, in which we of Quebec, we workers and students, we of the FLQ, still bring up the rear, because of some kind of false shame, stupid fear, or comfortable attitude of wait-and-see.

Hey, Georges! What are you waiting for to make up your mind? And the rest of you, Arthur, Louis, Jules, Ernest? On your feet, lads, and *all together:* to work! We'll have another glass of beer when we've done something besides talking and always putting the blame on other people. Each of us has his little share of responsibility to assume and to turn into action. The sooner we are united, lads, the sooner we will win. We have already wasted too much time in vain recriminations. Now we must go on to action.